Critical Muslim 14

Power

Critical Muslim is published quarterly by C. Hurst & Co. (Publishers) Ltd. on behalf of and in conjunction with Critical Muslim Ltd. and the Muslim Institute, London.

All correspondence to Muslim Institute, CAN Mezzanine, 49-51 East Road, London N1 6AH, United Kingdom

e-mail for editorial: editorial@criticalmuslim.com

The editors do not necessarily agree with the opinions expressed by the contributors. We reserve the right to make such editorial changes as may be necessary to make submissions to Critical Muslim suitable for publication.

C. Hurst & Co. (Publishers) Ltd., 41 Great Russell Street, London WC1B 3PL

ISBN: 978-1-84904-490-5 ISSN: 2048-8475

To subscribe or place an order by credit/debit card or cheque (pound sterling only) please contact Kathleen May at the Hurst address above or e-mail kathleen@hurstpub.co.uk

Tel: 020 7255 2201

A one year subscription, inclusive of postage (four issues), costs £50 (UK), £65 (Europe) and £75 (rest of the world).

The right of Ziauddin Sardar and the Contributors to be identified as the authors of this publication is asserted by them in accordance with the Copyright, Designs and Patents Act, 1988.

A Cataloguing-in-Publication data record for this book is available from the British Library.

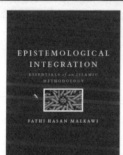
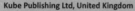

HALAL FOOD FOUNDATION

Halal Is Much More Than Food

The Halal Food Foundation (HFF) is a registered charity that aims to make the concept of halal more accessible and mainstream. We want people to know that halal does not just pertain to food – halal is a lifestyle.

The Foundation pursues its goals through downloadable resources, events, social networking, school visits, pursuing and funding scientific research on issues of food and health, and its monthly newsletter. We work for the community and aim at the gradual formation of a consumer association. We aim to educate and inform; and are fast becoming the first port of call on queries about halal issues. We do not talk at people, we listen to them.

If you have any queries, comments, ideas, or would just like to voice your opinion - please get in contact with us.

Halal Food Foundation

109 Fulham Palace Road,
Hammersmith, London, W6 8JA
Charity number: 1139457
Website: www.halalfoodfoundation.co.uk
E-mail: info@halalfoodfoundation.co.uk

@HFF_UK

Halal Food Foundation

The Barbary Figs

by

Rashid Boudjedra

Translated by
André Naffis-Sahely

Buy a copy of Rashid Boudjedra's *The Barbary Figs* at
www.hauspublishing.com or by calling +44(0)20 7838 9055
and a recieve a copy of Khaled al-Berry's memoir
Life is More Beautiful than Paradise free.

RASHID AND OMAR are cousins who find themselves side by side on a flight from Algiers to Constantine. During the hour-long journey, the pair will exhume their past, their boyhood in French Algeria during the 1940s and their teenage years fighting in the bush during the revolution. Rashid, the narrator, has always resented Omar, who despite all his worldly successes, has been on the run from the ghosts of his past, ghosts that Rashid has set himself the task of exorcising. Rashid peppers his account with chilling episodes from Algerian history, from the savageries of the French invasion in the 1830s, to the repressive regime that is in place today.

RASHID BOUDJEDRA has routinely been called one of North Africa's leading writers since his debut, *La Répudiation*, was published in 1969, earning the author the first of many fatwas. While he wrote his first six novels in French, Boudjedra switched to Arabic in 1982 and wrote another six novels in the language before returning to French in 1994. *The Barbary Figs* was awarded the Prix du Roman Arabe 2010.

CM14

April–June 2015

CONTENTS

POWER

ARTS AND LETTERS

REVIEWS

ET CETERA

CRITICAL MUSLIM

Subscribe to Critical Muslim

Now in its third year, *Critical Muslim* is the only publication of its kind, giving voice to the diversity and plurality of Muslim reporting, creative writing, poetry and scholarship.

Subscribe now to receive each issue of Critical Muslim direct to your door and save money on the cover price of each issue.

Subscriptions are available at the following prices, inclusive of postage. Subscribe for two years and save 10%!

	ONE YEAR (4 Issues)	TWO YEARS (8 Issues)
UK	£50	£90
Europe	£65	£117
Rest of World	£75	£135

TO SUBSCRIBE:

CRITICALMUSLIM.HURSTPUBLISHERS.COM

41 GREAT RUSSELL ST, LONDON WC1B 3PL
WWW.HURSTPUBLISHERS.COM
WWW.FBOOK.COM/HURSTPUBLISHERS
020 7255 2201

POWER

INTRODUCTION
SEARCHING FOR POWER

Ziauddin Sardar and MerrylWyn Davies

Muslim attitudes to power are like everything else about the contemporary *ummah*: complex; contradictory and chaotic. Everywhere power is the lodestone sought with passionate intensity yet everywhere it is as elusive as the legendary alchemical element. When any portion of its rare and delicate properties is grasped, the golden elixir inevitably melts to dust. Power will not stay still in Muslim hands and never delivers its yearned for promise. Yet, power is seen and conceived as the answer to all the ills of the Muslim world.

But let us be fair. It is not just in the *ummah* that power, and those with power, have gone mad. The whole damn world is complex, contradictory and chaotic. It is the spirit of our time, the postnormal condition, where everything seems to be sliding out of control and very little actually makes sense. A point well made by the English film maker, Adam Curtis. His famous documentary, 'The Power of Nightmares', drew parallels between the rise of Islamist extremists and the emergence of Neoconservatives in the US and argued that both needed the myth of a dangerous enemy to sustain their power base. In his short film, reflecting on the events of 2014, Curtis declares that 'so much of the news this year has been hopeless, depressing, and above all confusing'. To explain what is happening, Curtis begins with Vladislav Surkov, an advisor to President Vladimir Putin. Surkov, Curtis suggests, has imported 'ideas from conceptual art into the very heart of politics' with the intention of undermining 'people's perception of the world so they never know what has really happened'. Surkov sponsored all kinds of groups, Neonazi skinheads as well as liberal human rights campaigners, including parties opposed to Putin, to create 'a ceaseless shape-shifting that is unstoppable because it is indefinable'. The strategy was also used in the invasion of Ukraine to produce a 'non-linear war', where you never know who the enemy are let alone what they are up to – 'not to win the war but to use the war to create a constant state of destabilised perception in order to manage and control'. Curtis then goes on to suggest:

> Maybe we have something similar emerging here in Britain. Everything we are told by journalists and politicians is confusing and contradictory... there is an odd non-linear world that plays into the hands of those in power. British troops have come home from Afghanistan. No one seems to know whether it was a victory or a defeat. Aging disc-jockeys are prosecuted for crimes they have committed decades ago while practically no one in the City of London is prosecuted for the endless financial crimes that are being revealed there. In Syria we are told that President Asad is the evil enemy but then his enemies turn out to be even more evil than him. So we bomb them, and by doing that we help keep Asad in power.

> But the real epicentre of this non-linear world is the economy. And the closest we have to our own shape-shifting, postmodern politician is George Osborne. He tells us proudly that the economy is growing but at the same time wages are going down. He says that he is cutting the deficit but then it is revealed the deficit is going up. The dark heart of this shape-shifting world is quantitative easing. The government is insisting in taking billions of pounds out of the economy through its austerity programme yet at the same time it is pumping billions of pounds back into the economy through quantitative easing. The equivalent of £24,000 for every family in Britain. But it gets even more confusing, because the Bank of England has admitted that those billions of pounds have not gone where they are supposed to. A vast amount of the money has actually found its way into the hands of the wealthiest five per cent of Britons. It has been described as the biggest transfer of wealth to the rich in recent documented history. It could be a huge scandal comparable to the greedy oligarchs in Russia. A ruthless elite siphoning off billions of public money. But nobody seems to know – it sums up the mood of our times, when nothing seems to make any coherent sense.

The world is indeed becoming contradictory and confusing, full of uncertainty. What Curtis says about Britain is equally true of other countries. The US is never tired of espousing the rhetoric of 'democracy and human rights' yet, as the Senate Committee report on CIA torture reveals, the bastion of freedom engages in 'gruesome and widespread' torture. The 'security' of the US is absolute; but the security of other states is irrelevant. In the quest for its own 'security', the most weaponised country in the world, has made Iraq, Afghanistan and Pakistan the most insecure states in the world. The second most weaponised state in the world, Israel, feels constantly threatened by totally powerless people, the Palestinians, who are imprisoned in a territory it controls. US multinationals build efficient and sophisticated infrastructures and networks that lock other countries in long-term dependencies in collusion with the government, yet claim to be independent – even occasionally taking their own government to court. Democracy is projected as an essential ingredient for economic prosperity, yet the most successful economies of the last decade – China, Russia, Singapore, Qatar, Saudi Arabia – are unburdened by democracy. India, the biggest democracy in the world, touted as an emerging superpower, is in danger of turning into a 'Hindu State'. Violent Hindu extremists belonging to Rashtriya Swayamsevak Sangh and the Vishwa Hindu Parishad, given a boost by the election of Prime Minister Narendra Modi, are forcing Christians and Muslims to convert. Their 'home coming' campaign has been used to engineer conversions on a mass scale; and they plan to 'finish' Christianity and Islam in India by 2021. Contradictions are deeply intrinsic to capitalism, which 'has become too complex, too interconnected, too contradictory, too steeped in deep uncertainty and ignorance to be anything else but chaotic' – yet, it is still defended and projected as the panacea for a global system perpetually in crisis.

While Vladislav Surkov may have made his little contribution to the state of affairs, the blame for creating a 'non-linear' world cannot be laid on his door, as Curtis seems to suggest. While there may be spectacle and illusion there is nothing postmodern either. Postmodernism is as dead as the dodo.

The contemporary times are best characterised as postnormal, where what we conventionally accepted as normal is rapidly evaporating. It is a product of accelerating change in a highly complex, networked, globalised world where old, conventional orthodoxies are dying, and new ones have yet to be born. It is a period 'where facts are uncertain, values in dispute, stakes high, and decisions urgent'. As Curtis rightly points out, 'a constant vaudeville of contradictory stories' makes individuals and communities feel 'powerless, unable to challenge anything because we live in a state of confusion and uncertainty'.

Like much else in postnormal times, power is in a state of flux. It is shifting from the West to the East, from presidential palaces to public squares, from the states to colossal corporations and non-state actors, from men to women. Wealth and power can move at great speed and can be accumulated by individuals and corporations almost overnight. Today's start-up can become tomorrow's multi-billion corporation. A street demo can go chaotic and bring down a government. But while shifts in power can lead to toppling tyrants, and dislodge monopolies, it can also, as Moises Naim demonstrates in *The End of Power*, cause chaos and paralysis. Power has become simultaneously omnipresent and cynical as well as illusive. And there is little or no accountability.

In postnormal times the venality of the enemy, real and imaginary, justifies all. Even failed leaders get to be rhetorically prescient and aphoristically correct in seeing political power as emanating from the barrel of a gun; and brutality rules okay. Of course, it is not okay – but despite all the lip service given to the moral high ground, upholding ethical standards of behaviour and remaining true to enduring values of civilisation, the potent power of fear makes us all equally compromised. We are merely standard bearers for keeping ourselves secure by whatever means possible in a frighteningly precarious world.

The contemporary chaotic, complex and contradictory nature of the *ummah* should be seen in this context. Muslims do not exist in isolation from the rest of the world – even though some think they do. But the chaos that predominates as the condition of the *ummah* has a particular character. The majority of the world's refugees are from Muslim states fleeing conflicts fuelled by sectarian strife, ethnic antipathies, political dissent or the brutal grip of authoritarian oppression. There are wars and rumours of war that spread dearth and blight the lives and aspirations of entire societies. There are places where the curse of war passes down the generations who know nothing but its unending misery. Elsewhere there are discontents milling beneath the veneer of calm. There is the scourge of poverty and underdevelopment encouraged by debt swelling around islands of excess where wealth is poured into ostentatious projects designed to aggrandise those in power. Money circulates to bolster the grip of ideological power, to boost blocks of continuing antipathy, and fuel future antagonisms. And everywhere in Muslim majority countries and among Muslim minorities west, east, north or south there is a yearning for the power to create order, to regain balance, to establish the *deen*, the way of being of Islam. This desire sees Islam itself as the foundation of power – the engine of harmony, the source of command over the vicissitudes of life, the ideology that puts everything in its proper place, and, once again, returns worldly power in the hands of Muslims. But the desire for order is not solely benign; it has taken brutal life that does not shrink from mayhem and murder to become sheer depravity and brazen barbarism that seeks to legitimise itself in the name of Islam while visiting its indiscriminate vengeance most liberally, though far from exclusively, on Muslim victims. Hardly surprising then, that nowhere is there agreement on how power is to be accessed and actualised. The path to power is everywhere complex and contradictory because all meanings and means of power are themselves in dispute - hence the chaos.

Chaos, however, is no straight forward matter. The conventional understanding of the term as total confusion or disorder well expresses the feelings evoked in the generality of participants in and observers of the Muslim scene. However, these feelings are not the subject of chaos theory which more fully enables us to consider the predicament that confronts the world today. Chaos theory deals with the problems of predictability in complex systems and has a great deal to do with the limitations of our understanding of what constitute set patterns and how they work. Chaos theory seeks to comprehend how complex systems respond to minute differences in initial conditions which never repeat and vastly affect the outcome. Complex systems are complex because of the multitudinous interactions of which they are composed all of which are in continuous motion – nothing stands still. Yet what the world is waiting for and wants is a stable platform, a regular, predictable, knowable Muslim world, the reliable partner kind of Muslim World that does the expected kind of things. The trouble is such coherent agreed definitions neither exist nor are sufficiently widely accepted across the increasing diversity of Muslims societies. The standard Muslim responses of self-definition are, in reality, encrusted within and without by varied traditions and their accompanying myths, legends and flights of fancy. The most basic requirement in approaching chaos is acquiring some grasp on what constitutes reality.

Muslim reality is a conundrum appearing through the lens of apologia, nostalgia, romanticism, hagiography, as well as the extensive library of Orientalism and Islamophonbia according to one's origin, interest, affectation or predilection. Muslim reality is out there somewhere, largely beyond the major conventions through which it is perceived and discussed by Muslims and non-Muslims alike.

Chaos is not fashioned from nothing; it arises from complexity and complexity is the legacy of history, the inexorable accretion of events and ideas. History is that most human of endeavours, a game of whispers fashioned from diverse ways of communicating and remembering things past, that shapes attitudes and actions in the present and visions of the future. Muslims like people everywhere live among the wreckage with the weight of history bearing upon them. More and more it is the way Muslims rummage through the debris of their diverse histories that define the complexity of their differences and construct factions, tendencies, groupings and persuasions. History has become the most contentious issue where Muslims are concerned, none more so than how they should understand and operate the history of the origin of Islam itself. History provides an almost infinite variety of initial conditions from which the construction of contemporary Muslim identity, persona, aspiration and action is inspired. In today's *ummah*, history is power, the presumed power of authenticity, a power sought after, jealously guarded and not infrequently wielded with malign intent to harvest ever more potent power.

The relationship of Muslims to their history has two inescapable aspects. The most basic definition of a Muslim is one who believes in the revelation of Truth in history: that of Truth is contained in the Qur'an and exemplified in the life of the recipient of revelation, the Prophet Muhammad. Secondly, the history of Muslim civilisation charts the immediate accession to worldly power by the first generation who gave allegiance to the Qur'anic revelation. History records the spread of empire and influence by their succeeding generations: the ideal phase of the 'Rightly Guided Caliphs', the 'Golden Age' of the Abbasids, the mighty power of the Ottoman Empire. Then, we have the inexorable falling off from power as Muslims gradually relinquished control over their destiny. After their glorious rise, Muslims everywhere lose the knack of worldly success. These two aspects of history intrinsically shape Muslim ideas about the relationship of identity and power.

Consider, for example, the recent surge of neo-Ottoman nostalgia in Turkey. The main stalwarts of the Islamist party that rules Turkey, President Recep Tayyip Erdoğan and Prime Minister Ahmet Davutoğlu, both suffer, to use the words of Mohamed Bakari, 'from delusions of grandeur which stems from nostalgia for the Ottoman past'. Erdoğan started as a pragmatic Mayor of Istanbul. But that pragmatism evaporated with successive terms as Prime Minister, after which he, following in the footsteps of Vladimir Putin, installed himself as President with real power. One can look at his attempts to revive Ottoman culture and heritage with favour but the restoration of status-obsessed political Pasha culture is another matter. It has led to the obscene $615 million Presidential Palace outside Ankara, thirty time larger than the White House, complete with one thousand rooms. The Ottoman Empire, Barnaby Rogerson notes, 'is a human edifice to be desperately proud of if you are Turkish' but its spiritual and moral foundations were rather dubious. 'The Ottoman Empire was a conquest state pure and simple', writes Rogerson, 'based on the very successful military formula of balancing the élan of Turkish tribal cavalry from Central Asia with a salaried army of professional engineers, musketeers and artillerymen recruited by enslaving the boys of the Christian minorities'. It had 'no historical links real or imagined' with the Prophet Muhammad or his teachings.

Was the success of Muslim Empires the product of a direct correlation between belief and power? Is political power, governance over populations, irrespective of their race, creed, colour, language, ethnicity or communal history, the proper and necessary concomitant of true belief? For the Islamists of various ilks the answer is clear and precise. Power belongs to those who are pure and true believers; and everything can be justified to gain and maintain power, no matter how horrendous. This is not just the creed of the psychotic followers of Islamic State of Iraq and the Levant (ISIL), who glory in beheading innocent people, or the Taliban, who massacre innocent school children, or Boko Haram, who kidnap school girls and sell them into slavery – it is the basic dogma of all puritans. This is how the Saudis justify their rule and power and the Iranian Ayatollahs rationalise their theocracy. It has been the mantra of the Muslim Brotherhood of Egypt and the Jamaat-e-Islami of Pakistan, the two movements that, according to Abdelwahab El-Affendi, have cornered the

'Islamism' market. All Islamists, Sunni or Shia, Salafi or Wahhabi, Brotherhood or Jamaat, have a 'rigid and non-flexible agenda', based on True Belief, that 'leaves no room for dialogue, let alone negotiations of any kind', notes Najah Kadhim. What this means is spelled out by El-Affendi: 'in the age of ISIL and similar mega-terror groups, the lines between violent dysfunctional and non-violent varieties of Islamism get blurred. The Brotherhood wants to re-establish the caliphate, but never gets there. ISIL does establish the caliphate, but its success appears worse than the Brotherhood's failure'.

But what is this Caliphate that these puritans seek? 'The whole mesmerizing edifice of the Caliphate, that world-wide medieval super-power of yore', writes Rogerson, 'is one of the most potent dreams for anyone interested in a revival of Muslim culture. It is also the oldest curse, the most persistent heresy'. Rogerson takes us through the Umayyad, Abbasid and Ottoman Caliphates to show that there was nothing there but imperial power. Even during the period of the Right Guided Caliphs – 'a time of true heroes, when sovereign rulers cared for the poor, orphans and widows of the community as much as they directed the affairs of the state. When they shopped for their own households in the market place, darned their own clothes, led the prayers and theological discussions, fasted the hardest during the month of Ramadan, led the prayers as Imam and could chant the whole (yet unwritten Qur'an) through the night, and remember the traditions better than any scholar' – there was, Rogerson finds, no Caliphate as such. Indeed, he warns that 'we must begin to detach these rulers from the bloody soaked human glory of the imperial conquests of the Arab Caliphate'.

Indeed, it is 'comically absurd to think' that the Prophet Mohammad 'was interested in systems of government, the title and powers of rulers, their governors, judges and administrators'. 'There was no Empire, no Caliphate declared or dreamt about during his lifetime'. The whole notion of the Caliphate is a manufactured pipe dream.

But the Caliphate is not the only grand illusion in the pantheon of the *ummah*. There is also the Sharia. The idea that Islam is law is the greatest shibboleth whose pervasive grip has drained Muslim societies of their humanity. Every evil known to humankind can be, and often is, committed in the name of the Sharia. The quest for the power of purity invariable resolves itself into the notion that what Muslim society everywhere is lacking is Sharia and the thing that alone will usher in pure Muslim existence is the institution of this legal code as the ground plan for the entirety of political, social and economic life. The great question is what is Sharia? The shorthand answer is always that Sharia is 'God's law' with the implication that it is fixed, known, invariant and hence vital to Muslims' existence. Yet, any basic introductory guide to Islam, the kind of booklet one would give to a youngster, would state that Sharia is derived from Qur'an and Sunnah. They are also likely to be introduced to four key principles by which this law works: *ijma*, consensus of the learned; *qiyas*, reasoning from analogy; *ijtihad*, independent judicial reasoning; and *adab*, customary practice which is deemed not to contradict anything contained in the primary sources. All of which should, yet somehow fails, to draw attention to the salient point that Sharia exists only as a human construction. This way of making law – with its accretion of power to religious elite, outmoded logic, and incorporation of tribal norms and customs – was developed and established by great jurisprudents of yore, whose names are blithely appropriated to 'schools of law' though their constructive function in this process is overlooked. The human reasoning that went into the process and the attention given to fashioning reasonable rules and regulation to take account of context and circumstance also become incidental items of forgetfulness. The word Sharia itself implies an active path, a way to a watering hole. Thus by all tests Sharia is unequivocally the work of human interpretation seeking God's pleasure. Since no human being can in honesty be certain of attaining the mind of God, Sharia can only be a human approximation and never can be fixed in time. Yet when Muslims clamour for the power of purity they clamour not for the responsibility of shaping Qur'anic principle and the example of the Prophet to order society today in light of contemporary circumstances but rather to impose a human construct, a set of laws made as best they could manage to serve other times, other places and other problems. When they speak of Sharia most Muslims actually mean fiqh, the body of jurisprudence fashioned to serve the ethic of empire, full of the accretions of imperial times.

Sharia does not descent ready-made from Heaven. It is has to be made and remade by humans, through continuous effort and intellectual rigour, in every epoch according to the circumstances and certain principles (*maqasids*). Far from being an outmoded romantic notion that takes us back to distant mythical history, it should be a pragmatic answer to the demands of a changing world that takes us forward to a feasible future. Or, as Malise Ruthven put it, citing the scholar of Islamic law, Wael Hallaq, Sharia constitutes 'a colossal project of building a moral-legal empire whose foundational and structural impulse is summed up in the ever continuing attempt to discover God's will.' The project entails 'dialectic between the sociological and the metaphysical, between the Community as a worldly society and its persistent attempts to locate itself in a particular moral cosmology'. It is an on-going realist effort focussed on the real world that in history 'was always placed in a metaphysical context, just as this metaphysics was constantly teased out in the realism of mundane existence'. Moreover, historically the Sharia's moral and ethical imperatives had nothing to do with the State – they operated outside the confines of political power. Those who equate the Sharia with the State are in fact totalitarians. Their claim that 'sovereignty belongs to God' is actually a claim that they are the representatives of God on earth.

The history that is used to justify puritan ideologies is essentially romantic hagiography. Even the life the Prophet is presented as idealised stories lacking human weakness, and thus devoid of humanity. But as Rogerson shows, the Prophet led a community where discussion, different viewpoints and disobedience were common. His contemporaries saw him as 'both fallible about the affairs of this world, whilst at one at the same time being revered beyond all men as the mouthpiece of the divine'.

Indeed, 'there never has been a golden period of hallowed political obedience in Islam, not then, not now'. The idealised norms that we are presented with, Kecia Ali points out, diverge from earlier norms in striking and unrecognised ways. For example, the widely accepted notion that power in a household belongs to the man, who are breadwinners and head of the family, actually rewrites the past. Ali examines the relationship between Muhammad and Khadija, his first wife, which is conventionally presented as an ideal monogamous marriage. Yet, as she notes, 'this emphasis on Muhammad and Khadija's marriage diverges sharply from premodern Muslim accounts of his life'. While 'Khadija played a pivotal role at key moments in Muhammad's life, she was absent from the bulk of the material transmitted about him. His public leadership of the community in Medina transpired after her death, and so relatively little of the hadith corpus concerns her. To read certain books about Muhammad's life, one would think Khadija was his only wife'. Ali argues that 'the triumphalist narrative of Muhammad's egalitarian marriage to Khadija', inadvertently strengthens 'a model of male/female coupling and nuclear family life that excludes those who are single by choice, couples who cannot or do not have children, and especially gay people from its vision of the good family'. To redress the balance of power we have to retell 'the stories about our sacred figures' anew.

Hagiography of first generation Muslims obscures the undeniable fact that their ranks were riven with dissent and burgeoned into bloody civil wars. Diversity of interpretation among the first generations of Muslims produced fundamentalist literalists who while proclaiming God alone should decide on matters that governed the fate of the Muslim community nevertheless excelled in denouncing all who disagreed with them as infidels (*kafirs*) whose blood could be shed legitimately. The bloodletting self-appointed Islamic warriors of today have ample historic precursors from whom they draw their horrific inspiration. And such groups of religious maniacs have re-emerged down the centuries. Muslims cannot glibly rest content by saying this is not Islam, which means peace. They cannot complacently answer that these aberrations have been settled in history, militarily defeated, and intellectually denounced by great scholars long dead. The challenge posed by fanatics recurs in every epoch; and has to be tackled by every generation - before the fanatics persuade young men and women to think they are warriors of Islam purifying the world by creating charnel houses.

The problems with history thus reach back to the original formation of everything Muslims take to be religion and their religious identity. History as tradition encrusts how Muslim religious discourse is structured. Tradition as instituted over time has become a source of power and authority which now regulates and constrains Muslim debate. Muslims seek power by deferring to tradition without questioning what tradition has become, or inquiring into the competence of the bastions of tradition – the religious scholars. In the complex networked world, most Muslims are content to hand their children to obscurantists Mullahs to 'teach them the Qur'an', leaving them without the faculties of interpretative reasoning. The masses are happy to bow down to the sole authority of traditional scholars who have become the clerical professionals Islam is supposed not to possess. Authority and power is invested in a 'scholarship' which is ultra-conservative and preservative, agile on the head of numerous pins, ever ready to offer an answer even to the most stupid questions rather than genuinely educate the masses to accept individual responsibility for the moral and ethical choices they have to make in their daily lives. Nostalgia for an imagined prefect history of perfect men who made perfect decisions during the formative phase of Islam makes Muslims compliant sheep following religion as a series of dos and don'ts. Or in contradictory mode it generates schizophrenic believers who exist in bifurcated worlds, of religion and normality, that are uneasy companions constantly giving birth to unresolved insoluble questions.

Idealised stories and history are the main instruments through which Islam is turned into an ideology. It all amounts to a desperate attempt to define what is essential, what has been lost, what must be implemented to regain the lost levers of power which generate and guarantee self-determination and genuine authenticity – so that Muslims can resume wielding earthly power once again. Power, control over things has somehow become an essential proof of right belief, a prerequisite of marching on to power. The best illustration of how Islam has been used as an ideology of power is provided by Pakistan, a state created in the name of Islam. The various factions, from the Jammat-e-Islami to the Taliban, fighting for their puritan versions of Islam in Pakistan is a spectacle that is as astounding as it is sinister. But the true defender of Pakistan's ideology is the military, which has carefully crafted its Islamic image. The military, writes Hussain Ahmed, is 'the ultimate patriarch, the symbol of Pakistani masculinity, the most-*sadiq* (truthful) and most-*ameen* (trustworthy) – traits traditionally used to describe Prophet Muhammad'. Without the army, it is argued, both Pakistan and Islam are doomed. 'Therefore as guardians of the state, the army must be permitted to act as it deems fit so that both physical and ideological boundaries are protected'. As a result, the military's dominance and control of society, economy and politics is absolute – 'and it defends its hegemony through a combination of real and imagined power'.

But it is not just Pakistan's military that behaves in this manner. The military's dominance over politics and society is pretty evident in most Muslim countries – from Egypt to Indonesia. Far from being the defenders of the state, the military is often the biggest hurdle to progress and progressive thought. What Pakistan illustrates is that when Islam becomes an ideology acutely preoccupied with power it turns easily to totalitarian ruthlessness and brutality involving all segments of society. As Ahmad points out, military dominance is coupled with 'colluding elite, naked profiteering' and 'a blissfully ignorant young middle-class'. It is a reality, Ahmad concludes chillingly, that has been 'carved indigenously and terrifyingly', in the name of Islam, 'through a willing acquiescence of the citizenry'.

The citizens are totally baffled by our chaotic, complex, and interconnected world. They exist within a framework that is simple, unitary and uniform: God is One, all Muslims are a single community distinct from all others, Islam is a total way of life which covers all aspects of existence. How then to come to terms with proliferating diversity? How do sectarian divisions come to mean so much? Why are Muslim societies so diverse in their cultures and ways of being? Where is the uniformity that should surely characterise everything from how to trim a beard to how women should or should not be covered and hidden from public gaze? How should they react to the ideologues who promise earthly order through instituting Islam as power? How do Muslims debate what are presented as inflexible certainties, enduring traditions that are the only basis for establishing the autonomous independence of being they are told should be theirs by birth right? The conundrum of a pious personal life is that it cannot cope with complexity – the hallmark of contemporary existence.

Consider, for example, the issues of governing a nation state. As the Muslim Brotherhood discovered in Egypt, the modern state is a formidably complex entity. Those in power have to deal with different vested interests some of which may be armed, an all-powerful army, entrenched institutional frameworks, unruly judiciary, an economy that may not be in good health, a health system that may be falling apart, an international system that may place its own demands, and a citizenry with a long string of grievances. It is not just a question of many different and diverse parts, but how these parts interact to produce a complex nation state. The complexity is well illustrated by Bosnia-Herzegovina. The Bosnian government, Sejad Mekic tells us, 'is a three-headed hydra, with a presidency that consists of representatives from three "constituent peoples": Bosnian Muslims (Bosniaks), Croats and Serbs. The Dayton Peace

Agreement, signed on 14 December 1995, divided the country into two mini-states: the Serb Republic and the Bosniak-Croat Federation. The two semi-autonomous entities are united under a parliament and three-member presidency. Despite the efforts to build up the powers of the central state, both entities are still highly autonomous, with separate political, police and financial structures'. Governing a complex structure of this nature itself requires a complex controlling mechanism – not an easy task. Indeed, this is why even matured and established democracies, such as Britain and France, are finding it difficult to cope with the complexity of governing a modern state. As the rate of change accelerates, the issues of governance will become even more complex.

Of course, one way to deal with complexity and diversity is simply to suppress it – and store up even more complex and wicked problems for the future. A benign way of looking at the dominance of military in politics and the emergence of Islamist authoritarianism in the Muslim world would be to see it as a mechanism of avoiding complexity. Nazry Bahrawi highlights another device: using Islam to construct racialism, which makes races into foundations of Islamic and political identities. Thus, to be Malay in Malaysia is by definition to be a Muslim (of a specific type), which in turn means you subscribe to the political concept of *ketuanan Melayu*, or Malay supremacy. In Brunei the formula is '*Melayu, Islam, Beraja*', which translates as 'Malay, Islam, Monarchy' – by being Malay and Muslim you automatically pledge allegiance to an obnoxious and absolutist monarchy. A similar pattern has emerged in the Gulf, as Hassan Mahamdallie points out in his review of Miriam Cooke's fascinating book, *Tribal Modern*. Here the blood purity of a tribe, rigorously policed, determines the purity of your faith and your righteous claim to power. But no matter what sinister mechanism you use to suppress diversity, what instruments you use to banish complexity, they are not going to go away. They are here to stay; and set to increase rapidly.

Uniformity, let alone unity any sense of the concept of the *ummah* might imply, is a palpable fiction, a cruel and cynical lie. Muslims are divided by language and history derived from their colonisation as much as colonialism divides them from and distorts their relationship to history. Modernity confounds Muslim societies because it appears invariably in the guise of westernisation and becomes a questioning of authenticity, of autochthonous potency and power, the ability to derive their own future from their own ideals and authority. Muslim nation states owe nominal allegiance to supra national Muslim/Islamic organisations while being members of a variety of other groupings depending on their divergent status as client states of former colonial powers or new Empires. The reality of naked power relations disenfranchise as much as they disadvantage the citizens of Muslim societies. Muslim minorities living within western societies find the complexities of their existence even more disturbing. They are confronted with the plethora of ways to accommodate and be within the supposedly permissive acceptance the West offers yet also acutely conscious that their Muslim identity is suspected to be beyond the acceptable bounds of liberalism.

The complexity shaped by history makes Muslim existence profuse in contradictions. Muslims find themselves confounded by quandaries at every turn, embroiled in contemporary existence where all meanings admit of so much different and diverse implications and interpretations. Power is the question at the top of the agenda and their most common vantage point on power is the embrace of victimhood. Muslims are victims of the historic insult of colonialism, and victims of the pernicious gaze of western society which views them through the distortions of Orientalism or the more naked prejudice of Islamophobia. Muslim are victimised by their inability just to be themselves however they understand that to be. Muslims are victims caught between tradition and modernity, everywhere powerless and constrained by the failings, corruption and complicity of their governments. Muslim nation states lack democratic legitimacy even where elections are held. Their governments are implicated in the policies of western imperialism, craven clients of foreign powers.

Victimhood is so well rehearsed it has become routine. It has become a powerful tool to mould and mobilise popular dissent especially where people lack the conventional outlets of a thriving civil society. Muslims routinely cast themselves as pawns in the hegemonic game of real power; and thus see venality everywhere. The venality of the enemy, real and imagined, is then used to justify their own venality expressed often as religious piety and moral superiority. The asymmetry of power that casts Muslims as victims has inured people to a tacit acceptance that this legitimises terrorism as the weapon of the weak. With creeping horror the depredations of such violent response has become ever more pervasive and brutal in Muslim societies and around the world. Terrorism most effectively victimises the victims of victimhood – most often it kills maims and destroys the living and livelihood of Muslims. Caught in the complexities of decoding and disentangling the abuses of hegemonic power and power politics here, there, and everywhere the Muslim response is mindless violence or quietism. The majority disown egregious actions and declare it has nothing to do with the peaceful ethos of Islam. Quietism is never an effective answer to the real complex issues of power, more usually it amounts to passing by on the other side attempting to be oblivious to the substantive problems. In the face of the many ideological movements, violent and non-violent, that are the modern reality of the Muslim world simply taking the alternate position that Islam means peace is a very public washing of hands – a disclaimer designed to distance people from guilt by association with those who pursue naked power. However sincere a statement of unshakeable belief the definition of Islam as peace may be for what one hopes constitutes a majority of Muslims, it is nevertheless a way of disowning rather than resolving a very obvious problem within Muslim societies.

Overburdened with a sense of victimhood, Muslims dream of power and the invariant relationship of power to purity as proof of right religion. And thus they are lost. It is too easy to blame hegemonic politics and spout the mantra that Islam is peace. It is too easy to wallow in nostalgia, romanticism and hagiography which amount to little more than apologia in a variety of disguises. It is far more difficult, not to say complex, to lift your gaze from misplaced nostalgia and a sense of victimhood and look at the real sources of contemporary power: culture, education, and engagement with the diversity of the world.

A major problem with the quest for purity as the source of power is that it wipes out culture and diversity. When culture and its diversity are removed all that remains is the arid rigidity of *fiqh*, the literalist letter of the law. Islam, as Kadhim points out, is reduced to a 'crude mathematical equation': 'Islam is equal to *fiqh* (jurisprudence) and *fiqh* is equal to Islam'. However, the Qur'an itself is explicit and profuse in its insistence that religion as values and ethics is an operative force that must be at the heart of culture and society in all its myriad human diversity. A purist approach to religion denatures humanity and de-cultures what the Qur'an insists are essential vessels of our purposeful creation. When you abandon culture, or look down on its highest expressions, you forego power to shape history. It is through culture that we untie the knots of social, ideological, and political power. Indeed, the culture of power itself can only be tamed through the power of a thriving culture. People without culture are powerless nonentities.

Underpinning all varieties of cultural power is the Word which, as Boyd Tonkin argues 'may now shine brighter as a shield than as a sword'. The Word is the major 'tool of transformation' in postnormal times: it can 'hold complexity and contradiction in a stable suspension without any "irritable reaching" after certainty. Its power, writes Tonkin, 'lies in unending, self-revising curiosity - a winding path of tests, variations and adaptations to match its own narrative of natural selection'. The power of the powerless comes, as Czech writer and dissent Vaclav Havel demonstrated, not from quietism and passivity but from 'living in truth': 'the daily practice of honesty and integrity in thinking, writing and personal conduct'. 'The true word spoken, written and above all performed will bring a "repressed alternative" to fruition'.

When culture is combined with education an understanding emerges of the complexity of the contemporary world providing us with the capabilities to tackle the issues of power. As Jeremy Henzell-Thomas shows so effectively, education is a source of multiple powers: 'the power to recognise the full extent of human powers and faculties'; 'the power to arrest fragmentation, resolve conflict and transcend narrow definitions of identity'; 'the power to ask searching questions, root out our own prejudices, and resist indoctrination'; 'the power to amass a body of knowledge, to marshal evidence, and to resist conditioned, biased and one-dimensional thinking'; 'the power to reach for a universal vision of excellence which encompasses truth, meaning, purpose and what it means to be fully human'; 'the power to keep on inquiring and learning' and 'opens our minds and hearts to the source of all knowledge and its infinitely generative power' and 'the power to reach for the sky, and to join heaven and earth, the transcendent and the immanent, in the love of God and "all that moves on the face of the earth"'.

Education also confers, Henzell-Thomas tells us, 'the power to relate and to know the "other", and by so doing to enrich and improve ourselves'. Many Muslim problems, including the issues of power, are deeply intertwined with their inability to relate to Others – including the Others within Islam. Just as Muslims dehumanise themselves by suppressing culture and diversity, so they dehumanise Others by seeing them as distinctly different, a product of corrupted religions and false worldviews. And, as such, at best to be shunned. Yet, without engaging with the other, without seeing the Self in the Other, without interacting with other notions of Truth, we cannot appreciate the true diversity and complexity of the world. This is the true god-shaped hole in our hearts; the true source of our helplessness. Engaging with the Other, as Rahel Fischbach and Rachel Friedman demonstrate, can be discomforting. When Muslim, Christian and Jewish postgraduate students meet in a classroom at the Mohammed V University, Rabat, bewildering and outrageous questions are raised. 'Do you really believe in all the doctrines of your religion?' Wasn't Paul an imposter? But 'the lines that divided us were not simply religious but also cultural, educational, geographical, and especially epistemological', write Fischbach and Friedman. There were contradictory and contending conclusions. Eventually though there was enlightenment once the power of engagement came to the fore: there was understanding to be had of 'ourselves and others'.

Engagement, education and culture are not only sources of power they also provide us with the essential instrument for navigating the chaotic, complex and contradictory world of today: critical acumen. Everything we know about power and its misuse points towards the need for robust, open, and critical Muslim debate about our misconstruction of the very idea of power. 'Every time you erect an authority figure', Rogerson writes, 'who thinks on behalf of other humans, who decides what is wrong and right, you weaken the first and essential purpose of Islam, which can usefully be imagined as an electrical charge connecting humans to their God'. History, including Muslim history, attests that power derived from brute force, through the imposition of the Sharia, through terrorism, through military dominance of politics, or any other insidious, barbaric battery of means human wit can contrive, does not produce progress and never peace on earth. So long as Muslim societies truncate, obfuscate, and censor critical debate about their formative history and the relationship of religion and power they will place the subtle seduction of the gun and the scimitar before the demands for positive change and enlightened progress. It is time for Muslims to take responsibility for their own times, unafraid to engage with others and openly critical of themselves. The only real power that can redeem Muslim communities is the power of critical reasoning, the power of education, the power of engagement, and the willingness to honestly address the shortcomings of our present way of being Muslim. It is the only way to fit enduring values and ethics of Islam to the needs of our complex times. It would be a powerful way to go.

DREAMING OF THE CALIPHATE

Barnaby Rogerson

It was during Saddam Hussein's disastrous annexation of Kuwait in 1990 that I had an idle daydream of what a tired old tyrant sitting on the throne of Iraq might be persuaded to do towards the end of his life. Like many observers I realised that the organised looting of the wealthy suburbs of Kuwait City by units of the Iraqi army was not playing well to the newly 'liberated citizens of the 19th province of greater Iraq' or to the other Arab states stretched along the Persian Gulf. It looked shoddy, the operation of a bored mobster, a gangster up to his eyebrows in debt without imagination, style or finesse.

And then in an instant I knew what council a Machiavellian Vizier should whisper into the ear of Saddam, if he was going to successfully cloak his crimes and gather to himself the mantle of history. As his first troops crossed the frontier posts he should have simultaneously unfurled the black banners of the Abbasid Caliphs from Baghdad and the ruins of Samara. He should have sent out a public invitation to all the Muslim community leaders of the world whilst appealing to each Islamic nation to send one delegate for every million of their people, and so gather together to elect and acclaim a new Caliph. To complete this propaganda coup he would then publicly resign as President of Iraq and then publicly recite the humble oath of the first Caliph Abu Bakr in the courtyard of his hometown mosque at Takrit whilst modestly stepping forth into the television cameras as a mere Emir — allowing others to make what they would of his newly adopted name of Saladin and the gift of an ancient cloak-like mantle. His armies would have also been renamed after the first great Arab generals: such triumphant heroes as Khalid ibn al-Walid, Saad ibn Abu Waqqas and Amr ibn Al-As. The long wireless whip cords of the tank columns would be decorated with black and green silk pennants and their sides painted with swirling calligraphy and loaded down with cheering children and ululating women. National frontiers within greater Arabia would be abolished and his armies told not to stop until all the oil pipelines of Arabia had been switched off, in advance of negotiating a fair, pre-1967 physical frontier between Israel and Palestine. Brotherhood would be declared between Sunni and Shia, who would have been acknowledged as the fifth school of the Sharia tradition. As an act of contrition for the foolish border wars with Iran he would penitently be filmed walking barefooted across the land of Iraq to serve as floor sweeper in the shrine-mosques of Najaf and Karbala. The equality, egality and universalism of women with men, black with white, south with north, Arab with Turk, Muslims with all the peoples of the book would be declared as the cornerstone of every state wishing to claim to be Islamic. Oil revenues would be poured into a brand new worldwide Bayt al Hikma foundation, setting up free hospitals and universities with a network of hospitable courtyard library-schools which would be open to all who walked in with the open mind of a scholar or the tattered cloak of a dervish. Eternal Jihad would be declared against just three enemies: ignorance, disease and poverty....

And then I switched back to reality, to watch Japanese televisions, Korean freezers and Chinese dishwashers being loaded onto American trucks by units of the Iraq army driving through the streets of Kuwait in European made armoured-cars. The day dream of a charismatic renaissance of Islam was replaced by the grubby reality of oil states capable of waging high tech warfare but not yet capable of building and designing their own pan-Arabic bicycle let alone car. A surge of annoyance flowed through my veins, but then came a trickle of a smile. For I began to examine each cherished detail of my absurd historical fantasy and slowly realized how much they all owed to pride and glory, and nothing to either the example or teaching of the Prophet.

The whole mesmerizing edifice of the Caliphate, that world-wide medieval super-power of yore, is one of the most potent dreams for anyone interested in a revival of Muslim culture. It is also the oldest curse, the most persistent heresy. But first let us remind ourselves of some of the attractions as we settle back and think of all the stirring examples of the glory of Islamic culture as represented by the Caliphate. But don't be too focused, for it is best to let your eyes dwell on the soft focus of centuries of grand mosque architecture, beautifully illuminated Qur'ans and walled palace gardens. And the glory of those maps that chronicle the vast extent of the Imperial Caliphate all coloured in attractive shades of ever expanding green. Then allow yourself to feel a bit maudlin for the abolition of the last Caliph in 1924 before settling down and fingering a period that can usefully be considered an example for our contemporary world. The Ottoman Caliphate? This is a good start surely, the community that defended the heartland of Islamic culture from the cannons and the battleships of all the most aggressive European states for 500 years. It is a human edifice to be desperately proud of if you are Turkish, but grounded on exactly what spiritual or moral foundations? For the Ottoman Empire was a conquest state pure and simple, based on the very successful military formula of balancing the élan of Turkish tribal cavalry from Central Asia with a salaried army of professional engineers, musketeers and artillerymen recruited by enslaving the boys of the Christian minorities. This modern Sparta had no historical links real or imagined with Arabia, the Arabs, the founders of Islam, let alone a saintly scholar, or the family of the Prophet Muhammad or his teachings. It arose from out of a hotchpotch of emirates that squabbled over the border badlands between the old Byzantine and Seljuk Empires. It was a dynastic kingdom par excellence based on a Darwinian like code of the survival of the fittest often assisted by the murder of the brothers of the ruler. Each new generation princes were bred from captured concubine slaves – which in no way could be seen to be following the open, family-centred example of the Prophet's household. The Ottomans did not even bother to claim the Caliphate until the eighteenth century, though they were proud enough of having destroyed its last medieval traces when they conquered the Mameluke Sultanate of Egypt in 1516 and dispatched the last heir of the Abbasids to Istanbul.

So let us look instead at the Abbasids, surely a role model for a modern Islamic dream of a Caliphate. Descended, so their genealogists assured us, from an uncle of the Prophet Muhammad and stretching in a grand chain from the eighth to the thirteenth century. But once again it is best not to look at the details too closely. For the Abbasids first rose to power as capable warriors fighting on behalf of the true family of the Prophet Muhammad. But there was a satanic double-standard at the heart of this state, revealed in the story of how the first Abbasid Caliph left a key to a secret treasury to his heirs. These subterranean vaults were found to be stacked full of the neatly labelled corpses of all the members of the Prophet's family that had been poisoned and secretly assassinated whilst the Abbasid state had publicly espoused their cause as their most loyal supporters. This habit would continue until all of the Prophet's descendants were killed or had escaped to far distant lands. While even the most sympathetic historian cannot make much of the first eponymous founder of this dynasty, for Abbas the uncle of the Prophet is not a hero of early Islam. He was however rich, clever and well connected, and so he made his peace with Islam, and cut his deal as a canny survivor, once he realised his nephew was on the point of victory after a bloody eight year struggle between Mecca and Medina.

So let us look further back, to the Omayyad, that first dynasty that conquered an Arab Islamic Empire that stretched from Spain to Central Asia. Perhaps they represent our ideal polity? Their monuments, such as the dome of the Rock, the Great Mosque of Damascus and the Great Mosque of Cordoba remain powerful totemic symbols of Islamic culture. They led a broken patchwork of tribes from one of the poorest regions of the ancient world and established from this one of the greatest Empires that our world has ever known. An Arab can indeed take great pride in this masterly human achievement, and look over the Omayyad Empire as a true equal to the conquest Empires of Alexander the Great and Turkic Tamburlane. But like these two blood-soaked military geniuses, the Omayyad can make no claim to any spiritual value. Indeed they are to an almost comic extent, the bad guys of early Islam, desperately keen to maintain the Arabs as a race apart, fed by a tribute of bullion and slaves from the conquered races and nations. With one notable exception they certainly had no interest in converting their subjects to Islam and making of them a near equal to the ruling warrior caste of Arabs. While the traditional histories remembers how they waged war on the Islamic heartlands, opposing such heroes of real Islam as Ali, his son Husayn and even destroying the Kaaba when they besieged holy Mecca. To add a further graft of villainy, this dynasty is of course descended from Abu Sufyan and his witch-like wife Hind who were the great motivators of the pagan opposition to the Prophet Muhammad in his lifetime. So despite their Arab armies riding west into France, south into the Sudan and east into the borders of China no one could ever seriously contemplate the Omayyad caliphate as a role model for true Islam.

Which takes us back right towards the origin of the story. To the first four Caliphs: Abu Bakr, Omer, Uthman and Ali who ruled for less than thirty years from 632-661. This was indeed a time of true heroes, when sovereign rulers cared for the poor, orphans and widows of the community as much as they directed the affairs of the state. When they shopped for their own households in the market place, darned their own clothes, led the prayers and theological discussions, fasted the hardest during the month of Ramadan, led the prayers as Imam and could chant the whole (yet unwritten Qur'an) through the night, and remember the traditions better than any scholar. But even as we venerate this age of fully engaged moral leadership, we must be careful to do one thing. We must begin to detach these rulers from the bloody soaked human glory of the imperial conquests of the Arab Caliphate. Think of Ali, of the endless stories that circulate about his bravery and self-sacrifice as a young soldier fighting during the lifetime of the Prophet but yet nothing is attached to him of a military nature during the period of conquests. For it seems clear through a proper study of the traditions and early historians that their arena of personal authority, their role of direct supervision was centred on the two cities of Mecca and most especially Medina — even if Omar did once famously make the journey to Syria to inspect the garrison bases and even if Abu Bakr did present the armies of Bedouin Arabs with their lance-standards as they rode out of the oasis of Medina. While the first armies of Arab conquest were always led by a very different stamp of man, such vaultingly ambitious, brave and clever generals such as Khalid ibn al Walid and Amr ibn al-As. These two generals might remain role models of Arab masculinity, political dexterity and ferocious bravery but no-one remotely familiar with the early histories can see them as guiding lights of Islamic morality or spirituality. Once again it is useful to recall, that Khalid ibn al Walid and Amr ibn al-As were the chief commanders of the pagan resistance to the Prophet Muhammad before they converted to Islam - just when they recognized that the tide was about to turn. While the early historians also record for us such scoundrels who did so well for themselves from the early days of Empire, the Zayyad's and Mughira ibn Shuba's of the early Arabic Empire, who in their bare-faced sensual self-advancement can only be usefully compared to Flashman or a Maupassant anti-hero. While at such cities as Basra the traditions correctly remember that the first Arab conquests of southern Iraq were often led by their tribal sheikhs, with only a very sketchy sense of connection to the Islamic heartland. So that side by side with the advance of Arab armies with an Islamic banner about them we must also imagine a more nuanced scenario, the disordered migration of Arab clans and tribes into the shattered lands of the Persian and Byzantine Empires. This would have had much in common with how the German tribes, the Franks, Vandals, Anglo-Saxons and Visigoths pouring over the Rhine and occupying the provinces of France, Spain, North Africa and Britain once the formal power of the Roman Empire through its legions had been broken. A fascinating epic indeed, but not for one second was it a conscious attempt to make a heaven on earth.

So what does all this ancient history tell a Muslim looking for a historical role model for a future Islamic state. Be proud as an Arab of the Arab Empires, of the Caliphates of the Omayyads and the Abbasids, just as the Turks will be proud of the vigour of their ancestors carving out the Ottoman and Seljuk Empires, and just as modern Uzbeqs raise statues to Tamburlane and Mongols to Genghis Khan, and the British and French cherish their own violent history of Imperial conquests, but let us all be clear that all this talk of Empires and Caliphates is emotive blood pride and has nothing whatever to do with religion.

And then we must make the final step towards knowledge, and remind ourselves of the political situation at the end of the life of the Prophet when the Caliphate was first forged. Muhammad was interested in all of human nature and linking it with a permanent achievable morality upheld by a compassionate, forgiving conscious universe. His teaching, his moral example, his revelations were all about this direct connection between humankind and the unitary deity. He brilliantly brushed aside the intermediary role of divine kings, priests, temples and acolytes to connect the Arab speaking humans of his day towards the single, moral centre of the universe. Seen in this bright white revolutionary light it is comically absurd to think that he was interested in systems of government, the title and powers of rulers, their governors, judges and administrators. This is borne out by the example of his life. There was no Empire, no Caliphate declared or dreamt about during his lifetime. Indeed Omar and most of the Companions believed that they were the last generation and that the world would end before the Prophet died.

It is true that the Prophet appointed commanders for some three dozen military expeditions and embassies, but this was as an essential need of both warfare and the Arabian Desert. And it is clear that once they returned to the oasis, just like the Emir of a trading caravan, they surrendered this authority on their safe return to the oasis. For the whole frame of Muhammad's teaching was to break these fences between man and the deity, and in the process make each and every human responsible for their own moral choices. Each time you erect an authority figure, who thinks on behalf of other humans, who decides what is wrong and right, you weaken the first and essential purpose of Islam, which can usefully be imagined as an electrical charge connecting humans to their God. Who is closer to you than their jugular vein.

But to remind oneself of true early Islam, it is always useful to follow the actual day by day narrative of the Prophet's life. By the time he undertook what is known as the Farewell Pilgrimage (631 AD) it seems clear that he knew that his life was coming towards its end. This pilgrimage drew together the largest concentration of sincere Muslims of Arabia that he was likely to ever address. So does he use the occasion to delegate authority, appoint a succession council, create a hierarchy of officials, in short sort out anything of a political, financial or administrative nature. No, he does not. Because he does what he thinks most important, which is to recite the Qur'an in its entirety twice and make a skilful, quick summary of his teaching in his very public Farewell Sermon. Half way back on the journey from Mecca to Medina at the campsite near the rock pool of Ghadir Khum, he makes some sort of declaration in favour of his son-in-law Ali as the male head of his household, which was obviously not considered by his contemporaries at the time to have any political bearing. For all its subsequent importance in Shiite theology this declaration was also something of an afterthought, made after the whole Pilgrimage was over. It is also a very understandable and practical decision for Ali was not only the father of Muhammad's only male grandchildren, his cousin, first disciple and close confidante, but was also the son of Abu Thalib,

Muhammad's uncle who had been the recognised sheikh of Muhammad's own Hashim clan throughout the Prophet's early life.

Then very shortly after Muhammad returns home to Medina he makes an appointment that is bitterly resented by most of his followers, for out of loyalty to his adopted son and ex-slave boy Zayd (killed in a disastrous recent battle on the Syrian frontier) he appoints Zayd's own son, the very young and inexperienced Usama, to be the leader of the next military expedition. In the grumbling from the clan chiefs about this appointment (the most important tactical one in Muhammad's gift) we have not evidence of treason but a wonderfully revealing instance of how the Prophet was considered by his contemporaries, to be both fallible about the affairs of this world, whilst at one at the same time being revered beyond all men as the mouthpiece of the divine. In this one instance one can emphatically see the clear division between temporal and spiritual authority in the early Islam. It was whilst trying to sort out this squabble that the Prophet went one night to pray over the dead in the cemetery, 'O people of the graves! Happy are you that you are so much better off than men here. Dissensions have come like waves of darkness one after another the last being worse than the first.'

Once again crucially revealing evidence that the Muslim community was, even in its heyday of being led by the Prophet, also full of discussion, multiple view points and disobedience. There never has been a golden period of hallowed political obedience in Islam, not then, not now. After this prayer session the Prophet was caught in the grips of a mortal fever, but in the mosque that morning despite being visibly ill he continued to try and urge his followers to march out and place themselves under young Usamahs' command. This was only half-heartedly achieved by his most obediently loyal followers who then drifted back to the oasis once the news of the seriousness of his fever became better known. Indeed the fever so overwhelmed him that for the next ten days he was cared for in Aisha's hut. In this period of devastating weakness he asked Abu Bakr to lead the prayers but revived enough to lead them himself on Monday morning. It was his last public action.

Abu Bakr had been relieved to see the Prophet attend the dawn prayers that Monday and so left Muhammad's courtyard in order to visit one of his wives, Habiba bint Kharidja, who lived out in a farmhouse in the Medina hamlet of al-Sunh. By midday he – and everyone in the entire oasis - knew something had gone terribly wrong. The scattered hamlets of Medina were filled with the screams of men and the wails of the women (no matter that the Prophet had detested too public a display of emotion). By the time that Abu Bakr returned to the mosque courtyard the place was in total uproar. Abu Bakr slipped through the hysterical displays of grief and quietly entered his daughter Aisha's hut. A thick cloak covered in the embroidery of the Yemen was draped over the still body of Muhammad. He raised the cloth to kiss the forehead of the dead Messenger of God and murmured, 'You are dearer to me than my father and mother. You have tasted death as God decreed: a second death will never overtake you.' Then he pushed his way through the crowd and tried to interrupt Omar, who was ranting at the crowd outside, threatening them with the direst punishments if he heard any more rumours about the death of the Prophet. He promised to cut off both the hands and feet of any man who dared whisper that Muhammad was dead. Omar tried to explain to the crowd 'he has gone to his Lord as Moses ibn Imran went and was hidden from his people for forty days, returning to them after it was said that he died. By God, the apostle will return as Moses returned…' Perhaps he also imagined the reborn Prophet leading them to a triumphant military victory, just as the tribes of Israel had been allowed to enter the Promised land only after the death of Moses. Much later he would confess to another hidden belief: that the Prophet would not die until he had prayed over the grave of the last of the believers.

Nothing that Abu Bakr could do, neither tugging at his clothes nor trying to whisper in his ear, could halt the passionate flow of Omar's rhetoric. Abu Bakr gave up this unequal struggle and moved away to another corner of the courtyard where his calm, measured voice gradually summoned some of the people over to listen to him.

'O people. To those who used to worship Muhammad, Muhammad is dead. But for those who used to worship God, God is alive and can never die.' He reminded the crowd of the Prophet's own Qur'anic recitation of his mortality, 'Muhammad is but a messenger, messengers the like of whom have passed away before him. Will it be that, when he died or is slain, you will turn back on your heels?'

Omar's passion dried up at this sound. In his own recollection, 'directly I heard Abu Bakr ...my feet were cut beneath him and I fell to the ground.' If this was the reaction of Omar, most steadfast and iron-willed of believers, the panic that filled the hearts of other Muslims can be readily imagined. One contemporary recalled the mood of that day as being 'like sheep on a rainy night'. It was ironic that old Abu Bakr, known to be a highly sensitive man, not strong of voice and given to tears when he recited the Qur'an, should have yet emerged as by far the strongest character at this critical moment.

Then a messenger came hurrying to Abu Bakr and Omar to inform them that a meeting of some of the chieftains of the Medina clans had been called. Although many commentators like to give a whiff of treachery to this gathering, they had every right to assemble. The population of Medina had made a highly personal oath of loyalty to the Prophet Muhammad, who as their appointed judge-like arbitrator had not only ended the recurrent civil wars of the oasis but had led them from victory to victory. They had no desire to sink back into civil war, and now that their chosen chief had gone, they were in need of another guide. Undoubtedly the man who had called them together, Sad ibn Ubada of the Beni Sadah clan, had political aspirations, but these might have only extended to a recognised position within oasis politics. Omar had by now recovered his poise and bravely insisted that he would lead a delegation of the Meccan Muslims – the Muhajirin – to this critically important meeting of the Ansar – the Muslims of Medina. They were met by 'two honest fellows' who advised Omar to call his own meeting of Muhajirin and leave the men of Medina to their own deliberations. Omar characteristically brushed this advice aside and forcibly declared, 'By God, we will go to them.' They arrived at a critical moment but they were also clearly impressed by the implicit Muslim faith that governed the actions of every speaker. Omar was incensed to hear the Muhajirin described as just another clan who had been welcomed into the Medina oasis, and was preparing a suitably proud and invective reply when Abu Bakr lent across, lightly touched his arm and whispered, 'Gently Omar.' Abu Bakr was right: an aggressive speech from Omar at this juncture would have backfired. As Omar later described it, 'He [Abu Bakr] was a man with more knowledge and dignity than I, and by God he did not omit a single word which I had thought of but he uttered in his inimitable way better than I could ever have done.' So in a measured, calm and tactful speech Abu Bakr repeated the Prophet's praise for the men of Medina but insisted that now that Islam had become an Arabian-wide phenomenon they would have to choose a candidate from out of the Prophet's own Quryash tribe from the city of Mecca if they wished to retain the respect of the great Bedouin tribes, the kings of Yemen and the borderland chiefs in Syria and Oman. Abu Bakr, who was of venerable age, finished by proposing two candidates for the assembly to choose from. He made no mention of himself. A clamour of excited voices soon filled the hall as Abu Bakr's ideas were debated by the rival clan chiefs of Medina. A respected old sheikh called out, ' I am the rubbing post and the fruitful propped-up palm' (a traditional oasis idiom which asserted that he was a greybeard whose good advice had proved fruitful over many a long year) and then suggested that the men of Medina elect one ruler and the men of Mecca another. This intriguing suggestion was broken by Omar who roared out, 'Who will willingly take precedence over the man that the Prophet ordered to lead the prayer!' It was an unanswerable assertion. Omar made use of the brief silence to quickly seize the hand of Abu Bakr and pledge public allegiance to him. One by one his example was followed by the small delegation of Muhajirin that accompanied them. The solemnity of the occasion swept the clansmen of Medina along in a surge of emotion and they soon too plighted their troth. In the process Sad ibn Ubada (who seems to have weakened by fever) was pushed aside and smothered.

The next day at the dawn prayers this accidental coup was formalised. As the worshippers filed into the mosque, Abu Bakr was already sitting in the pulpit and led the prayers. Immediately these were over, Omar got up and addressed the packed ranks of the assembled faithful. He repeated his oath of loyalty (the *bay'a*) and described Abu Bakr to the congregation by quoting from the Qur'an 9:40, 'the best of you, the Companion of God's Messenger, the second of two when they were both in the cave' (when they fled from the persecution at Mecca). With one voice the congregation acclaimed Abu Bakr as 'Khalifat Rasul Allah', the successor to the Messenger of God. The title Khalifa can also be translated as 'Vice-regent' and by long-established usage is customarily rendered 'Caliph' in English.

Thus was the first Caliph acclaimed, by acclamation of the assembled faithful at the end of the morning prayer after a highly confusing succession of events. Abu Bakr's reply to the congregation took the form of an oath in exchange, just as Muhammad had replied to that first midnight pledge of faith to the people of Medina at Aqaba. It should be engraved in stone on the gates of every Presidential palace and in the public reception hall of every Muslim monarch. It should be stamped on the front of every identity card and passport so that the police and security forces of the Muslim world are daily reminded of this great and noble contract between the governed and the governor:

> I have been given the authority over you, and I am not the best of you. If I do well, help me; and if I do wrong, set me right. Truth consists in loyalty and disregard for truth is treachery. The weak amongst you shall be strong in my eyes until I have secured his rights, if God wills it: and the strong amongst you shall be weak with me until I have wrested from him the rights of others, if God wills it. Obey me for so long as I obey God and His Messenger. But if I disobey God and His Messenger, you owe me no obedience. Arise from your prayer, God have mercy upon you!

Ali had clearly been too preoccupied by the burial of the Prophet to take part in the discussions over the succession. As a thirty year old young father he may not have wished to be nominated as the political successor to Muhammad – indeed when encouraged to put forward his candidature by both his uncle Abbas and the old leader of Mecca, Abu Sufyan, he indignantly rejected the suggestion. But he most certainly expected to have been consulted and listened too. He was certainly the most conspicuous of the Muslims to abstain from joining in the oath to Abu Bakr in the subsequent few months. During this period Ali had withdrawn to his house where he now heard with a leaden heart the last whispered conversation that had taken place between the Prophet and his daughter Fatimah. She had been seen to weep and then to laugh. She now explained to her husband that she had wept when her father had warned her that he was about to die. 'Then he told me that I would be the first of the people of his house to follow him' and therefore I laughed. This was to be Ali's heritage: the death of his beloved wife just a few months after the death of his adopted father, his cousin, his mentor, his father-in-law, Muhammad the Prophet of God. To make things worse, an unpleasant row had developed between the ailing Fatimah and Abu Bakr. As Aisha would explain to later generations of Muslims, the Messenger of God died without leaving a dinar, a dirham, a sheep or a camel to his name while his battle armour was in pawn to a Jewish merchant for thirty measures of barley. His family did not expect anything other from a man who so passionately taught that every believer had a duty to care for the poor, the old, the sick, orphans and the needs of travellers. However they did expect that his lands – especially those in Khaybar and Fadak oasis – would pass onto them. Abu Bakr refused to allow this, quoting as his evidence a remembered saying of the Prophet: 'We do not have heirs, whatever we leave is alms.' All that Abu Bakr allowed the surviving daughters and grandsons to directly inherit was a parcel of property in the oasis: seven small garden plots that had been left to the Prophet in the will of a childless Jewish convert (from Medina's Beni Nadir clan) to Islam who had died at the battle of Uhud. These little gardens were made into an endowment that was jointly administered by Ali. Fatimah was furious and Ali quoted the Qur'an in her support, for 26:16 gives the clear example of how the prophets of old had heirs: 'Solomon became David's heir and Zachariah said who will inherit from me..' It was to no avail. While Fatimah was alive the row was impossible to heal. Only after her death was Ali able to explain his position in a face-to-face meeting with Abu Bakr. Ali declared, 'I know well your pre-eminence. But you did confront us with a thing accomplished, leaving us no say in the matter, and we felt that we had some claim as the nearest in kinship to the Messenger of God.'

No one can find a blueprint that sets up a God-ordered system of Islamic government, a Caliphate, from out of this chance succession of events. It was messy, full of compromise and accommodation, like all political life. But these good men persevered in attempting to live a good life, and in the process preserved the message and example of the Prophet Muhammad. In this they are heroes. But as a Moroccan friend once confessed to me, with both laughter and sadness in his eyes, 'I know history is but day-dreaming and that our real life is in our actions but that is also our greatest freedom because no-one can prohibit them, and the angels do not record our dreams.'

ISLAM AND THE STATE

Malise Ruthven

In his engaging and perceptive book *The Crisis of Islamic Civilisation*, the former Iraqi minister Ali Allawi tells a story that goes to the heart of the problematic relationship between the idea of Islam, as manifested historically, and the modern state. In the early 1980s a group of modestly affluent British Muslims – most of them converts – determined they should exercise their right as Muslims to migrate to a place of their choosing in *Dar al-Islam*, the land of Islam. After considering a number of Muslim majority countries they chose the United Arab Emirates and headed for Abu Dhabi. Here they arranged to meet the chief *qadi* – a venerable and erudite *'alim* – to whom they presented their petition to settle in the UAE. Their aim, they explained was to perfect their religion: Did not Islam enjoin the believers to leave *dar al-kufr* – the land of unbelief – and migrate to *dar al-Islam*? The chief judge was sympathetic, and asked them to wait while he consulted the authorities. A week later, he met the group again. With tears in his eyes, he informed them their request had been denied. They returned to Britain, disappointed. 'The country to which they had wanted to emigrate, the UAE, had turned them down', comments Allawi, 'citing impossibly restrictive and discriminatory immigration policies. The whole notion of an Islamdom (*Dar-al-Islam*) where a Muslim can travel and settle freely had been thrown out of the window.'

The concept of *Dar al-Islam* sits uneasily with the reality of the modern state, with its right to restrict the movement of people across its frontiers (unless, of course, it has agreed to suspend those rights under treaty, as in the currently contested and contentious case of the European Union.) The days are long past when the fourteenth century traveller Ibn Battuta could ride in caravans or dhows from Tangier to China and back, calling in on the Maldives to serve as a judge, because of his prestige as a Muslim learned in Arabic. Yet the legacy of a millennium or more when territorial boundaries were not yet fixed, and political power was calibrated through human filters disposing of varying degrees of force and legitimacy, is not so easily erased from the collective memory, from what the late Mohamed Arkoun called the 'social imaginary'. The modern national state with its fortresses of walls and fences, its armies of border guards, its currency of passports and visas, and its claimed monopoly over the use of lethal force, is a recent invention. Moreover, as Wael Hallaq, a leading scholar of Islamic law argues, its provenance is European.

In his somewhat polemical book *The Impossible State: Islam, Politics and Modernity's Moral Predicament*, Hallaq takes issue with Islamists who seek to re-introduce or impose a form of Sharia governance on the basis of modern state power. The overwhelming majority of Muslims, he acknowledges, wish for a restoration of the Sharia as a spiritual resource, a connection with the divine and a way 'to discipline the inner self'. His claim is supported by research which suggests that there are solid majorities in favour of establishing the Sharia among Muslims in the Middle East and North Africa, sub-Saharan Africa, South Asia and Southeast Asia including 71% of Muslims in Nigeria, 72% in Indonesia, 74% in Egypt and 89% in the Palestinian territories. Under modern conditions, however, this aspiration poses a central difficulty. Historically the Sharia was not applied as state law: it was the law to which Muslim rulers – whose powers were much more restricted than those exercised by modern governments – were themselves subject, in theory, if not always in practice.

> Islamic governance (that which stands parallel to what we call 'state' today) rests on moral, legal, political, social and metaphysical foundations that are dramatically different from those sustaining the modern state. In Islam it is the community (*ummah*) that displaces the nation of the modern state. The Community is both abstract and concrete, but in either state is governed by same moral rules…Whereas the nation-state is the end of all ends, knows only itself, and therefore is metaphysically the ultimate foundation of sovereign will, the Community and its individual members are a means to a greater end. This implies that the Community itself neither possesses sovereignty nor does it have – in the sense the modern state has – an autonomous political or legal will, since the sovereign is God and God alone.'

Hallaq's views about divine sovereignty chime in with those of Sayyid Qutb, the Muslim Brotherhood intellectual executed by President Nasser in 1966, and those of Abu Ala Maududi, the Indo-Pakistani ideologue and founder of the Jamaat-i Islami movement and party. Both of these influential Islamist thinkers argued that the 'sovereignty of God' should have primacy in matters of human governance, though they differed in detailing how the idea of divine sovereignty could be given practical effect. For Hallaq the Sharia constitutes 'a colossal project of building a moral-legal empire whose foundational and structural impulse is summed up in the ever continuing attempt to discover God's will.' The project, if one may call it such, entails a 'dialectic between the sociological and the metaphysical, between the Community as a worldly society and its persistent attempts to locate itself in a particular moral cosmology.' This realism about the world, he concludes 'was always placed in a metaphysical context, just as this metaphysics was constantly teased out in the realism of mundane existence.'

Drawing on the rich and varied critiques of the Enlightenment by the likes of Michel Foucault, Christopher Lasch, Charles Taylor, and John Gray, Hallaq sees the modern state as a fundamentally amoral structure whose agendas of economic growth and well-being have been emptied of transcendental meaning. Despite its claim to be founded on Enlightenment principles of liberty and rationality, the modern state has signally failed to prevent social injustice, social fragmentation and the 'Project of Destruction' by virtue of human agency. In short, the modern state is incompatible with Sharia morality. Since 'there can be no Islam without a moral-legal system that is anchored in a metaphysic' and 'there can be no modern state without its own sovereignty and sovereign will', the modern state 'can no more be Islamic than Islam can come to possess a modern state.'

One may conclude from Hallaq's analysis that Islamists who seek to impose the Sharia through the coercive apparatus of the modern state system are committing a category error. 'For Muslims today to adopt the positive law of the state and its sovereignty means in no uncertain terms the acceptance of a law emanating from political will, a law made by men who change their ethical and moral standards as modern conditions require.' Whereas in the past, the 'discursive world of Islam and its forms of knowledge were pervaded by oral prescriptions and by Sharia-prescribed ethical behaviour', its modern applications are 'permeated by positivism, politics and the political, by concepts of citizenship and political sacrifice'.

Historically, the Sharia's moral imperatives were effected outside the domain of the state: 'The political absolutism that Europe experienced, the merciless serfdom of feudalism, the abuses of the church, the inhuman realities of the Industrial Revolution, and all that which made revolutions necessary in Europe were not the lot of Muslims', who, comparatively speaking, 'lived for over a millennium in a far more egalitarian and merciful system and, most importantly for us, under a rule of law that modernity cannot fairly blemish with critical detraction'. Yet, unlike many western critics of the modern state system and the Enlightenment assumptions that underpin it, as well as theorists of globalisation who question its future viability, 'modern Islamist thinkers and scholars take modern state for granted and, in effect as a timeless phenomenon'. An egregious example of this thinking cited by Hallaq is a 2011 statement by the Muslim Brotherhood which insists that the modern nation-state

> does not stand in contradiction with the implementation of Islamic Sharia, because Islam is the highest authority in Muslim lands, or so it should be. With its mechanisms, regulations, laws and systems, the modern state – if it contains no contradiction to the founding and indubitable principles of Islam – does not preclude the possibility of being developed ...[so that] we can benefit from it in achieving for ourselves progress and advancement.

The ousting in July 2013 of Mohamed Morsi, the first elected Muslim Brotherhood President of Egypt, in the military coup masterminded by his defence minister 'Abd al-Fatah al-Sissi – now president – could well be seen as proving Hallaq's point. The Brothers and their 'moderate Islamists' supporters believed, during the turbulent months that toppled Mubarak, that they could take over existing state institutions on the basis of their electoral strength, with the aim of Islamising society once they had consolidated their power. Lacking a strategic sense, however, they scared and antagonised not only the secular parties who wanted to end the regime, but also the Salafist al-Nour party, a group that could have been their allies. The Salafists were frustrated by what they saw as the deliberately weak representation of their party in Morsi's cabinet, and the Brotherhood's tendency to monopolise the Islamist discourse. Instead of cooperating with other parties to achieve a broad consensus on a post-Mubarak constitution, the Brothers sought to defer the drafting of a new constitution till after the parliamentary elections they believed would enhance their leverage.

In his searing critique of Morsi's year in office, Ashraf el-Sherif shows how Brotherhood's reluctance to share power with the other anti-Mubarak forces lay at the heart of its failure to govern successfully, enabling the old regime to reassert itself on the basis of the popular Tamarod protests in July 2013. The failure seems surprising, in view of the restraint that the Brotherhood and other Islamist groups, including the Salafists, had exercised in the course of the tumultuous demonstrations that preceded the toppling of Mubarak in February 2011. As many observers noted at the time, Islamist slogans such as 'Islam is the solution' were conspicuous by their absence in Tahrir Square. As el-Sherif notes,

> Brotherhood leaders were aware that the protests were not dominated by Islamist ideas but rather oriented toward the broad goals of freedom and social justice. They were also aware that other political groups and movements were instrumental in mobilising demonstrators and writing the narrative of the uprising. As a result, Brotherhood leaders were careful not to alienate other protesters by expressing their Islamist views too overtly.

Once in power, however, the picture changed drastically. Instead of seeking to rule by consensus in co-operation with other parties, both Islamist and secular, the Brotherhood relied on a combination of its own system of governance and the 'deep state' apparatus it inherited from Mubarak. To the consternation of those who thought the Brotherhood's inclusion in the political process would lead to its democratisation and moderation, it sought instead to achieve a position of political dominance by using the electoral clout it enjoyed by virtue of its suburban, rural and provincial constituencies. In the heady days of the revolution that led to Mubarak's downfall

> The Brotherhood viewed the unrest as a heavenly gift that rewarded the group for its past sacrifices and eradicated all constraints that Mubarak had placed on it. Brotherhood leaders were therefore totally occupied with how to seize this golden opportunity, maximise their political gains, and dominate the post-Mubarak political sphere — regardless of the implications of their approach on the prospects for Egypt's democratic transformation and even their own long-term interests. But given the magnitude of past government failures and

the Brotherhood's own lack of a genuine political project, voluntarily opting to take full responsibility for the post-Mubarak political system was political suicide.

The model often advocated by the Brotherhood and its supporters was that of Turkey's 'Islamist' Justice and Development Party (AKP) led by its founder Recep Tayyip Erdoğan since 2001 and Turkey's Prime Minister from 2002 till his elevation to the presidency in 2014. When Erdoğan visited Cairo in September 2011, he received a rapturous welcome, with thousands of Egyptians holding up posters and carrying him shoulder high among the crowds. It seems doubtful, however, if Egyptian or indeed other Arab supporters of the 'Turkish model' were fully conversant with that country's modern history. For all its historic claims to Islamic legitimacy, the AKP de-emphasises its Islamist roots, regarding itself as a 'pro-Western mainstream party with a "conservative" social agenda and a firm commitment to liberal market values.' Indeed Erdoğan himself raised some Islamist hackles when he told Mona al-Sazly of Dream TV that he favoured 'secularism' for Egypt. The secularity of the Turkish state - whereby religion and government occupy separate spheres - has deep foundations, going back to the *tanzimat* (administrative) reforms undertaken by the Ottoman rulers in response to pressure from their Russian and Austrian rivals and to the rebellions by their Greek, Bulgarian, Serbian and other European subjects that shook the empire throughout the nineteenth century, culminating in the Arab revolt (1916-18). As el-Sherif points out, the situation of the AKP in Turkey is completely different from that of the Brotherhood in Egypt. In Turkey, Sufi, social, religious, and educational movements became the backbone of the broader Islamist movement developed in the course of nearly a century of secular government forged by Ataturk, who himself was building on decades of Ottoman reforms in which religion became increasingly subject to state control.

Put briefly, the Brotherhood, despite their long drawn-out accommodation with the 'deep state' under Mubarak (with members permitted to sit in parliament as independents, although the organisation itself was banned), proved unfit to hold executive power. Given the parlous state of the Egyptian economy, an intelligent strategy would have been to form alliances with other parties, so they could share the burden – and the inevitable blame – for the administrative chaos and economic turmoil consequent on the revolution. Instead they tried to 'go it alone', following their instincts for top-down authoritarian governance.

> Organisationally, the rigidity of the Brotherhood's structure, which lacked meritocracy, inclusiveness, and transparent decision making, contributed to the movement's inability to adapt to a rapidly shifting political landscape. These combined failures made the Brotherhood end up seeming to many Egyptians as a vestige of the old system rather than a herald of a forward-looking new Egyptian polity.

The Brotherhood's failure, and inevitable unpopularity, made it all too easy for the old regime to restore the status quo ante on the wave of popular dissent it may have manipulated, but did not invent. The movement is now banned as a terrorist organisation. Morsi is in jail, on charges that include ordering the shooting of protestors and conspiring with Hamas, Hezbollah and Iran's Revolutionary Guard to commit acts of terror in Egypt. By contrast Mubarak is out of jail – cleared of all the charges of corruption and killings that arose from the brief revolution. For the time being, the counter-revolution – overseen by Sissi, a former chief of intelligence under Mubarak – seems complete.

'Counter-revolution' seems an obvious description, given that many observers have seen the Arab uprisings as comparable or analogous to the revolutions (and subsequent reactions) that took place throughout in Europe in 1848. A more useful analogy, however, may involve putting the clock back a further two centuries – to the 1648 Peace of Westphalia, widely seen as the landmark event that gave rise to the modern state system. The Latin formula *cuius regio, eius religio* ('who the ruler, his the religion') – adapted from the earlier Augsberg settlement (1555) that failed to prevent the bitter Thirty Years War (1618-48) allowed rulers of the principalities of the Holy Roman Empire to choose between Protestantism or Catholicism. By allowing the ruler discretion in the choice of religion it actually increased his leverage over his subjects, making state religion a reality. While individuals were permitted religious choice in theory, Westphalia effectively consolidated the notion that rulers could determine the religion of state. Formally speaking, there existed an element of toleration, of personal choice in religion. In reality, however the national interests and goals of states (and later nation-states) were widely assumed to go beyond those of any citizen or ruler. States became the primary institutional agents in what developed into an international system of relations.

The Peace of Westphalia is considered to have ended attempts to impose supranational authority (whether papal or imperial) on European states. The 'Westphalian' doctrine of statehood that emerged culminated in nineteenth century ideas of nationhood as 'imagined communities' whereby peoples such as Irish, Hungarians, Poles, Germans and Italians claiming a common ethnic, linguistic or cultural heritage demanded recognition as national states. The legitimacy of states as political actors shifted from widely held notions of rule by divine appointment or approval towards the doctrine that 'sovereignty' belongs to the people, to be exercised by their duly appointed representatives. Underpinning this idea is a concept of sovereignty based on property rights. The European states of the early modern period emerged in areas of high rainfall where peasants worked the land and where territory and property were coterminous. The social conflicts accompanying urbanisation and political advances brought about the great shift in sovereignty from 'God' to 'the people'.

Vestiges of older notions of divine sovereignty remain in the US pledge of allegiance to 'one Nation under God, indivisible, with liberty and justice for all,' and the English coronation ceremony where the monarch is 'anointed' with holy oil by the Archbishop of Canterbury, the country's chief cleric, using a special filigree spoon in a ritual so sacred that it cannot be filmed or photographed. Internationally speaking, however, the presence or non-presence of a divine element in a nation's conceptual make-up is immaterial to its behaviour as an actor on the world stage today. As Charles Tilly wrote in his seminal 1975 book *The Formation of National States in Western Europe* 'the Europeans and their descendants managed to impose that state system on the entire world,' adding that 'the recent wave of decolonisation has almost completed the mapping of the globe into that system.'

Part of the Westphalian process involves what might be called the 'domestication' or nationalisation of religion. The Peace of Westphalia ended the 30 Years War in Germany, a conflict fuelled by religious zeal and religious hatred, with both sides Catholic and Protestant, believing, as Diarmaid MacCulloch put it, 'that they could effectively eliminate those who took a different view of the Christian message'. A spirit of accommodation – of live and let live – was one of its longer-term outcomes. However, this spirit, exemplified by the 1598 Edict of Nantes granting freedoms to France's protestant minority, ran counter to the requirements of the newly emerging national states, where allegiance to crown or nation required a common ideology of ritual and feeling. The reformation and counter-reformation had led to an increase in the power of states, both Protestant and Catholic, helping to transform them from loose dynastic territories dependent on consent from barons and representative assemblies (in free cities) to tightly organised monarchies, such as the protestant monarchies of Sweden and Brandenburg-Prussia or the Catholic states of France, Spain and the Habsburg empire. Before the ideas of Enlightenment philosophers such as René Descartes or Immanuel Kant could take root, banishing religion from the public realm to the bunkers of private belief, the state appropriated religion as its primary source of legitimacy and demand for national allegiance. A critical moment was Louis XIV's revocation of the Edict of Nantes in 1685, in which the French king tore up the guarantee of tolerance granted to Protestants by his predecessor Henry IV. A monarch who claimed to have been chosen by God enforced religious conformity in order to remove all obstacles to obedience. Louis's action, which led to the mass expulsion of Huguenot Protestants from France (to the benefit of the English economy) may have been an extreme example, but generally speaking religious conformity was the norm until well after the French revolution. National churches (Lutheran in Prussia and Scandinavia, Catholic in France, Iberia, Bavaria, the Austrian empire, the Italian states and Poland, Presbyterian in Scotland, Anglican in England, and contested in Ireland, where attempts to impose Protestantism met Catholic inspired-resistance) were the norm outside of some rare pluralistic exceptions such as Switzerland and the Netherlands.

In contrast with Europe, Islamic pluralism has a long and venerable history. A kind of 'edict of toleration' between Sunnis and Shi'ites became normative from the ninth century. Chase Robinson, a specialist in early Islamic history, has pointed out 'Sunnis and what became mainstream Shi'ites agreed to disagree. Expressed in a variety of ways (including the hadith that 'disagreement in my community is a mercy'), it accommodated what had been irreconcilable positions taken by proto-Sunnis and Shi'ites on matters as grave as the succession to Muhammad himself.'

This does not mean that religious tolerance was universal. In the tenth century, Baghdad was already balkanised between Sunni and Shi'a quarters, with sectarian riots a frequent occurrence. But in comparison with post-reformation Europe, the record of tolerance – over a millennium or more – is impressive. Shi'ite dynasties who held power from the tenth century after the Arab empire foundered allowed Sunni systems of law to coexist alongside the Shi'ite versions. The most enlightened of these dynasties, the Fatimids, who ruled in Egypt, North Africa and Syria-Palestine prior to the Crusades, never imposed their version of Shi'ism as state ideology apart from requiring recognition of the legitimacy of their rule. The approach of Qara Qoyunka or 'Black Sheep Torcomans' who ruled in western Iran, Northern Iraq and Eastern Anatolia in the fourteenth and fifteenth centuries was one of studied ambiguity: coins minted for the Sultan Jahanshah have Sunni inscriptions on one side, Shi'a on the other. Even the dictatorial Asad regime, justifiably execrated for the brutality of its conduct in the Syrian civil war, had an impressive record of religious (as distinct from political) toleration prior to the demonstrations that sparked the current conflict in March 2011.

A natural question rises. If Muslims have a lengthy and generally creditable record of 'agreements to disagree' on issues of religious governance, with Sunnis (like protestants) holding strictly to systems derived from the holy texts, and Shi'as – more like Catholics – recognising the additional authority of 'unwritten spiritual verities' derived from the Hidden Imam and communicated by a trained cadre of religious specialists, why does the hideous spectre of religious conflict loom so vastly today?

While it might seem Eurocentric to invoke the Westphalian precedent, there may be a clue lying here: religious conflict is being exacerbated because Muslim rulers (despite some anti-Western or anti-colonial rhetoric) are following in the path of early modern Europe in enforcing religious conformity in pursuit of statist goals. There are plenty of Muslim precedents for international relations theory: the Qur'an (49:13) addresses humanity, stating 'We created you male and female, and made you into nations and tribes that you may come to know one another. The noblest among you in God's sight are the most pious'. Influential medieval commentators, such as Ibn Taymiyya accepted the plurality of separate states within the *ummah*, with the proviso that the Sultan (authority) had the duty of *hisba* 'to command the good and forbid the evil' with the good (*al-ma'rouf*) understood as the 'known' instructions issuing from divine revelation. Ibn Taymiyya may be the inspiration of modern Islamists who challenge what they regard as the corruption or infidelity of modern Muslim governments, but he can also be used to legitimise state authority. Wahhabism, drawing on the same Hanbalite tradition as Ibn Taymiyya, legitimises the authority of the current Saudi regime, putting forward (in Aziz Al-Azmeh's words) 'a model whose task is to subject local societies with their customs, authorities, devotions and other particularities to a general process of acculturation' in order to prepare them for membership in a commonwealth 'whose linchpin and exclusive raison d'etre is the absolute dominance of the House of Saud.'

It is not difficult to see in this a resemblance to the role of Catholicism under the ancient regime in France, with persecuted or under-privileged Shi'as (and marginalised tribes such as the 'Asiris) having the exclusionary role of the Huguenots. The same étatist logic may be applied to the Saudi's principal regional rival, Iran where Shi'ism has been erected into a state ideology. Here the Sunni minority (around 10 per cent of the population, based mainly in rural Kurdish regions, Lorestan in the west and Baluchistan on the south-eastern border with Pakistan, but with a presence in major cities) complain of persecution and marginalisation, with Sunni imams forbidden from leading prayers at the 'Ids.

Observers see the growing manifestations of sectarian violence in Iraq, Pakistan and of course Syria as being driven in part by the regional rivalry between Iran and Saudi Arabia. In March 2011 the Saudi government sent 1,200 troops across the causeway into Bahrain to assist the Sunni minority regime led by King Hamad bin Isa al-Khalifa, repress the mainly Shi'a movement of popular protest that erupted in the wake of the uprisings in Tunisia and Egypt. At that time the Saudi government claimed, unconvincingly, to be 'unable' to prevent volunteers from joining the Al-Qaeda affiliates in Syria and Iraq who were fighting what they saw as a legitimate jihad against infidel Shi'as backed by Iran. Young men, many of them from well-connected families, were being motivated by the same ideology that brought the Al Saud to power in the 1920s: Muslims not subscribing to the Wahhabi version of Islam – even children – were infidels deserving of death.

The same anti-Shi'a ideology, promoted by Deobandi seminaries in India and Pakistan, ideological bulwarks of the Taliban movement, motivates the violently anti-Shi'a Sipah-i-Sahaba ('Army of the Prophet's Companions') which aims to have Shi'as declared non-Muslims, following the precedent of the Ahmadiyya sect, disenfranchised in 1974. As Rana Tanveer, a Pakistani scholar and journalist observes: 'If Pakistani Sunnis were being radicalised through Saudi funding and patronage, in retaliation Pakistani Shi'as became increasingly sectarian under Iranian influence.' After the Taliban victory in Afghanistan in 1996 tensions increased exponentially, with leading Sunni scholars issuing fatwas declaring Shi'as to be infidels. In 2003, after a massacre of Shi'a Hazaras in Quetta, Balochistan, Hazara leaders managed to expose the anti-Shi'a fatwas previously issued from the major Deobandi seminaries. According to Tanveer 'no one took any notice.'

As many commentators have noted, ISIS or ISIL under its self-appointed caliph, with its penchant for beheadings and the slaughter of people it regards as enemies or infidels, its misogyny and re-adoption of slavery, closely resembles the Saudi culture that gave birth to it. The principal difference between ISIS and Saudi-based Wahhabism is that under the chaotic conditions of Syria and Iraq, groups such as ISIS and Jabhat al-Nusra are free from control by the modernising, decree-based system that now rules in Saudi Arabia itself.

In the more settled polities state religion is now becoming the norm. In Egypt, the Arab world's demographic heartland, the destruction of the Brotherhood vastly exceeds the scale of repression conducted by the Nasser regime after the attempt on the Egyptian president's life in 1954. The confrontations between the Brotherhood and the state, moreover, are happening in the context of violent militancy that was largely absent in Nasser's day. In August 2013 the security forces themselves suffered considerable losses when they cleared the pro-Morsi sit-ins in Rabaa al-Adawiya and al-Nahda squares in Cairo, killing around 1,000 protestors. Unlike the 1950s and 1960s, when Saudi Arabia provided refuge and hospitality for Brothers in exile, with university posts for its leaders, the gates of state sponsorship are closing. The crackdown was supported, if not inspired, by Saudi Arabia and the UAE, both of whom feel threatened by the challenge the Brotherhood poses as a well-organised political force capable of demonstrating that there exists a democratic Islamist alternative to systems of dynastic rule built around hydrocarbon royalties and inherited privilege. On 7 March 2014, Saudi Arabia included the Brotherhood on its list of terrorist organisations, strangling the group's local support in the country as well as aiming to suppress potential threats from jihadist fighters in Syria and Iraq. As el-Sherif explains 'the unwavering support for the Egyptian regime from Saudi Arabia and the United Arab Emirates reflects their fear of the Brotherhood's political and ideological ascendancy in the region.' After Sissi's coup Qatar, the only wealthy Gulf state to have supported the Brotherhood financially and politically via the al-Jazeera network, effectively terminated its support, offering sanctuary to some exiles but expelling others, while refusing money to the organisation for fear of alienating its powerful neighbour.

In the aftermath of the Brotherhood's debacle, Islamic legitimacy is being increasingly appropriated by the state. Al-Azhar, Egypt's foremost religious institution, has joined with the Ministry of Religious Endowments to curtail the religious space, appointing preachers and controlling the provision of charity. Preachers, who must be government-licensed, have to sign up to a code of ethics forbidding discussion of politics, with smaller mosques banned from holding Friday prayers. The state take-over includes some 7,000 Salafi-oriented mosques previously encouraged for their non-political, quietist approach, after reports of a sermon forbidding Muslims from buying interest-bearing government bonds. Themes for sermons to be delivered at permitted mosques are now standardised by the ministry – with hotlines provided for worshippers willing to denounce any preacher who voices dissent. Some 12,000 imams have been dismissed already. Though officials cite the lack of a required license as the reason, many see the dismissals as retaliation for Islamist connections. The ministry's new leadership has dissolved the boards of directors for mosques that the ministry installed under Morsi. Given the existence of hundreds of thousands of unregistered small mosques all over the country and the shortage of qualified preachers, it remains to be seen if al-Azhar and the ministry will succeed in a campaign that bears a striking resemblance to the crackdowns on religious dissent in early modern Europe.

The ongoing struggle between the transnational Islamic ideal that proceeded the era when the Ottomans imitated their imperial Christian rivals by ratcheting up the power of the state at the expense of Muslim freedom is far from limited to Egypt. Faced with the threat posed by its own jihadists angered at its support for the US-led coalition against the Islamic State (IS) in Iraq and Syria and from Muslim Brotherhood sympathisers outraged at its support for Sissi, the Saudi government is now planning to install centrally monitored cameras in every mosque. According to *The Economist*,

> Kuwait has long-installed tape recorders to monitor Friday sermons. Preachers in the neighbouring UAE need not write their own sermons. Except for a few trusted senior clerics they read instead from a text delivered weekly by the government department for religious affairs that also pays their salaries. 'Protecting Youth from Destructive Ideas' and 'Our National Flag, Symbol of Affiliation and Loyalty' provided two stimulating recent topics.

The same magazine states that Tunis's secular government – which omitted any reference to the Sharia in its new constitution after lengthy deliberations with all the parties, including al-Nahda, its Muslim Brotherhood affiliate – has restored state control over its mosques, while neighbouring Morocco televises Ramadan sermons by the king who claims the title of *amir al-mu'inin* – Commander of the Faithful.

The state control of Islam is an ongoing project. It is failing where the political order is being disrupted, as in Syria, Iraq, Yemen and Somalia, and will continue to fail so long as there are significant numbers of unemployed, alienated or disenfranchised youths – in Muslim majority countries, or in Western diasporas – who are drawn to the utopian vision of a transnational caliphate where Muslims can range freely across the vast territories of the *ummah* without the constraints imposed by post-Westphalian territorial system, with its rigid barriers and controls. The doctrine that sovereignty (*hakimiyya*) belongs to God as distinct from 'the people' – an attitude widely shared by jihadists as well as advocates of the Islamist state, such as Qutb and Maududi – can of course be dismissed as a demand for totalitarian power on the part of those claiming to be God's representatives, as manifested by those Shi'a mullahs now holding sway in the Islamic Republic of Iran. But it can also have other, more positive resonances in a world facing global warming and a growing battery of environmental threats. Anthropologists who have studied segmentary societies where pastoralists use the land at different seasons have shown how the holy men who 'speak for God' act as mediators in disputes over land-use. In transhumance societies the idea that the 'earth belongs to God' can be structurally meaningful, a tool for social and ecological management. It seems ironic that in the rush for development so many Muslim governments have come to neglect the rubric that the 'earth belongs to God', or have turned it on its head, by using modern technologies to defy the limitations of an environment once deemed to have been subject to the divine order.

The vision of divine sovereignty is all the more vibrant as modern electronic communications tend to de-couple cultures from their territorial bases, creating the illusion of frontier-free world. Freed from the bonds of nationality, people may come to enjoy more free-ranging lifestyles not unlike those described by Hallaq or by Marshall Hodgson in the sections on medieval Islam in his great trilogy *The Venture of Islam*, with the added advantage of modern conveniences. Such a vision, however distant from the present, would offer a more attractive version of a revitalised Islamic world than the cruel, misogynistic and puritanical versions apparently on offer from today's Islamist militants. In the longer term, the subjection of Islam to state power may prove a temporary phase. Like state control of religion in Europe it may be a holding operation – a prelude to an Enlightenment where the bonds of religion are loosened and faith becomes individual and personal. Historically speaking religious toleration is the outcome of religious conflict: as the French philosopher Pierre Bayle (1647-1706), who was born a Protestant and converted to Catholicism, before reverting to Protestantism, put it: God is 'too benevolent a being to be the author of anything so pernicious as the revealed religions which carry in themselves the inexterminable seeds of war, slaughter and injustice.' But state religion is unlikely to be dispensed with as a prerequisite for the homogenisation beloved of nation-states. For good or ill, the nation-state is here to stay. As the Syrian-born political scientist BassamTibi explains, 'almost the entire world is now the dominion of secular nation-states on the Westphalian model that originated in Europe. This is a political reality, not as some Muslim scholars contend, a Eurocentric idea of international relations theory.' This seems to be the message proclaimed in mosques which preach 'Our National Flag, Symbol of Affiliation and Loyalty.'

ISBN: 9781849043014
£16.99 / Paperback / 288pp

Medina in Birmingham, Najaf in Brent

Inside British Islam

INNES BOWEN

Muslim intellectuals may try to define something called British Islam, but the truth is that as the Muslim community of Britain has grown in size and religiosity, so too has the opportunity to found and run mosques which divide along ethnic and sectarian lines.

Just as most churches in Britain are affiliated to one of the main Christian denominations, the vast majority of Britain's 1600 mosques are linked to wider sectarian networks: the Deobandi and Tablighi Jamaat movements with their origins in colonial India; the Salafi groups inspired by an austere form of Islam widely practiced in Saudi Arabia; the Islamist movements with links to religious political parties in the Middle East and South Asia; the Sufi movements that tend to emphasise spirituality rather than religious and political militancy; and the diverse Shi'ite sects which range from the orthodox disciples of Grand Ayatollah Sistani in Iraq to the Ismaili followers of the pragmatic and modernising Aga Khan. These affiliations are usually not apparent to outsiders, but inside Britain's Muslim communities sectarian divides are often fiercely guarded by religious leaders.

This book, of which no equivalent volume yet exists, is a definitive guide to the ideological differences, organisational structures and international links of the main Islamic groups active in Britain today.

'After a decade of fear-mongering, when Islam was portrayed as a unitary threat to the West, here comes a book that cuts through the hysteria. In this short and very readable volume, Bowen shows the complexity and nuances of Islam in Britain. This is a must-read for all people who want to understand the changing nature of Britain and its Muslim communities.' — Marc Sageman, author of *Leaderless Jihad: Terror Networks in the Twenty-First Century*

WWW.HURSTPUBLISHERS.COM/BOOK/MEDINA-IN-BIRMINGHAM-NAJAF-IN-BRENT

41 GREAT RUSSELL ST, LONDON WC1B 3PL
WWW.HURSTPUBLISHERS.COM
WWW.FBOOK.COM/HURSTPUBLISHERS
020 7255 2201

MUHAMMAD AND KHADIJA

Kecia Ali

We tell stories, and stories are powerful – none more so than stories about our sacred past. Told repeatedly, tales become truth. We forget that they were once told differently, or not told at all. Stories told and retold lead us to expect certain outcomes. Stories that break patterns may be rejected, or mis-heard, or ignored. But sometimes, told often enough, new versions of old stories take root. Stories help make sense of who we are and how we are to live in the world. Among other things, we tell stories about love, about mar-riage, about sex. Our stories reflect our deeply held values and deeply rooted and unexamined assumptions.

Stories about sacred figures are not the only tool we have in the quest to end persistent gender inequalities in families, communities, and societies. Historical knowledge helps. Muslim advocates for women's rights have pointed out, correctly, that Muslims have a wide array of expectations for men and women across space and time. There is no universal, trans-historical 'Islamic' role for women – indeed, no uniform set of laws governing Muslims across the globe now, or in the past. Take the example of children. The current fashion among many Muslims for describing homemaking and childcare as tasks for which females are biologically suited diverges from earlier ways of thinking. Classical thought about marriage foregrounded a wife's sexual duties. Caring for children was simply part of life – delegated to servants when possible – not a dedicated calling requiring a special temperament. In other words, Muslims today already diverge from earlier norms in striking and unrecognised ways. The neo-traditional vision of homemaker wife-and-mother and breadwinner husband-head-of-household pretends seamless continuity with an ideal Islamic past. In reality, it rewrites that past.

Muslim feminist scholarship criticises and historicises this neo-patriarchal vision. But as cultural critic and theorist bell hooks reminds us, it is insufficient to criticise the status quo; we must offer a compelling alternative.

CRITICAL MUSLIM 14, APRIL–JUNE 2015

To be convincing, that alternative ideal must draw from authoritative sources. Scholars, activists, and ordinary Muslim women's accounts of egalitarian marriage have two main touchstones. The first is the account of creation of spouses 'from a single self' or 'from a single soul.' (Qur'an 4:1) This reciprocal relationship, originating in sameness according to theologian Amina Wadud's now widely accepted interpretation, stands as a basis for much thinking about marriage. The second is Prophet Muhammad's marriage to Khadija.

Muhammad and Khadija are a compelling ideal for advocates of egalitarian marriages. Khadija was older, wealthier, and in a position of power: as Muhammad's employer, she was in no way subordinate or submissive, which was, we hear, despite the patriarchal environs of sixth century Arabia. Theirs was a long-term monogamous marriage; so long as she lived, his biographers tell us, he took no other wife. She was the only woman to bear him children who survived infancy. At her death, he was devastated by grief. Though he remarried, Khadija remained the ideal – to the jealousy of at least one of his later wives.

These particulars have long formed part of prophetic biography. Khadija's centrality to discussion of Muhammad's marriages is not ancient, though. For many centuries, Khadija the Grand was a focus of idealisation and devotion, the only one of Muhammad's wives among the four perfect women who will be housed in splendour in paradise. Yet she was marginal to discussions about the 'Mothers of the Believers' in the Qur'an, in the hadith, or in jurisprudence.

One might assume that Khadija's new importance is a result of pro-female-equality readings of the last few decades. Certainly, she has been cited by Muslim women looking for a precedent for (elite) women's work outside the home or seeking support to limit polygyny. However, the changes that have brought Muhammad's marriage to Khadija to the fore in modern stories of his life came earlier and are in some respects deeply conservative.

Starting in the nineteenth century, Muslim biographies began to respond to Western criticisms by defending Muhammad's polygamy or, more precisely, polygyny. One strategy was to emphasise Muhammad's relationship to Khadija, dwelling on its length, its loving tenor, its offspring. The critical and polemical Christian focus on Muhammad's polygyny to which these biographies responded grew out of new ideas about companionate (and by default, monogamous) marriage which were circulating in Europe and elsewhere.

Today, many worldwide take for granted the married couple as the key social unit. Not everyone, and not everywhere, but many more places than was the case a few centuries, or even a few decades, ago. Louis-George Tin, the Martinique born French historian, recently published a book explaining 'the invention of heterosexual culture.' By this, he does not mean physical intercourse between men and women, which is obviously as old as the human race. He means instead the organisation of social and emotional life around sexual relationships between men and women. He argues that heterosexual culture arose in medieval Europe in courtly contexts outside of marriage, eventually, over several centuries, in a series of fits and starts contested by poets, clerics, and doctors, coming to be centred in married couples. In the twentieth century, he argues, the autonomy and centrality of heterosexual coupledom came to be taken for granted. People, he writes, 'had become conditioned to accept heterosexuality *a priori* as the natural expression of human sexuality as a whole and found it impossible to think of it as anything other than a way of life.'

Indeed, it is striking, given the historicisation of homosexuality, how little historicisation of heterosexuality there has been. There is a vibrant debate between those who argue for an essential 'homosexual' orientation or identity and those who argue that sexual orientation is socially constructed. Still, it is clear that the term homosexuality is a nineteenth century invention. An Abbasid courtier having sex with his male slave is not 'homosexual' in the same way as two long-term-partnered Canadian Muslim men seeking an imam to marry them. The men's physical acts may (or may not) be the same, but the meanings attached to them differ radically. This much most would grant – at least most who have read any of the copious writings on the history of sexuality.

Somehow, though, marriage between a man and a woman is discussed as though it were the same thing today as it was a millennium – or even a century – ago. A similar pattern prevails when Christian advocates of 'traditional marriage' attempt to draw a seamless line from biblical texts through to the present day. Yet, as Tin shows, it is not just the legal institution of marriage that has changed but the social ideas associated with marriage and coupledom.

The developments in the intellectual and, to a lesser extent, social history of Europe chronicled by Tin have important parallels with modern developments among Muslims. Modern Arab and South Asian Muslim discourses on gender and sexuality are intertwined with Western writings on the same topics. In a recent book, I discuss the changing ways Muhammad's life has been understood over the centuries by both Muslims and non-Muslims. I show that Muslims and non-Muslims today are actually much closer to each other in their ways of looking at Muhammad's life than either is to members of their own religious groups who lived centuries ago. The ways they talk about his life overlap. This is particularly the case for his marriage with Khadija and, to a lesser extent, with Aisha.

Khadija was once first in a long list of examples that Muhammad's critics used to illustrate his 'depravity'. For centuries, European polemicists wrote that he tricked her into marriage in order to take advantage of her wealth and social standing. In this way, they saw his first marriage as, like his later ones, motivated by ambition and politics. Within the last few centuries, that changed. Now, even Muhammad's detractors laud the marriage with Khadija, and contrast it to his later polygamous marriages, which they see as motivated by lust, more often than ambition. Contemporary polemical authors charge that Muhammad's morality declined as his power increased – thus, a positive view of his marriage to Khadija serves a new type of criticism.

Muslim and sympathetic non-Muslim writers not only share the positive view of Muhammad's marriage to Khadija, they also grant it disproportionate attention in their accounts of his life. This emphasis on Muhammad and Khadija's marriage diverges sharply from premodern Muslim accounts of his life. It is not that those accounts reported trials or tribulations, or denigrated Khadija in any way; far from it. Yet though Khadija played a pivotal role at key moments in Muhammad's life, she was absent from the bulk of the material transmitted about him. His public leadership of the community in Medina transpired after her death, and so relatively little of the hadith corpus concerns her. To read certain recent books about Muhammad's life, one would think Khadija was his only wife.

Khadija, the powerful, older, prominent woman who bolstered the Prophet when he was unsure of himself, who lent him her confidence when he lost his own: that woman is someone to tell stories about. Just last week, a young Muslim woman stood up in a forum on Islam and feminism I was attending to affirm unhesitatingly that Muhammad was a feminist. Her evidence? He married Khadija. A Pakistani biographer wrote that Khadija was divinely chosen to be the prophet's wife and his 'twin preacher' in order to demonstrate that God believes women may work outside the home. Her economic clout and personal involvement in commerce motivated a Saudi organisation supporting women's business to call itself the Khadija bint Khuwaylid Center.

Apart from her personal success, Muslim and non-Muslim authors alike have often come to distinguish between the marriage to Khadija, in which love and affection played a crucial role, and Muhammad's later marriages which were politically motivated. Far from seeing political motivation as reprehensible, as European interpreters at least through the early modern era did, people have come to see marriages motivated by political alliances as understandable, certainly more laudable than those motivated by lustful urges.

The contrast between a marriage built on love and a marriage motivated by pragmatic political considerations is one among many reasons people have begun to focus on marriages to Khadija and Aisha and to oppose them to one another.

The political motivation for Muhammad's marriage to Aisha is a story many times told. When the Anglican clergyman and polemicist Humphrey Prideaux told it in 1697, he lumped Aisha with Sawda and Hafsa and saw Muhammad's ambition as despicable, marrying to strengthen alliances with the powerful fathers of his brides. Prideaux was writing before anyone was concerned about Aisha's age. Like his peers before the nineteenth century, he was concerned with sexual debauchery rather than female oppression.

Contemporary Muslim and sympathetic non-Muslim stories about Aisha encounter and attempt to mitigate a victim narrative. Instead of a dangerous woman, powerful and controversial, Aisha is largely disempowered. One strand of storytelling attempts to reclaim her power and authority as a public figure who intervened in battle and who was sought after for legal and religious guidance. This celebratory if complicated narrative is attempted in a smattering of novels including, roughly in order of prestige, Assia Djebar's *Far from Medina*, Kamran Pasha's *Mother of the Believers*, and Sherry Jones's *Jewel of Medina*. Though Jones especially makes love a centrepiece of her historical romance, more and more authors downplay any emotional connection in Muhammad's marriage to Aisha, instead contextualising (or simply rewriting) her age. Thus, the focus shifts to the motivations for the marriage, which are assumed to be strategic (rather than religious) and business-like, rather than motivated by divine decree, lust, or anything else. This leaves authors clear to highlight, at some length, the role of love and affection in Muhammad's 'perfect' marriage to and 'happy family life' with Khadija.

To a striking degree, modern stories about Muhammad's marriages are apologetic or polemical – often less stories than arguments with invisible interlocutors. A story about jealousy between co-wives might once have been about elevating one faction in the internecine contests over leadership that followed Muhammad's death, even as it portrayed real human emotion. Today, it is typically a pretext for an excursus about the morality of Islam and its gender politics. Instead of an account of a few individuals in a challenging interpersonal situation, it is possible grounds for indictment of the religion of one fifth of humanity, and for summary judgment of their exemplar.

No wonder stories are so fraught.

Given the possibilities of misreading, criticism, and controversy in accounts of Aisha's life, or Muhammad's multiple wives, what could be less controversial than to emphasise Muhammad's marriage to the upright Lady Khadija?

It turns out that one can overpraise monogamy. In some Muslim circles, how one views polygyny is a litmus test for one's religious bona fides: one needn't practice polygyny, necessarily, but one must accept it as legitimate. For many Muslims, and sympathetic non-Muslim authors, Muhammad's marriage to Khadija represents the norm. His later marriages were exceptional, designed to fulfil pragmatic purposes. Intelligible in context, they are nonetheless not the best model for emulation. Historian Amira Sonbol presents a measured defence of this view when she writes, 'the example of the Prophet is always used to support the contention that men have the right to take multiple wives. This example is problematic because of the essentialist and final way it is presented: as an argument to end all arguments, for who can question the Prophet's actions? Yet the Prophet Muhammad's marital history is rather intriguing and can lead in a different direction. When he was married to Khadija, he never took another wife. Given her importance, which went beyond being his strongest supporter, she may not have been willing for him to take more than one wife.'

By contrast, in other circles – for example, the ummah.net online forum – the idea that 'monogamy is a *sunnah* too' still raises controversy. Some argue that because Muhammad had not taken up the mantle of prophecy when he married Khadija, that marriage does not count as a *sunnah*. Others respond that he remained married to her even after he began receiving revelation, so it counts.

Polygyny, in theory and practice, presents one set of challenges to the widespread idealisation of the monogamously married couple. In the United States, Muslims who live in polygynous relationships – mostly African American – explicitly reject dominant marriage norms. Not only are they rejecting monogamy, they reject, at least in part, the bureaucratic role of the nation-state in regulating their marriages. But one thing they are not rejecting is patriarchy. Indeed, one frequent justification for polygyny is that it enables men to uphold – and women to benefit from – male providership and authority in the household. This bolstering of patriarchal marriage and gender roles is, as noted earlier, ahistorical in crucial ways. But it also responds to deeply felt needs and anxieties about safety, security, and care that are not resolvable for everyone within the logic of the monogamous, companionate, nuclear couple-family which, following Tin, is often taken for granted today.

In addition to these conservative or traditionalist critiques of the triumphalist narrative of Muhammad's egalitarian marriage to Khadija, there is also room for a progressive critique. In seeking to do away with hierarchical and potentially polygynous models of marriage, some ways of reiterating the story of Muhammad's loving, lengthy, companionate marriage to the mother of his children unwittingly strengthen a model of male/female coupling and nuclear family life that excludes those who are single by choice, couples who cannot or do not have children, and especially gay people from its vision of the good family.

Here is the problem. Both feminists and queer activists insist, correctly, that dominant norms surrounding Muslim sexuality are unjust. In theory and in practice, however, gender-justice advocates and lesbian/gay/bisexual/transgender activists often work in ways, and with arguments, at odds with one another. Both feminists and queer thinkers oppose the version of male-dominated marriage (typically monogamous, sometimes polygynous) that flourishes in sanitised pamphlets and Saudi-subsidised books like *Marital Discord: Al-Nushooz*.

Some Muslim gay men and lesbians have fought to redefine religious marriage to include same-sex couples. Some, perhaps most, merely tinker with standard *nikah* – considering its strongly gendered legal provisions marginal to its symbolic importance (married coupledom, in a form Tin did not explore). In this way, they echo the behaviour of many Muslims committed to egalitarian married life and also the religious symbolism (or family expectations) of a *nikah* ceremony. On occasion, however, I have stumbled across gay Muslims, always male, advocating a new jurisprudence on marriage based on other forms of licit sexual relationship. Most often, they single out *mut'ah*, so-called temporary marriage allowed by Twelver Shi'a. Astonishingly, some mention *milk al-yamin*, slave concubinage, as an alternate form of relationship that merits exploration for its potential to yield new strategies for gay marriage.

I have insisted elsewhere that Muslims should acknowledge that our tradition considered slave concubinage lawful and normal for well over a millennium. I sought to build on the widespread rejection of slavery by 'right thinking Muslims everywhere' to insist that other things once taken for granted as acceptable can also be up for debate. If the vast majority of Muslims reject slavery, a practice present in scripture and prophetic *sunnah* as well as Islamic jurisprudence, as legitimate or viable in the contemporary world, other reforms and transformations are also possible – perhaps including egalitarian marriage laws or even same-sex marriage. Writing nearly a decade ago, I did not consider the need to wage intellectual combat against those, like Boko Haram in Nigeria and ISIS/ISIL in the Levant, who would seek to justify the practice of kidnapping, enslavement, forcible 'marriage,' and rape in terms of Islamic norms. But neither did I expect to have to explain to progressive gay men why it is offensive to try to reimagine consensual male-male relationships by drawing on the by-definition non-consensual relationship of enslaved woman to male master. Apparently male privilege means never having to say you're sorry for strategically appropriating an intolerable institution while ignoring its inherent misogyny.

I imagine a similar criticism could be made of straight women's continual invocation of male/female partnering by quoting Qur'an 4:1 and talking about Muhammad and Khadija. Though there is no parallel between the viciously unequal dynamics of concubinage and the long-term marriage of two beloved figures, what the latter lacks in obvious offensiveness it makes up for with constant repetition. The motivation, as noted earlier, for telling and retelling the now-conventional version of their marriage is to portray polygyny and/or deeply hierarchical marriage as marginal, and companionate monogamy as central and privileged: the 'true' *sunnah* of the Prophet. As a by-product, however, this retelling reinforces a narrative of male-female complementarity as created mates – often with bonus Qur'anic quotation – and promotes a model of coupled family life that excludes, in some cases undoubtedly unintentionally, childless couples, those who remain single by choice or otherwise, and same-sex couples.

In academic circles these days, the hot term is intersectional: identities, patterns, structures intersect. An intersectional analysis reveals the vital stake that queer Muslims have in feminism and that feminists have in supporting diverse sexual and gender identities and orientations. Our current stories are not doing this work. Muslim feminists typically shore up the institution of marriage while redefining its essential nature as companionate (and monogamous). And no surprise: the marriage to Khadija is a valuable tool in the toolkit of those who seek to reimagine heterosexual marriage in egalitarian ways. Straight feminists benefit from heterosexism just like gay men benefit from patriarchy. Muhammad and Khadija as the ideal couple, along with the Adam and Hawwa from a single soul version of the creation narrative (and not the hadith-based Adam's rib version), aim to uphold monogamy. In doing so they insist on and repeatedly reaffirm coupled heterosexuality as normal, natural, and divinely chosen.

Is there a way out? Must stories pit non-dominant folks against each other? Divide-and-conquer tactics have a long history. In the American context, the classic example is that of post-Civil War suffrage, where 'suffragette' abolitionists saw male African-American freed slaves get the (nominal) right to vote while female suffrage was delayed for decades. Similarly, women's participation in anti-colonial struggles throughout the twentieth century was often rewarded with nationalist rhetoric: thanks for your help; now is not quite the right time to focus on women's issues. Time after time, equality delayed has been equality denied. Both of these examples are about the delay and denial of female rights by male allies.

Among Muslims today, women's rights are the easier sell, while gender and sexual diversity pose stickier challenges.

To be clear, I am neither suggesting that feel-good stories about Muhammad and Khadija should not be told nor that promoting egalitarian marriages between men and women is an unworthy goal. I am insisting rather that these stories have a lineage, and they have effects. They are not unproblematic retellings of 'original' authentic stories, drawn straight out of foundational texts. They grow out of nineteenth century colonial visions of a narrowly envisioned couple and family unit. Which is not to say they have remained static as they have been told by new, often female tellers, in new contexts. Told anew, they generate new responses.

One of those responses ought to be a cry for more complexity, more nuance, and more variability in the stories we tell. Are we so limited in our vision about what forms of committed, companionate, loving intimacy can flourish? I believe in long-term monogamous unions between equals. Still, to value only this form of connection excludes those who thrive in other forms of union, or no union at all. It excludes those who want but do not find or cannot sustain a marriage tie. And it excludes those who marry but maintain their primary intimate (not sexual) ties with friends or others not related by marriage or by blood.

Love and intimacy can flourish in the bounds of marriage, as stories tell us happened with Muhammad and Khadija. Love and intimacy can also surpass and overflow those bounds. Where are those stories? Might they help us envision forms of connection, belonging and flourishing that include divorced women, 'spinsters,' those who do not fit neat gender binaries, those who lack sexual desire, those whose families are blended, and include foster and step children, taken in out of affection rather than obligation?

These stories are available for the telling. We need look no further than the same sources from which current stories are drawn: prophetic biographies and the Qur'an.

Muhammad's own family experience does not conform to the oft-touted Islamic family model. The standard biographies tell us that he was orphaned, fostered by another family, taken in by extended family, shuffled from relative to relative. He became a step-father before becoming a father, adopted a 'son' – a grown man whom he later disaffiliated, and then married that former son's former wife. He mourned the loss of parents and parent-substitutes, children, and more than one wife.

A few of these bits slip into standard stories, such as his grief at Khadija's death. But seldom do we linger on the strangeness of this account when compared to the idealised model of married couples who parent their own biological offspring, raising them to adulthood and seeing them happily married off in order to repeat the cycle. Muhammad's life story does not fit the model.

Strikingly, neither do the life stories of other prophets such as we find them in the Qur'an. There is no singular timeless Islamic family structure depicted in its chapters. Through analysis of four prophets – Adam, Joseph, Jesus, and Muhammad – Amanullah De Sondy has recently argued that there are various ways of being exemplary man. These men have diverse relationships to marriage and procreation: a monogamous bond (Adam and Hawwa), non-monogamous bonds (Muhammad and his wives), celibacy (Jesus) and 'restrained virility' (Joseph). Moreover, though the prophets may be in some key senses exemplary, they come from families that are, at times, 'dysfunctional.' Other Qur'anic stories have absent fathers, fratricidal siblings, complicated reproduction (barrenness, nonsexual conception). Between scripture and biography, there is plenty of material for telling stories.

A plurality of stories about marriage, about divorce, about remarriage, about family violence, about 'blended families,' about widowhood, and about loss and grief can challenge our smug certainties about marriage, about family, and about community.

Our lives, like those of the Prophet and his beloved Khadija, don't come in tidy packages. Neither should our stories.

THE POWER OF EDUCATION

Jeremy Henzell-Thomas

A recent 'World Exclusive' on the front page of *The Times* caught my attention. It reported that the British Museum had allowed part of the Elgin (Parthenon) Marbles to leave London for the first time by lending one of the sculptures to the Hermitage Museum in St Petersburg. Further articles on successive pages explored the implications of the surprise appearance of the artwork in the museum founded in 1764 by Catherine the Great to enable Russia to participate in the European Enlightenment. Of course, the venue is highly symbolic at a time when there are growing fears of a new Cold War between the Kremlin and the West. Neil McGregor, the Director of the British Museum, believes strongly that the relationship between museums as an example of the power of culture to build bridges between nations is all the more important in times of political stress and rupture.

The god-like figure loaned to the Hermitage is thought to represent the River Ilissos, one of the streams that flowed near Athens in ancient times. It was here, according to Plato (as Macgregor describes) that 'Socrates conversed with Phaedrus in the cool shade of the plane trees that grew along the banks, discussing the value of beauty and the morality of love.' As such, 'it embodies the central values of dialogue and discussion which underlie today's ideals of intellectual inquiry and political freedom', and is 'an eloquent symbol of the key values of both Ancient Athens and of Enlightenment Europe.'

Now, I do not want to carp or undermine McGregor's essential point about the sanctity of dialectic. On the contrary, I want to take is as a fundamental axiom in what I have to say about the power of education. Nevertheless, it is well to remember that Socrates was executed for being, in Plato's words, the 'gadfly' of the state, the irritant which stings the horse into action, the thorn in the flesh. 'Freethinkers', Ziauddin Sardar writes in the opening essay of *Critical Muslim 12:Dangerous Freethinkers*, 'are seen as dangerous simply because freethought challenges the conventional, the orthodox, and the dominant perspectives.' To be shunned and exiled, he goes on to say, is the unsurprising consequence of ruffling feathers. In the case of Socrates, prominent Athenians were made to look foolish by his paradoxical wisdom, and one of his capital 'crimes' as a philosophical, social and moral critic was judged to be 'impiety' (not believing in the gods of the state). But we need always to bear in mind that Socrates was not simply a self- promoting agent provocateur captivated by his own wit and cleverness, or the creative and radical obliqueness of his own insights, nor had he turned freethought itself into a dogmatic ideology through which it masquerades as a supposedly 'progressive' force against religion and 'superstition'. If he were with us today we would not see him in uncritical and servile genuflection to the triumphalism of 'Enlightenment values' or 'secular humanism' or 'scientific materialism' or any other 'fundamentalism', whether secular or religious. Socrates would also have been the last person to indulge in the narcissism of a selfie, for not only did he have not the slightest interest in status or popularity, but he also recognised the depth of his own ignorance. As Sardar affirms, 'the knowledgeable know that humility is a prerequisite for true understanding.' What unsettled the grandees of Athens was the way in which Socrates came up with a paradox in the face of a pronouncement by the Delphic oracle. Asked if anyone were wiser than Socrates, the oracle had responded that no-one was. Since Socrates himself believed that he possessed no wisdom whatsoever, he interpreted this as a paradox, and proceeded to test the riddle (in order to refute it) by questioning prominent Athenians with a reputation for wisdom. He concluded that while so-called wise men thought themselves wise and yet were not, he himself knew he was not wise at all, and this, paradoxically, made him the wiser one since he was the only one aware of his own ignorance. The oracle, he realised, had therefore been correct.

Plato's *Apology* eloquently describes Socrates' defence at his trial before 500 jurors. This 'defence' is actually not an apology at all, but, in the words of Russell Bosworth, a stirring affirmation of 'the merits of a life consciously dedicated to the care of the soul, the discovery of wisdom, and fidelity to the truth'.

Thomas Merton, the influential Christian political activist and literary figure, writes with great depth, insight and personal realisation on the need to embody what we think and what we know in the conduct of our lives: 'The activity proper to man is not purely mental, because man is not just a disembodied mind. Our destiny is to live out what we think, because unless we live what we know, we do not even know it.'

If you google the phrase 'Power of Education', one of the top ten hits of a half billion results delivered in less than half a second is a manifesto on the website Deutsche Welle which tells us that 'Education means more than acquiring knowledge. It empowers people to develop personally and become politically active. That's not always in the interests of rulers...' It adds that education is a fundamental human right and an emancipatory force for political development, democracy and social justice, empowering people to contest the abuse and misuse of power by authoritarian rulers and governments and to gain access to uncensored perspectives.

The key here is the juxtaposition of personal development with resistance to authoritarianism and action for freedom and social justice. The Qur'an makes it clear that the transformation of society and the wider world must rest above all on personal transformation: 'Allah does not change the condition of a people until they change what is in themselves' (13:11). The Prophet Muhammad is reported to have said: 'He who knows himself knows his Lord', and also (though not in the authoritative collections) to have described the greater jihad (*al-jihad al-akbar*) as the struggle against one's lower self. The Ancient Greek aphorism 'Know Thyself' was one of the Delphic maxims inscribed in the forecourt of the Temple of Apollo and also a guiding precept of Plato's Academy.

The top hit also included a quote by Nelson Mandela: 'Education is the most powerful weapon which you can use to change the world'. Other sites in the top ten include one which emphasises how education confers the power to 'change one's view of the world and how to live one's life', and another which explains how the 'transformative power of a great education can change everything'.

Now, the resources we derive from web searches are littered with quotations often taken out of context and reduced to little more than clichés endlessly replicated and reinforced across countless websites. Once something is attributed to someone on the internet it tends to be endlessly proliferated as Gospel Truth. This is of course one of the problems with a mode of instant learning which, despite the inestimable value of the immediate access to knowledge which it provides, can also favour the truism and mantra, the slogan, platitude or significant-sounding sound bite. It can also cement the popularity of a corpus of quotations through a self-fulfilling rating system based on the number of 'hits'. Yet, it would be mistaken to quibble with the idea running through the core of most of the maxims encountered in the top hits, a simple idea of the greatest importance – education has the power to change oneself and the world.

First and foremost, the best education should confer the power to examine, know and change ourselves, so that we might transform the lives of others.

Inquiry and Wholeness

That transformation is also a never-ending journey of open inquiry and lifelong learning rooted in the premise that there is always so much more to know. And that is true, of course, not only of the intellectual domain but also of the spiritual path. With each step taken towards a greater understanding of the truth, new paths continually unfold in all directions, for such is the infinitely generative power of the Creator. Such tastings bring ever-stronger certitude, but, paradoxically, also perplexity, for spiritual certitude is not the same as the false certainty bestowed by the closed mind in its narrow understanding of the closed book. A mystical parallel to the never-ending process of education can be found in Ibn 'Arabi's description of the state of divine bewilderment arising from the opening of the door of the Heart through the process of cumulative 'Self-manifestation'. Here, he describes how one's awareness of the revelation of the nature or activity of God in the world is a continually unfolding discovery of new implications, and through this one comes to realise, in his words, that 'this matter has no end at which it might stop'. The Qur'an tells us: 'And if all the trees on earth were pens, and the sea were ink, with seven more seas yet added to it, the words of God would not be exhausted....' (31:27).

We might find a partial analogy to the process of continual 'unfolding' in the opening of those nested Chinese caskets from the Song Dynasty, in which successively smaller caskets were placed one inside the other. The last and smallest of these caskets (the precursors of the later Japanese and more famous Russian *matryoshka* nested dolls) traditionally contained a single grain of rice. Now, there is of course a definite end to the unwrapping in the discovery of the smallest casket or doll which can be made to fit (given the obvious physical limitations of space and materials). But to take the analogy further, we can liken the single grain of rice in the final container to the Singularity, that is, the essence, the original dimensionless point, from which the ever-expanding boxes emanate, and from which 'this matter has no end at which it might stop'.

The physicist David Bohm defined what he called the 'implicate order' as an underlying and undivided whole that physical form constantly unfolds out of and enfolds back into, such that 'every part of the universe is related to every other part'. This is William Blake's holographic vision of 'seeing the world in a grain of sand' and it is not just a poetic fancy. The unity and interconnectedness of all things is also at the heart of the discoveries of John Stewart Bell. He showed that every particle in the Universe has a memory of every other particle because they were all originally 'entangled' within the Singularity. The diversity of forms is infinite and ever-changing but there is an immutable essence which is the source of everything, and our own point of arising and return. 'Everything have We created in pairs', the Qur'an tells us (51:49), and yet there is unity in multiplicity.

Bohm points to the pressing problems caused by our fragmentary form of thought which fails to see that underlying unity and connectivity. It generates unending chaotic and meaningless conflict, and a wide range of crises – social, political, economic, ecological, psychological – in the individual and in society as a whole. If anything, the fragmentation lamented by Bohm has only increased since his book was published in 1980. And of course Bohm might also have included religious conflict, as well as the rising tide of xenophobia. We do not have to look very far in the world today to see the debilitating and even devastating outcome of exclusivism, tribalism, triumphalism, and narrow identity politics in the distortion and misappropriation of doctrines and values for cultural, ethnic, religious, national or civilisational superiority, whether in the East or the West. Unity in multiplicity is not uniformity, any more than the Absolute can be equated with the crushing absolutism which obliterates all context.

Ibn Khaldun used the term 'asabiyyah (tribal partisanship, ethnocentricism) in both positive and negative senses. It can be a source of solidarity and social cohesion, but in its negative form it is that crudely jingoistic and smugly ethnocentric mentality which endorses tribal prejudice and parochial self-interest. The Prophet's reaction to boasts of ancestral glory was to warn those steeped in the arrogance of pre-Islamic pagan ignorance that Islam had abolished such tribalism, and that all human beings are descended from Adam. We are advised in the Qur'an (49:13) that there is no superiority of one over another except in taqwa, that consciousness and loving awe of God which inspires us to be vigilant and to do what is right. This verse is an implicit condemnation of all ethnic/racial, national, class or tribal prejudice, a condemnation which is made explicit by the Prophet Muhammad: 'He is not of us who proclaims the cause of tribal partisanship, and he is not of us who fights in the cause of tribal partisanship, and he is not of us who dies in the cause of tribal partisanship'. When asked to explain what he meant by tribal partisanship, the Prophet answered, 'it means helping your own people in an unjust cause'. Disapproval of tribalism is also germane to the Pact of the Virtuous, struck when Muhammad was a young man, and not yet a Prophet. In this pact, tribal leaders and members pledged that it was their collective duty to intervene in conflicts in the cause of justice and side with the oppressed against the oppressors, whoever they might be and whatever alliances might link them to other tribes. The Prophet's approval of the pact, in which he saw nothing that contradicted the values of Islam, confirmed that principles of justice, morality and the common good of society are not the exclusive domain of any one community, faith or ideology.

Education should confer the power to keep on inquiring and learning. Beyond that, it opens our minds and hearts to the source of all knowledge and its infinitely generative power. Education should also confer the power to arrest fragmentation, resolve conflict and transcend narrow definitions of identity.

Expanding Knowledge and Transcendence

I remember as a boy of twelve borrowing a three-inch refracting telescope from my local public library and spending six months mapping the night sky. I believe my parents were happy that the gargantuan task I had set myself would at least keep me out of mischief. I remember with awe when the planet Saturn swam into view. I could see clearly the three main rings with my amateur instrument, but large telescopes reveal eight rings, and orbiting spacecraft like Cassini can now bring thirty rings and the gaps between them into view. The total number of rings is actually unknown.

As the discovery of new rings illustrates, human knowledge advances and expands, and one of the most important factors in that expansion is the inestimable value of pluralism, cross-cultural encounter and exchange. As Ahmed Moustafa and Stefan Sperl noted in *The Cosmic Script*, three centuries had to elapse after the death of the Prophet before the invention of the Proportioned Script by the Abbasid *wazir* Ibn Muqla and the master scribe Ibn al-Bawwab in tenth century Baghdad. The horizon of knowledge encompassed by Islamic culture (and with it the scientific terminology of the Arabic language) had to expand sufficiently to include and absorb the advances of other, earlier civilisations. And this process of growing awareness is suggested in the Qur'anic verse: 'We will show them Our signs in the furthest horizons of the universe and within their own souls so that it will become clear to them that this revelation is indeed the Truth' (41:53). Here, as I understand it, the term horizons (*afaq*) refers both to the expanding range and maturation of human consciousness and to the varying domains of human knowledge, whatever their source may be. The first verses of the Qur'an to be revealed urge us to 'Read – for thy Sustainer is the Most Bountiful One who has taught mankind the use of the pen – taught man what he did not know!' (96:3-5). Muhammad Asad notes that the pen is a symbol for all knowledge recorded by means of writing, and that man's unique ability to transmit, by means of written records, his thoughts, experiences, and insights from individual to individual, from generation to generation, and from one cultural environment to another endows all human knowledge with a cumulative character.

And let us be very clear that cultural exchange is a process that works in many directions. If Islamic civilisation owes much to Greek philosophy, ethics and geometry, so Western civilisation owes much to what Muhammad Asad has eloquently described as the insistence on 'consciousness and knowledge' which permeates the Qur'an and which engendered 'that splendid era of learning and scientific research which distinguished the world of Islam at the height of its cultural vigour'. As Asad explains, the Qur'an gave rise to a culture of 'independent inquiry and intellectual curiosity' which 'penetrated in countless ways and by-ways into the mind of medieval Europe and gave rise to that revival of Western culture which we call the Renaissance, and thus became in the course of time largely responsible for the birth of what is described as the age of science: the age in which we are now living.' I am reminded here of the novelist Sebastian Faulks' dismissal of the Qur'an and Ziauddin Sardar's delicious riposte in *The Guardian*. Faulks had described the Qur'an (a subject, as Sardar states, that 'demonstrably exists well beyond his grasp') as 'very disappointing', 'one-dimensional', 'barren', a 'depressing book' with 'no ethical dimension'. As Sardar points out, if that were the case, 'how could it motivate the believers to develop science and learning, promote reason and experimental method, establish universities and research-based hospitals, and advance philosophical inquiry?'.

The dynamic impulse derived from the Qur'an was at once intellectual and spiritual. The civilisation it fostered encompassed the discernment of truth which, at its highest level, is knowledge of God, for no higher civilisation is worthy of the name if it fails to distinguish between disorientated intellectual curiosity (no matter how 'open-minded', 'original' and 'creative') and that quality of intellectual endeavour which is grounded in the highest ethical and spiritual values and which is itself a reflection of the transcendent.

With that in mind, it could not be more appropriate to refer to Pope Francis's address to the European Parliament in Strasbourg on 25 November 2014. He spoke of Raphaels' famous fresco, 'The School of Athens', in the Vatican. Plato and Aristotle are in the centre. 'Plato's finger', he said, 'is pointed upward, to the world of ideas, to the sky, to heaven as we might say. Aristotle holds his hand out before him, towards the viewer, towards the world, concrete reality.' (What a marvellous image, I thought, of a saying attributed to the Prophet Muhammad: 'I have two sides, one facing the world and the other Allah'). The Pontiff went on to say that the fresco struck him 'as a very apt image of Europe and her history, made up of the constant interplay between heaven and earth, where the sky suggests that openness to the transcendent – to God – which has always distinguished the peoples of Europe, while the earth represents Europe's practical and concrete ability to confront situations and problems.'

How visionary is his conclusion that the future of Europe depends on the recovery of the vital connection between these two elements. 'A Europe which is no longer open to the transcendent dimension of life is a Europe which risks slowly losing its own soul and that humanistic spirit which it still loves and defends.'

The Ancient Greek word *anthropos* (human being) may well have had the original meaning of 'he or she who looks up at the sky'. Our erect posture gives us that upward vision, that higher aspiration which reaches beyond the earth to the heavens, and positions us as a bridge between the two realms. We have within us, in our essential nature, a criterion (*furqan*) or compass that orients us to our origin (for both English words come from the same root, Latin *oriri*, 'rise', and the verb 'orient' originally meant 'turn the face to the east', the direction of the rising sun) – a touchstone that shows us the way to be fully human. If the Pope is the Pontiff, all humanity has the function enshrined in the root of that word, Latin *pontifex*, the 'bridge-maker', one who negotiates between God and man.

Education should confer the power to reach for the sky, and to join heaven and earth, the transcendent and the immanent, in the love of God and 'all that moves on the face of the earth'. Education should also confer the power to discern and appreciate the many sources and strands of human knowledge and their confluence in the development of human civilisation.

Pluralism and dynamic outreach

Many of us will know some version of the Biblical story of the Tower of Babel from the Book of Genesis (11:1-9) and even those of us who do not may be familiar with the metaphorical application of the word 'Babel' to denote a confused medley of sounds or the din of mutually incomprehensible speech. According to the Genesis account, the Tower of Babel was erected by the descendants of Nuh (Noah) in a presumptuous attempt to reach up to heaven. As a punishment for their arrogant hubris, God confounded them by making the builders unable to understand each other's speech; hence, according to legend, the fragmentation of human speech into the various languages of the world, and also the dispersion of mankind over the face of the earth.

The Qur'an, however, does not support the idea that the diversity of languages and races is a punishment or a burden placed on mankind. On the contrary, it ordains unity in diversity, not only in terms of culture, language and race, but also in religion. Pluralism, quite simply, is an aspect of the *fitrah*, the essential nature or primordial condition of the human being. In the words of Mahmoud Ayoub, human diversity is 'not due to the gradual degeneration of human society from an ideal or utopian state. Nor is it the result of a lack of divine guidance or human understanding. Rather, religious diversity is a normal human situation. It is the consequence of the diversity of human cultures, languages, races and different environments.' 'Revelation', writes Rabbi Abraham Heschel, 'is always an accommodation to the capacity of man. No two minds are alike, just as no two faces are alike. The voice of God reaches the spirit of man in a variety of ways, in a multiplicity of languages. One truth comes to expression in many ways of understanding.' And Nancy Kline is spot on when she asserts that 'Diversity raises the intelligence of groups. Homogeneity is a form of denial.'

Recent research suggests that one of the factors which contributed to the extinction of the Neanderthals was their lack of outreach. More of the Neanderthal brain appears to have been dedicated to vision and body control, whereas modern humans deployed more brain power for maintaining complex, extended social networks (useful for competing for scarce resources) and the more complex language this would have required.

The verses of the Qur'an which ordain pluralism are well-known but they cannot be repeated enough: 'We have made you into nations and tribes so that you may come to know one another' (49:13); 'If God had so willed, He could surely have made you all one single community, but He willed it otherwise in order to test you...' (5:48). The Qur'an also tells us that the diversity of human tongues and colours is a sign for people of knowledge (30:22) and Asad notes other verses which uphold that, in his words, 'the unceasing differentiation in men's views and ideas is not incidental but represents a God-willed, basic factor of human existence'. The Prophet Muhammad is reported to have said: 'The diversity of my people is a blessing'.

It is important to distinguish between pluralism as an active process of learning and the unchallenging mediocrity of mere 'tolerance'. Omid Safi reminds us that the connotations of 'tolerance' are deeply problematic, rooted as the word is in medieval toxicology and pharmacology where it marked how much poison a body could 'tolerate' before it would succumb to death. As Diana Eck has eloquently argued, pluralism is not the mere existence of 'plurality' or 'cosmopolitanism', an array of isolated encampments or separate enclaves. Without real engagement, she says, they are simply 'icons of diversity' not 'instruments of relationship'. Neither is pluralism a kind of wishy-washy or contrived syncretism devoid of commitment or a dose of comforting platitudes about common ground served up at an interfaith breakfast. It is a truth-seeking encounter, a process of mutual transformation which goes further than simply trying to understand the 'other' but reaches out to a new level of mutual self-understanding.

The fostering of relationship is at the core of that encounter. One of the most important ways to develop the capacity to form and sustain relationship lies in a broad and balanced holistic education which gives adequate space for the arts and humanities. This is especially important in view of their progressive marginalisation in the curriculum of mainstream schools. In educational systems at all levels within Muslim societies, such neglect may be even more evident. An education rich in the humanities would foster the development not only of critical and creative thinking skills, questioning, and open-minded inquiry, and effective communication skills through discussion and debate but also a range of other opportunities: engagement in the creative arts as a means to engage the soul, kindle the imagination, develop aesthetic awareness and stimulate the connectivity of the brain; multi-sensory exploration and direct experiential learning, especially in the beauty and majesty of natural settings; understanding the human condition through the study of history, geography, languages, literature and the social sciences; the cultivation of an open-hearted and compassionate outlook which values and respects diversity and actively fosters intercultural awareness; and the development of character, virtue, altruism and ethical values, whether applied to personal conduct, relationships, citizenship, business practice, charitable service, or the care of the environment, which is now such a pressing concern for us all.

Education should confer the power to relate and to know the 'other', and by so doing to enrich and improve ourselves.

The schooling regime

I have given some attention here to the importance of the related concepts of pluralism, diversity, cultural exchange, relationship, and the expanding horizons of knowledge because there is a clear connection between all of that and the role of talk, discourse, discussion, dialogue, dialectic and polylogue as lynchpins of any powerful and transformational educational process – that is, one which confers the power to change oneself, society and the world. Within the Western discipline of developmental psychology, Karl Riegel identifies the ability to accept contradictions, constructive confrontations, paradoxes, and asynchronies as the highest stage of cognitive development, and James Fowler associates dialectical thinking with the development of faith. It goes without saying that the dialectical process is not one either of compromise or loose relativism, but one of creative tension which ultimately transforms contradictions into complementarities, releasing the open-minded thinker from ingrained habits and conditioned patterns of thought, established affiliations, fear of change and instability, and reluctance to approach anything which may be threatening to one's sense of 'self'.

So, is there a talking culture in our schools? The Harvard educationalist Roland Barth reports the estimate of John Goodlad and others that 85 per cent of lesson time in American schools is taken up by a prevailing pedagogy based on teachers talking and students listening, occasionally interspersed with teacher-directed discussion. It might be hoped that with the same preponderance of teacher talk in our own schools in Britain, a good proportion of it might be directed towards the development of creative and critical thinking. Not so. In fact, a wide-ranging survey of British secondary schools has revealed less than ten percent of teacher talk is concerned with the development of higher order thinking skills. The vast majority of it is directed to control and management, including keeping order and giving instructions, and low-level transmission of facts and information. Most questioning of students is only geared to seeking recall of 'right answers' in relation to prescribed content as required by an intrusive testing and assessment regime rather than promoting discussion through which alternative viewpoints or other higher-order processes of inquiry or reflection might be explored.

An educational process that is disproportionately focused on teacher-centred transmission of information (what Barth calls 'Sit 'n Git') cannot encompass the awakening and nurturing of the full range of human faculties. In the terminology of Islamic education, over-emphasis on the instruction and training of the mind and the transmission of knowledge through teacher-centred instruction (*ta'lim*) at the expense of the broader nurture of the whole being (*tarbiyah*) compromises the integrity of the educational experience. The good teacher is not only a *mu'allim*, a transmitter of knowledge but also a *murabbi*, a nurturer of souls and developer of character.

There is a pressing need for the revival of genuinely holistic and qualitative principles in the face of debilitating utilitarian approaches derived from target-driven managerialism which reduce human beings to compliant consumers in the service of crushing materialism, unsustainable economic growth and environmental devastation. This modern schooling regime has been the object of various critiques, including John Taylor Gatto's powerful indictment of the assumptions and structures which underlie modern state schooling in the USA. Gatto exposes the same deadening utilitarian agenda which also informs British educational policy – an agenda geared to turning children into cogs in an economic machine, children who are dependent, conforming, materialistic, and lacking in curiosity, creativity, imagination, self-knowledge, powers of intellectual inquiry and reflection, and capacity for solitude. Neil Postman, the prominent American social critic, has also lamented the way in which today's schools promote the 'false gods' of economic utility and consumerism.

One of the most vital powers of education must be to enable us to resist indoctrination of any kind. Let me give a telling example. A report by the Professional Council for Religious Education has revealed that amongst secondary school students aged 11 to 18 those who enjoy Religious Education and see positive benefits for their own lives from studying religion outnumber by four to one those who are negative about it. The report also gives examples of statements by students which show that many students also like the subject because of the opportunities it gives for expressing opinions, improving communication skills, acquiring knowledge of other faiths, developing inter-cultural awareness and sensitivity, developing the skills of philosophical inquiry and reflection, and pondering the meaning and purpose of life. There may be very few other opportunities within the curriculum for such enrichment. This evidence contradicts the vocal ideological prejudices of those who categorically oppose religious education as 'indoctrination', such as the British philosopher A. C. Grayling who once described religious education as 'intellectual abuse' and faith schools as 'ghettoes of superstition'. While indoctrination and lack of critical/dialogic thinking may characterise certain aspects of the educational process in some faith schools, it is grossly misleading to equate such deficiencies with religious education in general. Such generalisations not only exhibit a disregard for evidence which is surprising in self-appointed champions of critical thinking but also an authoritarian disrespect for the experience of young people themselves.

While the association of indoctrination with religion may be mechanical and formulaic within certain culturally conditioned mind-sets, we need to understand that indoctrination to some degree is embedded in the mainstream educational system which we characterise as broadly 'secular'. In *The Golden Notebook*, Doris Lessing writes: 'We have not yet evolved a system of education that is not a system of indoctrination...Those of you who are more robust and individual than others will be encouraged to leave and find ways of educating yourself – educating your own judgements. Those that stay must remember, always, and all the time, that they are being moulded and patterned to fit into the narrow and particular needs of this particular society'. Hannah Arendt, the social philosopher, puts it like this: 'The aim of totalitarian education has never been to instil convictions but to destroy the capacity to form any.'

Education should confer the power to ask searching questions, root out our own prejudices, and resist indoctrination.

Narrative Fallacies and Misperceptions

We might add to the general category of 'ingrained habits and conditioned patterns of thought' the allure of 'narrative fallacies', those flawed but simple and compelling stories of the past which arise from our continuous attempt to make sense of the world. It is well attested that even the very 'rational' scientific community is susceptible to confirmation bias. In the same way, we know from the psychology of perception that the human mind tends to see what it wants or expects to see. Perceptual preferences are of course necessary and understandable. Without the rapid automatic routines generated by top-down processing we would not be able to function in the world, for we would have to analyse everything laboriously from the bottom-up as if we were encountering it for the first time. The survival benefits of rapid processing are obvious, and dichotomisation is itself embedded in us to some degree as a means to judge and act decisively. By contrast, the armchair philosopher who scrutinises the logical minutiae of every proposition, absorbs every qualification, respects every position, and agonises over every minor dissonance and nuance may never get out of his chair. But we surely have to distinguish between the positive dynamics of familiar 'stories' which help us to bestow coherence and order on the world and their negative repercussions in the ingrained human tendency to espouse one-sided tribalism, bigotry, and prejudice. Challenging the mechanical perseveration of one-dimensional thinking and divisive 'scripts' must be one of the most important functions not only of thinkers and researchers at the cutting edge of academe but also of responsible journalists, commentators, and cultural critics wedded to the disinterested pursuit of truth and the excavation, marshalling and critical evaluation of evidence. And this function is always greater than a merely adversarial one which seeks to subvert for its own sake or defend a position at all costs, but is rooted in that intellectually honest critical engagement with alternative views, competing arguments and contradictory evidence in the service of the cumulative refinement of human knowledge. One of the founding principles of Western civilisation rests on Plato's affirmation that the process of philosophical dialectic is utterly distinct from and immeasurably superior to rhetoric as a means of persuasion, and that holds true today as surely as it did in his Academy.

One of the top ten hits on my 'Power of Education' web search refers to the oft-repeated aphorism attributed to the seventeenth-century English philosopher and statesman Francis Bacon that 'knowledge is power'. The Latin in which he actually expressed this (*ipsa scientia potestas est* – 'knowledge itself is power') is found in his *Meditationes Sacrae* of 1597, where he clarifies the equation of knowledge with power by going on to say that knowledge is 'not mere argument or ornament'. In other words, as a consequence of his frustration with the established tradition of Scholasticism, Bacon wanted to reconnect knowledge with action, to produce practical knowledge based on empirical principles for 'the use and benefit of man'.

To that end, Bacon upheld, we must purge the mind of prejudice, conditioning, false notions, and unanalysed authority – what he called the 'idols of the human mind' which distort and discolour the true nature of things – and rely instead on direct experience, perception, observation, and 'true induction' as methods of gaining sound knowledge. Amongst the more specific examples of hindrances to understanding included in Bacon's 'idols' are: trying to make things fit into patterns, seeking evidence to support preconceived notions, seeing what one expects to see, believing what one wants to believe, generalising, favouring one outlook or perspective over another (e.g. antiquity over novelty, the part over the whole, differences over similarities, or vice versa), and failing to understand that words may have more than one meaning. This is a remarkable list which has such a modern ring to it, converging as it does so strikingly with many of the key modern findings in cognitive psychology and related disciplines about the nature of conditioning, prejudice, confirmation bias, and other impediments to learning.

As for the dichotomising tendency, it is as ingrained in educational contexts as in most domains of human thought and activity. Obvious examples include the common misconception that memorisation is somehow inimical to thinking and comprehension, or that creativity is somehow independent of existing knowledge. Another is the false notion that specialisation, the accumulation of a detailed body of knowledge, is somehow opposed to the breadth and cross-connections gained from interdisciplinary or multidisciplinary learning. Great polymaths (including those who have been an inspiration to me) are not dilettantes skating on the surface of many ponds, any more than specialists are necessarily suffering from tunnel vision which prevents them from seeing the bigger picture.

Let us turn now to another of the false notions highlighted by Bacon – the distorted perceptions of reality generated by fixed ideas and expectations, and the concomitant disregard of evidence. A poll recently published in *The Times*, and appropriately subtitled 'The ignorance index', came up with striking overestimations in various categories, including the number of immigrants and Muslims in fourteen countries. American respondents, for example, believed that Muslims made up 15 per cent of the population of the USA, whereas the true figure is only 1 per cent. People are constantly fed sensationalised messages in the media about what worries them and this induces a mindset prone to overestimation. Another example of gross misperception of reality is the overestimation of violence motivated by religion. It is worth noting that, contrary to the widely held misconception that religion has historically been the chief cause of violent conflict, it is estimated that, at worst, religious causes actually account for less than 3 per cent of the 248 million deaths caused in the ten worst wars, massacres and atrocities in human history.

Education should confer the power to amass a body of knowledge, to marshal evidence, and to resist conditioned, biased and one-dimensional thinking.

Realising human potential

I take it as an axiom that a truly qualitative education can only be based on a mature understanding of the full range of human powers and faculties – physical, sensory, cognitive, perceptive, imaginative, affective, moral and spiritual – bearing in mind that from a spiritual perspective all such powers and faculties are divine endowments and 'there is no power nor strength save in God alone'.

The concept and practice of holistic education is also integral to the comprehensive vision of human faculties in Islam. There are repeated exhortations in the Qur'an to use the faculties given to us to attain knowledge and discern the truth. These encompass the senses, which enable us to learn by direct observation and experience, as well as through instruction; the language-based deliberative or rational faculty (*'aql*) which enables us to think, inquire, analyse, define, discriminate, conceptualise, argue, and engage in the process of dialectic; the capacity for relationship and empathy which is the ground of that active engagement with the 'other' ordained in the Qur'an; the higher faculties of 'intellection' which combine mind and heart, including reflection and contemplation (*tafakkur*); the creative imagination which engages the faculties of inner perception and insight; the moral faculties anchored in a criterion (*furqan*) which enable us to distinguish right from wrong, and assume personal responsibility and ultimate accountability for our actions; and above all these, the superordinate faculty of consciousness or mindfulness of God (*taqwa*), that sense of loving awe and awareness of the omnipresence of God, and the desire to conduct one's life in the light of that awareness.

This is an integrated vision of human faculties which never separates the rational powers from that of direct experience, moral valuation and spiritual consciousness.

If you google 'Human Powers', the top hits include the following four sites: 16 People with Real Super Powers; 18 Mutant Superheroes; 9 Humans with Real-Life X-Men Mutant Super Powers, and 3 Ways to develop Powers. The latter, intended 'for those who being a normal human is just not enough', includes seeing in the dark, running over walls, jumping like a cat, shunning the need to breathe, becoming an expert at detecting lies, persuading others with subconscious techniques, reading auras, and developing clairvoyance, clairaudience, astral projection and psychokinesis. The impact of mass media and popular culture is only too evident here, but the fascination in super-heroes and super-powers is also indicative of a deep recognition of human potential. At the same time, one can argue that this is bound to flourish in an age when the full potential of the human being and the full extent of human faculties are largely unrecognised in the pervasive culture of generally low expectations that exists both in our education system and in wider society. Unconscious of the full extent of our potential, we can only project that unconsciousness onto imaginary and sensationalised powers and beings.

Education should confer the power to recognise the full extent of human powers and faculties and to enable us to take conscious control of their development within ourselves.

Excellence with a soul

In the 1992 film *Under Siege*, Tommy Lee Jones plays a rogue ex-CIA agent who had been involved in covert operations with Special Forces, and who hijacks a US warship. He is a totally amoral nutter, but the CIA, when asked why they had employed him, explain that he was a 'creative thinker' who can be especially useful. Here we see the disconnection between 'creativity' and any higher concept of human character. Creativity, instead of being an aspect of human excellence, is conceived as mere ingenuity, with no thought for the purposes for which it is used. In the 1987 film, *Wall Street*, the protagonist Gordon Gekko, played by Michael Douglas, utters some infamous lines: 'Greed is good'; 'I create nothing. I own'; 'We make the rules, pal'; 'It's all about bucks, kid. The rest is conversation'; and 'What's worth doing is worth doing for money'. In an interview with *Empire* magazine, Douglas recounts how young business students would flock to meet him and tell him, 'Gordon Gekko! You're the man, Gordon! You're the reason why I got into this money business!' Douglas shook his head and said: 'I'm sitting there saying, "No, no – really, no. Look at the film. I'm not the man you want to be like. I'm the villain." The guys didn't get it. "Yeah, Gordon! You're really great!"' Douglas continued: 'Now I wonder just how many of those young MBA students back then who thought Gordon was such a great guy are at the head of those very same companies now.'

There is an important distinction between professionalism and excellence. After all, we can talk about a professional hit man, but would it not be rather strange to say that Mario is an excellent hit man, unless we were members of the Mafia. The difference is that the heart of excellence is not simply about personal mastery of a skill or effectiveness in accomplishing a task but includes excellence of human character, and that has a moral and ultimately a spiritual dimension.

This is a fundamental concept in Islamic tradition. The vision of 'excellence' that is expressed in the Arabic word *ihsan* is in fact inseparable from goodness, beauty and virtue. In the domain of Islamic art, a pivotal distinction can also be made between two concepts of beauty: one which is subjective and ephemeral (*jamal*) and the other (*husn*) which encompasses not only the aesthetic sense of beauty in its homage to the 'due measure and proportion' invested in creation, but also the intimate equation between what is beautiful and what is good. Beauty is thus inseparable from the attributes of Divine Perfection, and from the moral virtue, spiritual refinement and excellence of character which are the human reflections of those holy attributes.

In the Qur'an the higher faculties are always intertwined in a holistic vision of what makes a fully human being. That completeness is the underlying meaning of 'integrity', which comes from Latin *integer*, 'whole, complete, entire'. From this perspective, thinking, for instance, is not just an analytical, logical and target-driven activity that goes on in the head and through which the end can even justify the means, but it is inseparable from an innate moral and discriminating capacity to distinguish truth from falsehood and right from wrong. True excellence is therefore embodied and actualised in principled conduct and beautiful behaviour (*adab*) as well as skill and effectiveness in mastering a domain of activity. The eighteenth-century poet and literary critic Samuel Johnson wrote 'the supreme end of education is expert discernment of things, the power to tell the good from the bad, the genuine from the counterfeit, and to prefer the good and the genuine to the bad and the counterfeit.'

This definition converges strikingly with Asad's translation of the Arabic word *furqan* – 'a standard or criterion to discern truth from falsehood and right from wrong.' The sense of moral valuation is also present in other Arabic words in the Qur'an which denote the faculties of discernment and insight. The word *al-a'raf*, translated by Asad as 'the faculty of discernment', carries the same connotation of 'perceiving what is right', as does the word *rushd*, 'consciousness of what is right'. The word *basirah*, denoting the 'faculty of conscious understanding based on insight' also includes that moral compass which provides the essential orientation for perceiving the truth. The 'intellect' (*'aql*) encompasses not only the language-based rational and deliberative faculty but also the higher organ of moral and spiritual intelligence and insight. In a detailed study of the concept of *'aql*, Karim Douglas Crow has noted the re-appearance of the term 'wisdom' in recent descriptions of human intelligence to connote 'a combination of social and moral intelligence, that blend of knowledge and understanding within one's being manifested in personal integrity, conscience, and effective behaviour'. He concludes that one of the key components of the concept of 'intelligence' expressed by the term *'aql* was 'ethical-spiritual'.

Discernment also goes far beyond what Guy Claxton has labelled as 'd-mode' (deliberation mode), the sort of intelligence concerned with 'figuring matters out, weighing up the pros and cons, constructing arguments and solving problems, a way of knowing that relies on reason and logic, on deliberate conscious thinking.' Claxton points out that growing dissatisfaction with the assumption that d-mode is the be-all and end-all of human cognition is reflected in various alternative approaches to the notion of intelligence, such as Howard Gardner's 'multiple intelligences' and Daniel Goleman's 'emotional intelligence'. One might add to these alternative approaches the work of scientists such as F. David Peat, who have synthesised anthropology, history, linguistics, metaphysics, cosmology and even quantum theory to describe the way in which the worldviews and indigenous teachings of traditional peoples differ profoundly from the way of seeing the world embedded in us by linear Western science.

In conclusion, I will refer to Harry Lewis's book, *Excellence Without a Soul*, a robust critique of higher education in America by the former dean of Harvard College. 'College campuses', he claims, 'have become perpetual parties and many people blame the students themselves, suggesting that this generation is lazy, entertainment driven and doesn't care about anything other than themselves.' According to Lewis, colleges in America 'have forgotten that the fundamental job of undergraduate education is to turn teenagers into adults, to help them grow up, to learn who they are, to search for a larger purpose for their lives, and to leave college as better human beings'. Lewis believes that because colleges have failed to offer students reasons for education – which forces students to wrestle with deeper questions of meaning and purpose – they are failing students and a country that desperately needs a well-educated citizenry. 'The old ideal of a liberal education', he writes, ' lives on in name only. No longer does Harvard teach the things that will free the human mind and spirit.'

Let us be clear about the status of Harvard College. It is one of two schools within Harvard University granting undergraduate degrees. Founded in 1636 in Cambridge, Massachusetts, it is the oldest institution of higher learning in the United States. Cambridge University in England, founded in 1209, is of course much older, but much older still are the University of Al-Qarawiyya in Fes, Morocco, founded in 859, and Al-Azhar in Cairo, Egypt, established in 970. In 2015, Harvard came fourth in the QS World University Rankings and second in the THE rankings, while Cambridge came second and fifth respectively. The top university in both rankings was an Institute of Technology in the USA – Massachusetts in QS, and California in THE. The top university in the Muslim world, according to this ranking system, was Universiti Malaya (UM) in 151st place, and there was no university in the Arab world in the top 200.

Such statistics are often marshalled in lamentations about the intellectual stagnation and dearth of knowledge production in the Muslim world, even though justifiable reservations about the validity of the rankings have also been voiced. Despite those reservations, the rankings are a widely recognised measure of the quality of education at university level and an indication of a profound crisis within Muslim societies. Even so, critiques such as Lewis's are important correctives to the assumption that the panacea for education in the Muslim world is the uncritical emulation of Western models, as if the main criterion for 'success' in 'catching up' amongst 'lame-duck' Muslim institutions is improvement in their global standing as defined by international ranking systems and criteria.

One of the powers of education itself is to give us the depth and breadth of vision that enables us to see that the advancement of human knowledge is not a one-way street. It is not the assimilation of one culture or worldview into another either through Westernisation or Islamisation. Rather, it is the integration of the best there is in every culture and civilisation.

Education should confer the power to reach for a universal vision of excellence which encompasses truth, meaning, purpose and what it means to be fully human.

ENLIGHTENING ENGAGEMENT

Rahel Fischbach and Rachel Friedman

'Why study other religions if you do not expect them to yield theological truth?' Our professor asked this question in all seriousness, giving words to the thought at the forefront of the minds of many students in the class-room. Immediately, the students were abuzz with reactions. Their level of nervous excitement was palpable, adding heat to the already sweltering June day in Rabat. For many of the Muslim students sitting on the edges of their seats, so to speak, this was their first face-to-face confrontation with real live Christian and Jewish people. Their lifelong preparation to defend their religion bubbled forth, undermining the professor's question rather than giving positive answers.

The location was a religion classroom at the Mohammed V University of Rabat, Morocco, and the professor was Paul Heck of Georgetown University. The students – Muslim, Christian, Jew, all graduate students in theology and religion – were embarking on a course that constituted a venture into *suhba 'ilmiyya*, the Arabic term for scholarly companionship. The class was a mosaic composed of Moroccan Muslims sitting for the first time in their lives with Western-educated Jews and Christians – an eclectic group whose nationalities were American, German, Hungarian-French, South-African – counterparts in a new and experimental programme of religious study. All of the Moroccan students in the course were Sunni Muslims of various stripes: currents of Sufi, Wahhabi, and Salafi ideologies came together in the students, not always harmoniously. There was significant diversity among their brands of religious conviction, but all had enrolled in the religious studies graduate programme out of a strong religious commitment. We were part of the small group of 'Western' graduate students at US universities, equally diverse in our religious convictions, yet also united as children of our secular societies. We were engaged in study with the graduate students in the Rabat religious studies programme as part of an initiative called 'The Study of Religions across Civilizations' (SORAC). For three hours each day, we convened to study excerpts of the Gospel of Matthew, an ethical treatise by the Andalusi Jewish scholar Yaḥyā ibn Paquda, and texts by Thomas Aquinas and John Wesley. Moroccan students took the lead in giving lectures on hadith (Prophetic traditions) that included lexical explanations and interpretations of the hadith's importance to Islamic doctrine. Heck instructed the course on Christian and Jewish texts, eloquently leading the class in Standard Arabic sometimes punctuated by pointed uses of colloquial Moroccan Arabic, and was one of the co-organisers of SORAC along with the Rabat programme's head, Muḥammad Amīn al-Ismāʿīlī.

Morocco's still-palpable Christian colonial history and challenge of combating Christian missionary activities made Heck's personal relationship of trust with Moroccan university administrators, professors, and students essential to his credibility as a scholar. Against the backdrop of post-colonial society, it was important for him to reassure them that he would not proselytise in any way. Missionary activity in Morocco is no peccadillo; it is a crime punishable by law. Only shortly before we arrived in Rabat, a group of Christians alleged to be evangelisers had been expelled from Morocco. The history of French colonial and post-colonial impositions in Morocco, in which Christian missionaries played their part, echoes in the active fear of proselytisers. Heck's goal was to create a scholarly dialogue across religious boundaries, without challenging the religious identity of any of the participants. But he knew his project would pose challenges. Whatever images the term 'interreligious dialogue' might bring to mind, of willing participants longing to bridge their differences and tell others about how they participated in prayer and ritual – this scene was the opposite. These Moroccan students were not interested in sharing personal stories that would lead to sympathetic responses or find common ground. There was common ground to be shared, but it became clear that the boundaries of this common ground were often imagined antithetically by the participants. Many of the Muslim students were studying religion with the intention of becoming *imams*, *murshidat* (female religious leaders), and other public religious figures. Some saw themselves as defenders of their religion and its history against mainstream urban Moroccan society, which they saw as too Westernised and too secular. Islam, for many of our

Moroccan classmates, was a righteous refuge from the decay of Western culture and its permeation into Islamic life. As our course started, we got the feeling that our Muslim peers considered this course to be an opportunity to tell us their own Islamic narratives and perhaps even convince us of their truth-value. This included handing out pamphlets of *da'wa*, the propagating call to Islam.

The Moroccan students were a keen, active, hard-working, intelligent group from across Morocco's social strata. There was Karima, who had already at the age of twelve rebelled against her father when she sneaked away to attend dawn prayer, unaccompanied. Eventually, the father accepted his insubordinate religiously-minded daughter. Karima made everyone laugh, and her stubbornness at times brought her into trouble with the older generation. There was Abdessamad who had graduated from a madrasa in Mecca and who dressed up in the Wahhabi garb, and shaved his moustache in a way that left no doubt about his religious affiliation, and who was always ready to engage in theological discussion about the 'absurdity' of the crucifixion of Christ. Yet he was also generous, welcoming, and always interested in a good joke. And there was Badruddin, imam of a nearby mosque, father of many children, who stressed family life over everything else. He could be charming in his refutations of the trinity. Humour and laughing in general were guaranteed ingredients of all discussions at some point, in defiance of the seriousness of the arguments.

Years after this experience, we are still often reminded of the questions it raised. As much as we thought about the difference between Muslim and non-Muslim students in the classroom, and as much as our engagement was framed in these terms, it became clear through the course of our study that the real, salient difference was much harder to characterise. The lines that divided us were not simply religious but also cultural, educational, geographical, and especially epistemological. We had entirely different conceptions of religion. The question became, how are Western academics to engage with counterparts from radically different systems of education and culture – across boundaries of tradition or viewpoint – in a meaningful way when such engagements are often overdetermined, eager to find the simplest common ground, and limited to those who tend to already be on board with expanding mutual understanding across religious lines? What of those – Muslim, Jew, Hindu, Christian, atheist – who are warier of new or foreign ideas – those who might not even participate in conventional interreligious dialogues or move in the types of circles where they would often interact with members of other persuasions? These voices may still be influential in their own communities and beyond. The questions they raise are, doubtless, evocative of common sentiments among the religious sectors of their society. The basis of our interreligious engagement with the Moroccan students was our belief that it is important to take such prevalent ideas seriously, even if they only seem to bring forth more challenges to mutual understanding. Ultimately, our experience was that along with these challenges came partnership. Not necessarily answers, but at least understanding of the types of questions that were in the minds of our peers in these discussions. Cultures differ in nothing as much as in the questions they deem important, we realised. Such is the power of engagement: when it is taken seriously, it marks you indelibly with the experience of the other.

On a scholarly level, our experience can be thought of as a study in the far-reaching traces of the past: histories of colonialism, religious interplay and defence, and hegemony echoed through the discussions that circulated in our religious studies classroom. Taking a closer look at these histories, our experience indirectly highlights the encounter of two models of the academic study of religion. The particular types of discussion and friction that arose in our Rabat classroom were symptomatic of the student groups' differences in training. To put it in the most general terms, the Western-trained graduate students tended to focus on contextualising the content of the texts, while the Moroccan students wanted first and foremost to know how to locate the ideas we were reading within their own worldview: were they true or false? In a sense, we were all doing what we had been trained, taught, and shown how to do. It was just that we had been taught different approaches. These approaches are products of wider societal ideas of what is valuable, true, and significant, in this case filtered through an application of these values to pedagogy. We learned about the implications of these differences first hand through experiencing each other's process of reading the texts at hand: what kind of questions came up, what features of the text were surprising or objectionable, and how this learning was integrated into our knowledge bases. Our experience in

Rabat brings into focus the implications of Religious Studies methodologies in Western academic programmes as well as in the post-colonial context.

The field of Religious Studies has continually come under attack for not being scientific or objective enough and for still not being emancipated from its faith-based counterpart, Theology. Religious Studies as a field arose in the West, and its beginnings lie in the anthropological study of so-called 'primitive' peoples and their rituals with the aim of discovering the origins of religion as a human activity through studying 'other' religions. Subsequent scholars rejected these methods' assumptions of European superiority and abandoned such scientifically unsound hermeneutics. In the wake of this development, the field of Religious Studies (among others) has been left with uncertainty as to how to deal with Eurocentrism and one's own Western heritage of exercise of power over other peoples and even whole textual systems. Tied up in this complex question of how scholars ought to be in relationship with those whom they study (particularly in the non-West) is the question of where to attempt to stand on the traditional divide between the scholar-observer and the participant or religious subject matter. Despite these concerns, which at this point are not new, the modus operandi of the field has predominantly been to continue to strive for neutral and objective research – itself an illusion, as post-modern critics have taught us.

The concept of interreligious dialogue is just as mired in histories of ideology. Scholarship has shown that it was also inspired by the West's interest in the so-called Orient and grew out of the development of Religious Studies itself. The impetus for modern interreligious dialogue, and many particular such dialogues, were initiated by Western Christian organisations, sometimes backed by governments, and are, as such, subject to the terms and biases of these organisations and the thinkers behind them. The 1893 Parliament of the World's Religions in Chicago, the event that led to the rise of interreligious dialogue, was called in celebration of the 400th anniversary of Columbus's 'discovering' the Americas, one thought-provoking cue of how the discipline is wrapped up in a Western history of power. Rather than abandoning interreligious dialogue because of this history, recent scholarly efforts have explored how to reformulate it and even the playing field, so to speak.

An important facet of interreligious dialogue that plays into such power dynamics is the language in which dialogue takes place. Dialogue partners who are not native Arabic-speakers, for example, seldom converse in Arabic, while it is often expected of Arabic-speaking Muslims in international settings of interfaith dialogue that they be capable of conversing in English. Similarly, although Religious Studies scholars are expected to learn non-European languages, and for Islamic Studies, Arabic, they rarely publish or present their research in Arabic. Even conferences on Arabic literature in the United States are held in English, a case unthinkable for, say, German literary studies. The hegemony of English in academic discourse silences from the outset those scholars without the necessary language training. Thus many academic venues operate within a comfort zone for English speakers in which the linguistic structures for authoritative knowledge affirm and strengthen the geopolitical and often economic power structures.

While these issues are still hotly debated in Western academia, Religious Studies programmes have been established in non-Western contexts, including formerly colonised countries such as Morocco. The Religious Studies programme at Mohammed V University in Rabat is not simply a transplantation of a Western academic model into the Moroccan context but emerged out of a combination of influences, principally the Western Religious Studies model, the history of Islamic religious training in Morocco, and the tension between the Moroccan government and the religious establishment. Many elements of madrasa education continue to be significant in the contemporary context, especially for understanding the priorities, teaching methods, and obstacles in the Religious Studies programme in Rabat.

The Master's degree programme in Religious Studies at Mohammed V University in Rabat is formally called Māstayr al-Madhāhib al-'Aqdiyya fī al-Diyānāt (approximately, Master's in Doctrinal and Religious Schools/Confessions). As stated in the programme's handbook, the main goals of study are to reach understanding of religious doctrines so students can compare conceptions of divine unity in the different religions' scriptures and core texts, as well as comparing Islamic schools of thought (*madhahib*) with those in Judaism and Christianity. The professors are all Muslims, and the programme relies on detailed knowledge of Islamic doctrine and study of the so-called *adyan samawiyya* and *adyan wad'iyya*, roughly translatable as 'heavenly religions' and 'human-made religions' — the former referring to the Abrahamic religious traditions and the latter referring to the 'pagan' and other religions. The methods of instruction and learning in this programme differ from Western academic institutions' pedagogy. Most learning takes place in the classroom, where professors lecture from memory and students meticulously copy down these lectures, a practice of course also predominant in the French system. Students spend up to eight hours per day at school, and almost no work takes place at home or through reading texts directly. This method can be attributed to the privileging of the oral over the written and other factors such as household environments not conducive to concentration on reading and schoolwork. Students take more than a dozen courses at a time, each one allocated a few hours of lecture per week, and memorisation of class material is highly valued.

This emphasis on memorisation is consistent with the history of madrasa education in Morocco. Until the 1930s, the Qarawiyyin and Yusufiyya mosque-universities were the most prestigious institutions of Islamic higher education, attracting Morocco's intellectual and political elite. Reformist shaykhs (leaders or teachers) in the 1920s and 1930s expanded the curriculum there with the aim of making Islamic education relevant to contemporary society. These institutions were also centres of resistance to French colonialism, and when in the 1930s colonial rule was clearly becoming ineffective, the French tried to limit the mosque-universities' power through 'organisational' measures like regulating instructors. As a result, the schools' elite students fled, and the quality of religious education declined. French government schools became a popular option, and their graduates took the governmental and other prestigious jobs, thus diminishing the opportunities accorded by an education at one of the mosque-universities. The traditional body of Islamic knowledge that religious education provided was still valued on a popular level, nevertheless, and the post-1956 Moroccan monarchy recognised this fact. The Ministry of Education included a division to regulate Islamic schools, and student strikes led the government to formally recognise a religious education as an alternative to a secular one. A considerable number of departments of philosophy were transformed into Islamic studies departments, due in part to the Islamisation of the educational system. The philosophy department at the University of Mohammed V in Rabat is thus strongly influenced by its personnel recruited from Islamic Studies.

Aside from this fraught history, the strongest influence on the methodology and epistemology of the Religious Studies programme at Mohammed V University may be a particular strand of classical Islamic studies as it developed from within Islam. The 'religious sciences,' as al-Ghazali understood them, include Qur'anic sciences (its readings, recitation, exegesis), hadith studies (the transmission, content, and collection of Prophetic reports), Islamic jurisprudence (*fiqh*), creed and theology (including the study of various Muslim groups and other religions), Sufism, Islamic history (in the form of biographies, annals, chronologies, etc.), linguistics and language studies (including grammar, literature, and lexicography), logic, and philosophy. In their studies of non-Islamic religion, they apply a kind of scriptural criticism that can be traced back to the developments of classical Islamic scholars such as 'Alī ibn Aḥmad ibn Ḥazm and Muḥammad ibn 'Abd al-Karīm al-Shahrastānī who wrote from their own confessional perspectives. The Andalusian polymath ibn Ḥazm (d. 1064) recorded his thoughts on Judaism and Christianity in his treatise The Distinctions regarding the Religions and the Muslim Sects, a systematic and polemical work whose thesis is that the Zahirite sect of Islam is the only correct religious creed. The echoes of Ibn Hazm reverberated among the Moroccan students. Ibn Hazm is a towering figure in Islamic thought who produced brilliant work, yet he also had an arrogant, uncompromising attitude and quick temper and was generally troubled by any kind of pluralism. His concern for truth and the oneness of God led him to scathing judgments of prominent Christian figures. Thus, for him, St. Paul was simply 'the cursed one,' or 'the one who leads to error', Peter 'the abominable', Matthew 'the pig', John 'the neglectful', Mark 'the apostate', and Luke 'the heretic'. The Persian scholar al-Shahrastānī (d. 1153), author of the heresiological treatise *The Book of Religious and Philosophical Sects*, serves as a balancing voice to Ibn Hazm. Striving to provide a neutral account of all historical religions of his time, he differentiated between religions that have a 'Book' or Scripture and 'worldly' religions that do not – a distinction that is retained by the Moroccan Religious Studies programme. The approach of the programme thus takes place from a distinctly Islamic perspective that in practice is not separated from its participants' own beliefs.

For the students in Rabat, the study of religion constitutes a search for theological truth, and this is their starting point and most clearly articulated goal for their study of both Islam and other religious traditions. In this respect, the programme comes closer to what we know as a theological approach in the West. There is clearly an apologetic, or even polemic, methodology at work. For example, when asked what the main goal of the programme is, one student responded that it is 'the spread and defence of Islam'. This is not the official orientation of the programme but can be seen in the curriculum and in the direction that many of the classes take. For example, the main point of a session on Shi'ism was to demonstrate its wrongness and elucidate where it deviates (wrongly) from Sunnism. Because the body of Religious Studies students is on the whole committed to Islamic belief, this focus on truth made the question, one that the Moroccan students were not initially prepared to answer, echo constantly through our classroom: 'Why study other religions?'

Heck termed his approach of bringing together the US and Moroccan graduate students *al-suhba al-'ilmiyya*—'scholarly companionship.' *Al-suhba al-'ilmiyya* is based on the premise that knowledge is best acquired through studying together, conversing with each other, discussion and 'dialogue,' which can be understood as a negotiation of meaning. It prioritises scholarly engagement over sharing personal experience, yet with the understanding that this focused encounter leads to broader conversations. The goal is to learn together through focused textual study that inevitably leads to discussion, argument, and friction meant to bring about concrete engagement. At the core of *al-suhba al-'ilmiyya* lies the search for a nuanced understanding of another religion as a phenomenon in flux that has its own logic and complex tradition. It constitutes a move away from a solely text-based acquisition of knowledge that does not allow other scholars' perspectives to refine and deepen understandings of these texts. *Al-suhba al-'ilmiyya* accommodates the openness that religion as an analytical category contains by refusing to specify its identity too rigidly. It holds that Religious Studies must be put on its own epistemological terms, and that religious knowledge, even knowledge about a religion, cannot be acquired as other sciences can. It allows for the notion that, as scholars, we are always in a dynamic relationship with what we study and holds that knowledge would be useless if it did not leave an imprint on the scholar.

Wilfred Cantwell Smith, the Canadian scholar of religion, claimed that the best way to approach the study of others' religious traditions is in relation to one's own faith or at least as analogous to it. For all the valid critiques that can be levelled at this approach, it has the benefit of acknowledging the scholar's own subjectivity. Yet *al-suhba al-'ilmiyya* neither entails an identification with the subject matter one studies, nor with the person one converses with. The reciprocity of the religious debate between scholars from different faiths, cultural upbringings, and academic and geographical backgrounds in Morocco exposed both the scholars and the subject matter to critique, discussion, and questions, thus avoiding a situation in which a scholar can compromise the data at her mercy. Rather, the constant struggle served as a corrective in the participants' own thought.

Careful reading of texts formed the foundation of the classroom curriculum in Heck's course, and each class session was based around a piece of writing by a Christian or Jewish thinker. After a student read a passage aloud, Heck led the class in a discussion of the important issues in it, emphasising that the goal was not to memorise but to understand and to ask questions of the text. This collaboration became the basis for the Moroccan and Western students getting to know one another and staying for discussions after the daily class session ended. In the (slightly) cooler air in the courtyard outside our classroom, lingering discussion about the day's class session mingled with the beginnings of friendships and laughter.

Friction arose when the two groups of students' different epistemological frameworks came into direct conflict. Sometimes, the type of response to Judaism and Christianity that we saw arose from misleading sources and misinformation. At other times, it was a genuine theological concern based on quality scholarship. One of the Moroccan students' main points of contention regarding Judaism was the Jews' belief in their own status as a 'chosen people.' If Jews are God's chosen people, they asked, and Jews believe they have the truth from God, why do Jews not want to share their privileged status and religious truths with others? The students also raised theological issues based on their understanding of Jewish doctrine. For example, why did God rest on the seventh day after six days of creating the world? God is omnipotent, and tiredness arises from weakness, which is in conflict with the Divine attributes. Additional questions included the status and treatment of women in Judaism. Regarding Christianity, what was most outrageous, in the Moroccan students' minds (besides the trinity and the two natures of Jesus, of course) was – one may gasp in surprise – that Paul allowed the abolition of circumcision as a religious obligation. Again and again, hands shot up in class and the questions were raised: 'How could a true apostle of God do such a thing?' and 'Is it not the clearest sign that Paul was an impostor that he violated the divine law of God in such a way?' These questions provoked bewilderment at best among the Christian students, who could not fathom how this particular practice was so central to the general argument over the truthfulness of Christianity. The hermeneutics of raising questions can be a mysterious thing. The discussions that arose from questions like these were often challenging and left us grasping for words, but it was earnest engagement that caused all parties involved to challenge their own understandings of the relevant issues and think about them in unfamiliar ways. It goes without saying that Western academic study is equally plagued by biases and assumptions the scholar brings to her subject matter.

Why, indeed, did God rest after six days of creation? We repeated this question aloud one evening as the two of us sat on our mattress in our small Rabat apartment. The question about divine omnipotence, raised earlier in our class, was still on our minds. Neither of us had encountered this query, or an answer to it, in our own religious upbringing or education. And though some of the Muslim students in our class would ask such questions as part of a learned rhetoric of religious polemic, others asked out of curiosity. This was something we could answer by consulting trusted sources. A question more difficult in a different way awaited us in class on another day. A Muslim student asked Rachel: 'Do you really believe in all the doctrines of your religion?' It was hard to know what to say to this question, we felt. Aside from the complexity of the answer any one of us Western students might have given in a different setting, we were taken aback by this question in an academic setting.

Wrestling with the discomfort of our classroom discussion, we tried to find a model for understanding our reactions to it. If it is possible to reach understanding of a subject matter and the discussion partner's position, the highest possible degree of understanding should be aimed at, and we suggest that in regards to the acquisition of religious knowledge, *al-suhba al-'ilmiyya* is one of the most fruitful methods. And yet it forced us to confront questions that struck us as more 'personal' than those we were used to hearing in academic settings, such as whether we truly believed in a particular religious doctrine. In class discussions, Moroccan students brought up one single quest again and again: to arrive at the truth. Today's Western academic mind-set is rather uncomfortable with this goal, since the acquisition of knowledge through field research holds the risk of hermeneutic inaccuracy when the lines between one's data and one's interpretative tools are blurred. However, acknowledging the influence of the 'object' of study as a productive part of scholarship is not new. For the German philosopher Hans-Georg Gadamer (1900-2002), there exists a truth that can be uncovered through a process of questioning and ongoing conversation. He differentiates between the position a person takes and the person herself, in order to come to an understanding of the subject matter one chooses as the subject of inquiry. This is exactly the intention of *al-suhba al-'ilmiyya*: it entails struggling sincerely over texts and their meaning, a meaning that is always dynamic and shifting given the different approaches and backgrounds of the dialogue partners. The open form of discussion does not only shed light on the subject matter at hand but opens up room for new questions and directions a study might take due to the hermeneutical and creedal differences of the various interlocutors.

It is through conversation that we come to understand ourselves and others. Conversation, according to Gadamer, is not necessarily about understanding the other person but about cognising what the other person has to say. Gadamer's hermeneutics to explore understanding requires that 'each person opens herself to the other, truly accepts her point of view as valid and transposes herself into the other to such an extent that she can understand not the particular individual, but what she says...and thus... relate the other's opinion...to our own opinions and views.' Gadamer cautions the interpreter to focus on a particular subject matter beyond all distractions and projections originating in every interpreter constantly. The process of understanding a particular subject matter is the result of a fusion of horizons, places where people's visions overlap. Each person articulating her own position on certain issues aims to adopt 'the right horizon of inquiry for the questions evoked by the encounter with tradition.' Every tradition or perspective, according to Gadamer, is an ongoing process of fusion of different horizons.

The American theologian and ethicist William Schweiker has developed Gadamer's theory of a hermeneutics of understanding further. For Schweiker, truth is not simply the outcome of demonstrative deduction, although we sometimes like to see it that way. Rather, truth emerges through the encounter of the subject matter as well as through self-reflection that occurs with that experience. Schweiker's understanding of arriving at truth can thus be characterised as a participatory act in which the interpreter is as important as the subject matter. The responsibility of the interpreter can therefore not be overstated. Research most often does not evolve out of an eye-to-eye dialogue based on an equal footing. In particular, scholarship on religion is often left to the mercy of the scholar who has 'the power to construct and control a subject that has little opportunity to contest either the interpretation or the terms of the discourse; the power to dictate the parameters of the field.' In a direct encounter over a longer time, through sincere and scholarly cooperation and struggle, the interlocutors can straighten out what they perceive as corrupt interpretations of a subject matter. The corrective value of Habermas's notion of language as a tool for domination suddenly gains new relevance. Habermas stresses the necessity of the dialectical nature of understanding and a fair power balance between the interlocutors. This notion elucidates the usefulness of al-suhba al-'ilmiyya in the course of which the respect for the agency of all interlocutors is especially important. One may never be completely able to overcome a power imbalance, and one can hardly stand objectively outside of a discourse that one is a part of, in one way or the other. Yet one can be aware of this fact and aim at a fair approach.

The conversant method of *al-suhba al-'ilmiyya* holds great potential for arriving at an understanding of the material that is being discussed and religion as being in flux and developing. The advantage of direct dialogue is that misunderstandings can be corrected directly. At the same time, we must remain aware of the rhetorical component any dialogue exhibits. A special component of *al-suhba al-'ilmiyya* is that the scholar is not merely observer, but is also the observed at the same time, which heightens her awareness of sensibilities concerning the subject under study and makes her research vulnerable to critique outside of her comfort zone. It is, of course, in the hands of the participant to which extent she allows for such vulnerability. The moment of answering 'Do you really believe all the doctrines of your religion?' can feel like a moment of huge decision.

During our scholarly encounter in Rabat, neither the Moroccan students nor the Western students' approach was given precedence: instead, we relied on *al-suhba al-'ilmiyya*, a text-based approach that focused on discussion arising from textual interpretation that all participants undertook together. This academic practice of careful reading differentiates *al-suhba al-'ilmiyya* from other types of interreligious engagement that may have a broader thematic or personal framework for discussion. This approach can be seen as an alternative to the main model of interreligious dialogue we often see in the West where the participants are often self-selecting individuals who are already open to others' religions and eager to understand, and where conversation is most often based on personal experience with religious practices and experiences and avoids difficult questions. When interreligious dialogue only includes participants already invested with finding common ground, when it limits its scope to non-incendiary issues, when it deals with personal experience to the exclusion of foundational texts, it runs the risk of becoming too tame to undertake the difficult work of real change. It allows participants to protect their own comfort zone, but at the expense of meaningful progress in understanding. As a methodology, *al-suhba al-'ilmiyya* could be the basis for all sorts of configurations of interreligious engagements. What if the programme we participated in had included American Muslims? Shi'ites? Atheists? Arab Jews and Christians? Whereas in our experience the most salient contrast was between Moroccan/Muslim and Western/Christian and Jewish students, a move to expand the identities of participants would result in an interesting kaleidoscope of affiliations and identities within the classroom. Ultimately, though, each participant brings his or her own experience, education, outlook, openness, and goals to the discussion.

About a week before the end of our course in Rabat, a conference on the theme of Abrahamic religions was convened, and students were given the opportunity to show off their research. The conference was well-publicised, but we were still surprised to see the lecture-rooms filled to capacity on the morning it began. On one panel about Judaism's attitude toward other religions, a Moroccan pupil presented her research, clearly the product of polemical books demonising Judaism. The idea of Jews as a chosen people was twisted into a framework for arrogance and condescension toward other religions and their followers. As the student's presentation progressed, we grew more and more uncomfortable. The information in her presentation was clearly wrong and damaging, but the student was sincere and thought she had done responsible research. When she finished speaking, the panel moderator spoke up, rigorously and spiritedly condemning the wrongness of the ideas she had presented. He ardently lamented Moroccans' lack of knowledge about Judaism today. In the past, he explained, Jews and Muslims lived side by side, and stereotypes about Jews never took off or became prevalent. Today, when so few Muslims know Jews personally, misinformation goes unchecked. After the panel was over, the student who had given the presentation approached Rachel, tearful and inconsolable. 'I'm so, so sorry,' she said. 'I did not mean to mischaracterise your religion in this way. I did research and these are the ideas I found in books... What should I read instead?'

Rachel didn't know what to say. The ideas in the student's presentation were offensive and had no basis. But for readers who can only access Arabic-language texts, there is a shameful lack of quality resources out there. Rachel was continually troubled by hardly ever having a good answer for students who came to her asking for good scholarship in Arabic that could explain to them the basics of Jewish ritual and doctrine. The project of correcting this lack seemed so important and yet so daunting. Even finding the words to explain how some Jews could consider themselves 'chosen people' without looking down on their non-Jewish neighbours was a complicated conversation. Rachel had never been asked to explain it before. So she took a deep breath, gave the student a hug, and tried to explain. The dominance of Western languages in research suddenly seemed so costly.

The *al-suhba al-'ilmiyya* of our study in Morocco made interreligious engagement more uncomfortable in a friction that was at once challenging and productive. The text-based nature of the approach anchored class sessions and allowed students to come together over questions that, even if left unanswered, shed light on meaningful questions. Locating such uncommon ground nurtured a true appreciation for the complexities of others' viewpoints while challenging participants to articulate and interrogate their own. The power of engagement surprised us by leaving us without many answers in an immediate sense but rather questions that have stayed with us in our subsequent work – work in the largest sense, encompassing doctoral study, personal relationships, and engagement with the world through activities as quotidian as reading the news. Struck by our inability to articulate satisfying answers to our classmates' queries that summer in Rabat, the questions still echo in our minds as we engage with all these facets of our world.

THE TURKISH MEDICI

Mohamed Bakari

The exposure of alleged corruption in the AKP government by a leading Turkish newspaper, *Today's Zaman*, created a tectonic shift in Turkish politics. It led to the resignation of four ministers in the government of the then prime minister, Recep Tayyip Erdoğan, on 17 December 2014. The exposure was seen by AKP as part of a larger game plan by its erstwhile allies the Hizmet Movement to discredit it and its government. Stacks of shoe boxes containing millions of dollars were found in the house of the prime minister's son, Bilal Erdoğan and shown on television and across other media. There was also alleged incriminating evidence of some ministers' personal finance compromised by kick-back harvesting. The Hizmet Movement is a powerful, unstructured organisation that is an important part of Turkish civil society. It is led by the charismatic religious leader, Fethullah Gülen, who has lived in exile for almost two decades. Partly to protect himself from the reach of his internal enemies, mostly an alliance of suspicious secularists, high ranking bureaucrats in the civil service, and the upper echelons of the military, he chose to go elsewhere. As a religious leader at the head of a civic movement, they saw him as a potential threat to the Turkish secular state. At the time of the media exposure, Erdoğan was an embattled prime minister who was trying to stem the tide of a burgeoning civil unrest through street protests and demonstrations that attracted ever larger numbers. The government mishandled the demonstration. The police tear-gassed, beat up, shot at and bundled protesters into police vans, at what started as a peaceful protest by a small group of middle class environmental activists, protesting the increasing gentrification of the less salubrious neighbourhoods bordering the prime areas of the central business district, home to hotels, and shopping areas frequented by endless streams of tourists, mostly affluent Middle Easterners. Erdoğan's cronies had apparently earmarked part of a public park (a *gezi*) – a place where people simply promenaded – for the construction of yet another shopping mall. This naturally angered environmental groups, such as Greenpeace, architects and other social activists. Disgruntled elements and malcontents also joined the fray.

In Turkey, demonstrations are not simply spirited mobilisations for social causes, they often have an underlying political motive. Initially they start off as genuine public spirited mobilisation for just social causes, until they are commandeered by hidden political forces that hijack them for their own ends. In the build up to the 2007 elections in Turkey, the foreign press, mostly American and British, was ecstatic about what they erroneously read as an inevitable impending defeat of the Islamist government led by Erdoğan. What misled the foreign press corps was their gullible reliance on one source of information, the Turkish secular press and their secular informant contacts, who steered them towards the view that their nemesis was in for massive defeat. The short lived euphoria was followed by massive and orchestrated nationwide demonstrations that were well funded and hyped by the CHP, the Cumhuriyet Halk Partisi, Republican People's Party, a secularist party founded by Mustafa Kemal Atatürk in the 1920s to implement his *laiklik*, or secularist policies, that were modelled on an extremist version of French secularism. The demonstrations were given the widest coverage by the Western media because they fitted with their expectations for a strictly secularist Turkey, but which now had no basis in Turkish reality. What happened in Gezi Park was that there was crowd sourcing worthy of depiction in Gabriel Garcia Marquez's *The Autumn of the Patriarch*. In reality, the crowd was drawn predominantly from among the Alevis, a Shiite sect sympathetic to Syria's Alawite regime of Bashir Asad. They seem to dominate the CHP membership; indeed, the current leader of CHP, Kemal Kiliçdaroğlu, is himself an Alevi. Until very recently, the Alevis dominated the judiciary and the bureaucracy and also had a presence in academia, largely in state universities, where they made sure that they enforced the secularist dogma to the letter. Thousands of Alevis from all over the country and a sprinkling of other secularists were packed into buses and transported to Ankara and Istanbul to demonstrate against the AKP. The viewing public did not know that Erdoğan could in fact pull five times the crowd that showed up in demonstrations carrying distinctive flags, the familiar crescent and star against the red background of the Turkish national flag, only that this time, the flag had the head of Atatürk wearing an astrakhan, a symbol of resistance against invading allied forces during the Gallipolli war of independence. The irony is that CHP is as nationalistic and as xenophobic as the other nationalist party, the MHP (Milliyetçi Hareket Partisi), the People's Nationalist Party. When it suits its agenda, the CHP always appeals to the secular sentiments of Western societies to draw sympathy for their defence of Kemalist principles, and when it does not, it lambasts the West for its anti-Turkish postures. The failure of both nationalist parties has been their inability to find leaders with constructive and long term visions for their country. Both parties have consistently been led by lacklustre individuals whose sole purpose seemed to be self-preservation and aggrandisement in the positions they have entrenched themselves in. Not that these parties do not have talented members who could take the leadership mantle, only that the internal politics of self-preservation has become cut-throat and nasty, especially within the CHP. The party is stuck in the politics and policies of the 1920s, 1930s and the 1940s, in a country that has gone through breathtaking changes within the past two decades. The country had been so traumatised by internal oppression and extreme politics of exclusion, that the majority of the population saw themselves as onlookers in other people's politics of manipulation and rapaciousness. National resources were commandeered by a tiny political elite in the bureaucracy and the military to serve their personal interests and the interests of their cronies, of course at the expense of collective national development. The result, over the decades, was runaway inflation and national inertia, fear and anxiety about the future of the country. This was the perfect setting for the making of what a young Turkish academic Kerem Oktem called *Angry Nation*. The military intervened at will whenever it found it convenient to sabotage democratic aspirations of the civilians. In Turkish tradition, the military has always played a central role in national affairs, never straying very far from politics, a tradition that goes back to the Ottoman era. The military establishment has always seen itself as the guardian of the Turkish state, and in particular, the protector of its laicism, an ideology aptly described by Marc Fumaroli as 'the profane religion of happiness' in *When the World Spoke French*. Until recently, Turkish politics had been a game of musical chairs alternating weak civilian governments with strong military juntas. Most civilian politicians had been obsequious, obliging and diffident in their dealings with military strongmen. But the first democratically elected prime minister, Adnan Menderes, broke from this cycle, by engaging in the politics of brinkmanship, vis-à-vis the military. It had always been easy, in the name of saving the Turkish state, for military usurpers to ride roughshod over civilian administrations, while reminding them that they are in power only to do their bidding. This ruffling of the feathers was to have dire consequences for Menderes. He was overthrown in a military putsch, and from that fateful moment he became remorseful. The military took full advantage of his changed psychological state. Supine civilian politics came to an end with the advent of Islamist politicians, savvy to a man. In fact, the rise of Erdoğan's AKP is the result of the cumulative efforts of skilful politicians who knew how to choose their battles by weighing their political strength vis-à-vis the ever watchful politicians in military fatigues. Every previous Islamist politician learned from the missteps of the others and corrected their step in their inexorable march towards a putative Islamic New Jerusalem. Islamists had never forgotten the fate that befell the first Turkish politician who dabbled in Islamist symbolism, Adnan Menderes. A suave dandy, with a passion for beautiful women and a general *dolce vita* attitude, Menderes had no compunction in using Islamic symbolism in drawing votes. He was taken to the gallows when he posed a threat to the Kemalist dogma of separating religion from the state. His fate was sealed when he reversed the Kemal Atatürk edict that Turkish should replace the ancient Islamic tradition of calling the *muezzin* in Arabic. When AKP came to power Menderes was adopted as a martyr of Islam's first battle against creeping atheism.

The next prime minister to dabble in religious politics was Turgut Özal (1927–1993), a technocrat of Kurdish ancestry, hand-picked by the military as a safe bet when they decided that it was high time to create a facade of democracy by involving civilians. Turgut Özal led the ANAP, Anavatan Partisi (Motherland Party). Özal had the advantage of starting at the height of the Cold War, and the enlistment of religion to fight the godless ideology of Communism was considered the right thing to do. Özal did not take long before opening the political space for Muslims by embarking in liberal policies in politics and economics. In fact, the groundwork for the current Turkish economic and political take-off was partly laid during this Özal period, when he invested heavily in the much neglected infrastructure. His stint at the World Bank, and his professional credentials as a civil engineer, led his to the realisation that the country needed to be spruced up if it was to compete in the emerging global economy. He turned out to be a successful, if cautious politician, but the military were perennially wary of civilian politicians. He died under suspicious circumstances. The current AKP regime recently revisited the case by setting up a commission of enquiry to investigate the claim that his death was a result of foul play. Indeed, the preliminary findings pointed to the possibility that he might have been poisoned.

Özal was followed by Necmettin Erbakan (1926-2011). Born in the same city as the ancient eccentric philosopher Diogenes – Sinop in the Anatolian heartlands – Erbakan was a German trained professor of mechanical engineering who harboured economic and industrial ambitions for Turkey. He also wanted Turkey to reclaim its Islamic roots that had so far been gradually submerged by the secular political class. A mercurial and ebullient politician, Erbakan became, more than any other Turkish Islamist politician, an embodiment of Ottoman ideals. Very much given to Islamic enthusiasms, he was swept off his feet by the euphoria that engulfed the Islamic world in the wake of the 1979 Islamic Revolution in Iran. It was clear that he was thirsting for an Islamic utopia for Turkey, but the kind of utopia that included technological development and was located far from the stranglehold of Kemalist ideology. During the short lived coalition government led by him, a marriage of convenience between Tansu Çiller's (born 1946) Doğru Yol Partisi (The True Path Party) and his Refah Partisi (Prosperity Party), he embarked on quixotic adventures that were sure to provoke the military. His trips to embrace the Islamic Republic of Iran and a visit to Gaddafi, were, to say the least, reckless within the political climate of secularist Turkey. At the time, Turkey was the only Middle Eastern country with any ties with Israel. Although he did not dare to immediately make Israel an absolute pariah in the Middle East, the new political adventurism was already sending signals that there was a new Turkey about to be born. For an Islamist Party under the watchful eye of the military, Erbakan's party did well for itself, by garnering 21.3 per cent of the vote. This mandate, however small, gave him enough confidence to assume that he represented a serious constituency in the country. Interestingly, CHP, Atatürk's party, has never hovered beyond this 20 per cent threshold in all these years. Erbakan's audacious political escapades were buoyed by this electoral scoop. This bravado only led to threats from the military to force its hand in his premature resignation. But by the time he left government, the Islamists had been emboldened. The biggest gift that Erbakan bequeathed his party was his cultivation of a visionary younger leadership. Among those he took under his wings as a mentor were two young politicians of different temperaments, Recep Tayyip Erdoğan and Abdallah Gül. The former had the head of a foot soldier, while the latter was an intellectual strategist. During Erbakan's active political life, starting in the 1970s until his death in 2011, he belonged to a total of five political parties, all Islamist and mutating from a basic Islamic hydra. Islamist parties were repeatedly closed through legal injunctions, only to be resurrected again in yet another guise. The Islamist agenda in the parties was reflected in their choice of names, such as the Milli Nizami Partisi (National Discipline Party) 1970-71; Milli Selamet Partesi (National Salvation Party) 1973-81; Refah Partisi (Welfare Party), 1997-98 Fazilet Partisi (The Virtue Party) 1999-2003, Saadet Partisi (Falicity Party) 2003-11. The party names were straight out of Alfarabi's *The Perfect City*, which itself was indebted to Plato's *Republic*. The Farabi vision was reminiscent of St. Augustine's City of God. As Erbakan grew older, he became more cantankerous and more radical. All the while, the Islamist parties increased their electoral gains with each general election.

Abdallah Gül studied economics at Istanbul University, completing his doctorate under Sabahattin Zaim, an economist whose publications increasingly addressed issues in Islamic economics. Zaim and Gül both later worked for the Islamic Development Bank in Jeddah. Erbakan's radical politics did not suit the more sedate temperament of Gül who must have realised that the scare politics of Erbakan would only reverse any Islamist gains. This is perhaps why he teamed up with the populist Erdoğan to form what is now the AKP, Adalet ve Kalkinma Partisi, Justice and Development Party. It was formed almost on the eve of the crucial elections of 2002. Erdoğan and Gül, in their political alliance, were the two public faces of the AKP Janus. The two politicians complemented each other. Gül, the intellectual, lacked the shirt-rolling temperament of Erdoğan, and Erdoğan lacked the measured and discreet political style of Gül. Between them, Erdogn and Gül created a formidable party machinery that became like a big tent, welcoming all those disillusioned by the elitist politics or exclusionary postures of other opposition parties. The AKP was a coalition of Islamists and Kurdish elements who felt marginalised by the other parties. This smart calculation suddenly popularised the party. More intellectual elements were also brought into the party, including Ahmet Davutoğlu, then teaching international relations at Beykent University, in Istanbul. It was clear to Gül, like it was clear to Marx over a century earlier, that economics was the bedrock on which constructive politics can be built. On his part, it has been all along clear to the foreign policy guru, Davutoğlu, that good foreign policy, made for good politics and naturally good governance led to economic prosperity. He saw foreign policy as central to domestic policy success. The party went about recruiting Turkish talent both internally and overseas. Young economists like Ali Babacan and Mehmet Şimşek, who were among the best and the brightest, were brought in to test new ideas that would turn around the Turkish economy. AKP became the face of the emerging vigorous and vibrant new Turkey. The young and untried politicians were audacious enough to play ball with the IMF and the European Union, by implementing the economic measures and policies dictated by the two set ups. This turned out to be just the solution to turn around the economy. In its formative period, the AKP exuded unprecedented optimism. In comparison, the older and more established parties looked geriatric, or like the Soviet Politburos of yesteryear. They were led by ancient men with bushy eyebrows, hair sticking out of their noses and ears, tired and worn out by futile internal squabbles. In contrast, AKP's political line up was relatively youthful and ready to go. Above all, AKP pursued the politics of inclusion, a new experiment in Turkish politics, where virtually all existing parties were predicated on one exclusionary ideology or another.

The biggest dilemma facing the new triumphant political party, which the electorate did not take into account when voting, was the relative inexperience of the AKP leadership. Although many had served in different capacities, virtually none had the experience of running a government. Recep Tayyip Erdoğan may have been a successful mayor of Istanbul in the 1990s, but that was not the same as running a government. For over eight decades the secular parties, those in the judiciary, the bureaucracy, and the military had been grooming either their own children or those of their allies to take their places, generation after generation. Their children had easy access to scholarships in universities in Europe and the United States. Also, after retiring from the military or the bureaucracy, the same people joined their natural political parties, mostly CHP, and became members of parliament, cabinet ministers and presidents of the republic, thus perpetuating their grip on power. The profiles of CHP members of parliament still betray the old system of patronage. It is no surprise that owners of the party resented, and still resent the leadership of Kemal Kiliçdaroğlu, who is viewed as an outsider and a social upstart. When he was manoeuvred into power, it was with the unspoken understanding that he was a 'passing cloud', a walking stopgap measure before a 'real' leader emerged. No wonder Kiliçdaroğlu instituted unprecedented changes in the party to the annoyance of party old-timers. This patrimonial hold on the party gave it a general perception that CHP was the exclusive party of old, moneyed and connected families, largely an Aegean and Mediterranean party, with urban colonies in Istanbul's Kadiköy, Beşiktaş and Şişli areas, with virtually no presence in Anatolian heartlands, except Zonguldak. By the 1990s, CHP was perceived as Turkey's own Nasty Party. In this context, the AKP positioned itself as the champion of those who had been victims of the political aristocracy dating back to the founding of the First Republic. The party members, either as Kurdish cultural nationalists or Islamists had at one time or another felt wronged by the ruling elite. Among those who had chips on their shoulders was Erdoğan, thrown in prison for reading a poem that mentioned minarets. The minarets were as scary to the Turkish secularists as they still are to the Swiss, Danes, Norwegians and other Europeans. The draconian laws that guard the secular state have been used time and again to keep politicians and writers on the straight and narrow. Although CHP espoused, as they claimed, the ethos of the democratic left, it was divisive and alienating in its practice.

The manpower shortfall of AKP, through serendipity, was filled by their new allies, the strong, well organised and well educated cadres of the Fethullah Gülen movement, the Hizmet. The movement's members were drawn from the Islamist intellectual elites from universities, the private sector, the media, and civil society. The network of institutions which they set up outside the mainstream enabled them to exercise a certain amount of autonomy and independence. Fethullah Gülen and his followers were persecuted, hounded and harassed constantly and were generally perceived as the fifth column. Like all groups pushed to the corner, they developed a sense of solidarity and loyalty. Many of their members had directly benefitted from the informal membership of the movement through participating in free tutorial classes in preparation for the gruelling and dreaded university entrance examination. The network of cram schools, similar to those found in Japan, gave its alumni a sense of camaraderie when they went to universities. They collectively read the works of the reformist theologian Bediuzzaman Said Nursi (1877–1960), which gave them a sense of group identity with certain puritanical views about how they should live their lives. Many became voluntary members of the movement, and in the spirit of noblesse oblige, rendered services in the Hizmet institutions. Over the years, the Hizmet, through smart public relations, has managed to establish credibility globally. Fethullah Gülen has even been voted one of the world's leading 100 intellectuals. To the followers of the movement he is a spiritual superstar and the proverbial prophet who finds honour outside his own country. One of the crucial institutions set up by the Hizmet movement was the Abant Platform, a forum that provided space to debate sensitive, but important national issues, such as the marginalisation of minorities in Turkish society, democratisation, press freedom, constitutional processes, shameful atrocities and human rights violations. The Abant Platform, named after the town where the events are held on a half-yearly basis, has influenced the direction of politics in the country especially in bringing together people from opposing ideological positions to come and debate issues frankly and openly but with civility. The central agenda for Abant has been dialogue between groups with different political positions. Participants are also invited from abroad to witness Turkey's political maturity and civility. In an Abant gathering, it is not uncommon to find Islamists sharing the platform with Kemalists, Turkish ultranationalists, Alevis, members of the Kurdish minority opposition BDP, atheists, freethinkers, Israeli representatives, and members of right-wing institutions such as The New America Foundation and American Enterprise. The discussions are broadcast online and the public is encouraged to engage through Twitter. Hizmet is not so much a movement as an informal brotherhood. Turkish Islam is more spiritually inclined towards one form of mysticism or another and virtually all Turkish Muslims are associated with one religious organisation or another, a *tariqat*, all headed by a spiritual leader who demands and is given unconditional allegiance. This also influences the nature of politics and administration. The leaders of political parties or institutions have an imperial style, and expect unquestioning loyalty, reading any contrary behaviour as insubordination. Parents expect obedience from children, teachers from students, and heads of political parties expect all members to toe the party line – absolutely. This is a slippery road to despotism.

In the euphoria of the 2002 election win, AKP recruited vast numbers of Hizmet members to fill administrative and political positions in the government. The movement suddenly found itself represented in key positions in the country. This was part of AKP's reward for waging common battles against their nemeses in the military, the bureaucracy and the judiciary. The long drawn 'Ergenekon trials', a series of high-profile trials of 275 military officers, journalists and lawyers alleged to be members of Ergenekon, a clandestine secularist organisation, were only possible through the pressure of the Islamist and pro-government media. These trials consolidated Erdoğan's position as the unrivalled sultan of Turkish politics: charismatic, courageous and an in-your-face politician. His emboldened followers were accused of policing morality in neighbourhoods populated largely by them. Erdoğan publicly berated adult citizens for wine consumption and public smoking. Consummate politician that he is, he did this to divert public attention from key national concerns that were at the centre of public debates. Erdoğan may have been saying these things with conviction, but he also had an eye on political manoeuvring. The secularists always fell into his political trap and Erdoğan managed to shift the agenda as and when he thought opportune.

Through personal charisma and political manoeuvring, he has managed to wrong foot his detractors. The main political plank that supported the secularists in their grip on power was the election of the president of the republic through Parliament. Erdoğan and his party strategists calculated that if they managed to get the president elected through a direct vote, it would seal the opposition's only loophole to access the presidency. The opposition leaders lacked the common touch and could never move the vote in their direction. This was the AKP strategy. Despite all the vicissitude that he had to go through, Erdoğan's ultimate goal was Çankaya, the seat of power, and the presidential palace from where Mustafa Kemal Atatürk went on to shape the Turkish nation in his image. Erdoğan has never disowned the Atatürk legacy. No one in Turkey can seriously do so. President Erdoğan sees himself, and is seen both by his supporters as well as his detractors, as the most successful leader since Atatürk. He was at the head of a team that turned around Turkish fortunes, from a struggling nation riddled with self-doubt to one that was self-confident and proud of its achievements. Turkey is one of the few Muslim countries where stark poverty is never in evidence, and one of the key indicators of this economic boom is the vibrancy of its construction sector. And wherever there is economic boom, opportunities for money grabbing and general greed are not too far behind.

Monumental infrastructural projects that few countries dare embark upon have been started with pomp and brio. The Marmaray undersea tunnel, the joint project of Japanese and Turkish engineers, for example, is one symbol of Erdoğan's political and economic teams. The ostentatious $615 million presidential palace outside Ankara is another. Corruption is a natural corollary to such monuments of arrogance. A short period before the general elections, senior police officers ordered a probe into the finances of key Erdoğan allies in his cabinet. There was also the scandal of stashed millions in Bilal's house. A purported audio recording was posted on YouTube in which a voice alleged to be that of Erdoğan is overheard telling his son to take the hush money elsewhere out of the reach of investigators. Naturally, Erdoğan got rather angry, accusing the followers of Gülen as the authors of this nefarious plot to destabilise his regime on the eve of the elections. He termed this probe an act of treachery on the part of those he had given complete trust. Gülen's followers were ubiquitous in the civil service and especially the police department and the judiciary. Erdoğan is a street fighter who grew up in one of the toughest neighbourhoods of Istanbul. He brought to bear his street smarts to fight the fight of his life. As an instinctive politician, he followed his gut feelings, and in a typically Machiavellian style immediately swung into action. His first action was to suspend the initial probe, and then reshuffle the police departmental heads, at all levels country-wide, thereby displacing those officers he suspected of colluding with his opponents in undermining both his authority and credibility. The seriousness of the accusations allowed him little room to manoeuvre. Tactically he knew that heads had to roll and realpolitik required that those in the cabinet who were mentioned in the probe had to honourably resign. He cleared the way for the vindication of their innocence before setting a commission of enquiry to replace the original probe team. He also purged the judiciary of those elements that were deemed to be loyal to the Gülen movement. He made it clear in public that there could not be two centres of power, that it was Erdoğan who had the mandate to run the country, and not unelected bureaucrats whose loyalty he suspected. He dubbed his opponents as the denizens of what he called 'a parallel state'. The use of the discourse of 'parallel state' was a newspeak lexicon to describe what had been notoriously understood in Turkish as '*derin devlet*' the 'deep state'. The putative deep state was previously associated with clandestine elements made up of an assortment of the local mafia, political malcontents, disgruntled ultranationalists and other criminal elements, who took it upon themselves to dictate the direction the state should take in internal and international politics.

Both the AKP and the Gülen movement are media savvy. Over the past two decades, Islamists have set up their own mass communication tools, or gobbled up those in existence, to ensure that their voices are heard as frequently and as loudly as possible. The Gülen movement, which had been accustomed to being vilified and demonised through state media under the control of secularists, already knew the value of cultivating one's own media. The Hizmet has built both a local and international network of newspapers and television stations to rival any organisation. The AKP, as the ruling party, also had ready access to government mouthpieces such as the TRT (Turkish Radio and Television), a parastatal media outfit that loyally serves the government of the day. The conglomerate of newspapers, satellite television and magazines, radio stations ensures that the media was the message, as MacLuhan had famously put it. The political feuds are fought on television talk shows lasting several hours with shouting matches between rival political pundits and in newspapers where columnists – many professors at the plethora of universities in Turkey – denounce and expose all variety of misdemeanours. It has all became over-heated, and dangerous. The opposition feels targeted, especially when Erdoğan goes out of his way in his public appearances to point an accusing finger at his detractors. This sends a shiver down their spines. Although there has been a squeeze on the media, opposition journalists have continued their relentless assault on the policies of the government. A cursory glance at the media in Turkey leaves one with the impression that things are only black and white. The 'you are either with us or against us' kind of atmosphere prevails on all sides.

Over the years, AKP has increased its electoral margin, from the earlier 37 per cent, to 47 per cent in 2007, to 49.8 per cent in 2011. A gruelling countrywide campaign to repair his battered image with the electorate, through a combination of rhetoric and appeals of innocence, enable Erdoğan to win over his captive audience, the hardcore Islamists who are mortally afraid lest the secularists come back with their past oppressive ways. The comeback kid managed to garner 51.79 per cent in the first ever direct presidential elections. His opponent, Ekmeleddin Ihsanoğlu, a Cairo born and Al Azhar educated seventy-year-old Turk, whose parents were driven into exile in the early Republican period, was the choice candidate for the combined opposition. Ihsanoğlu himself owed his high profile job as the Secretary General of the Islamic Conference Countries to Erdoğan, as part of his strategy of influence within the international Muslim community. Everyone knew that given Erdoğan's high pitched rhetoric, the low key Ihsanoğlu had no chance against a street fighter. Under the circumstances, the presidential election turned out to be a test of the real strength of Erdoğan. As it turned out, half the electorate decided to give Erdoğan a second chance, since Ihsanoğlu did not quite fit their idea of a reliable leader. Many in the Islamist camp viewed him at best as a political opportunist and a turncoat. Erdoğan may be flawed but he was still a safe bet. It was a measure of CHP's maturity as a reforming party that they even bent over backwards to accommodate a candidate of Ihsanoğlu's Islamist background. By that very compromise, it was an irrevocably changed party that threw away its stuffy and wooden image as the party of the Kemalist aristocracy and bourgeoisie. It was a revolutionary act on Kilinçdaroğlu's part. It also says something about his kitchen cabinet's resolve to shirk off its inflexible past and curve an image for itself as a party of change, just like AKP. Ironically, the fall out between Erdoğan and his former allies created an opportunity for CHP to do a bit of soul searching. It also made it possible for former Erdoğan allies to look for a political home in one of the established political parties. In this regard, one can argue that it was the anti-Erdoğan forces that created the tectonic shift between important Islamic political groups. In the universe of Islamic politics in Turkey, the Hizmet movement now seems to be on its own. Its media outlets have been raided, media executives and journalists have been arrested on charges of being members of a terrorist group. Arrest warrants have been issued for Fethullah Gülen who is now accused of leading a criminal organisation.

Other Islamist groups appear to be still within the AKP orbit. This group includes many *tariqas*, whose leaders give them a nod about who to vote for, in return for political and economic favours. The Nakshibandi order, at least its Turkish branch, will always vote with AKP supporters. The Hizmet movement's supporters differ radically from the profiles of other Islamic groups in emphasising education and general economic development, agendas that are closer to those of the AKP than the general run of Turkish *tariqas* that are often conservative, inward looking, parochial and often obscurantist.

Will the AKP continue with the Erdoğan legacy? This is unlikely for Erdoğan is no longer the party strongman. He may influence party policies from a distance, but is unlikely to have his suggestions taken up in their entirety. For one, the national constitution requires that the person elected president has to sever all ties to his or her political party and become non-partisan. Erdoğan aims to change the current political system into a presidential one on the American model. Even the way he conducts his presidential duties differs from the low-key presidencies of his predecessors, including his close ally Abdullah Gül. There seems little likelihood of the constitution changing to an American style of governance any time soon, given the political polarisation in the country. A party has to have a solid majority, or convince some other parties to support their agenda to transform the Turkish political scene. For all appearances of radicalism, Turkish society is still a deeply traditional society, cautious about changes that will put power in the hands of one person.

This is where Prime Minister Ahmet Davutoğlu can play an important role in balancing the needs of tradition with those of national development. Davutoğlu remained with Erdoğan in his trying times. Although Erdoğan takes most of the kudos for Turkey's economic performance, and early foreign policy scoops, much of the credit goes to Davutoğlu. An international relations theorist with a background in political economy, he has spent time looking at the Middle Eastern chessboard and tried to calculate moves that will best maximise Turkish gains. His main source of inspiration, if one is to go by his studies on international relations and interest in civilisations, is Ibn Khaldun. Like Ibn Khaldun, Davutoğlu is not only a theorist of civilisations but takes lessons from politics through active political engagement. Davutoğlu may be the only person in his party who espouses a liberalism of sorts, but this liberalism is Islamic liberalism, not the liberalism of the type emanating from the West. However, one must admit, that Davutoğlu's initial steps do not look very progressive. When he announced his first cabinet, some of us were shocked by the line-up – all male except for one woman member. He has also been accused of suffering from delusions of grandeur which stems from his nostalgia for the Ottoman past.

Davutoğlu's immediate task is to transcend the Erdoğan legacy, which is associated with press ganging and the cult of personality. His greatest contribution to modern Turkish democracy would be to consciously make Turkish political institutions greater than himself, so that his personality does not overshadow the rule of law. After all, democratic rights are for everyone.

RACIALISM IN THE ARCHIPELAGO

Nazry Bahrawi

Out there, in the realm of the abstract, can be found a theory of human nature that has existed for aeons. It purports to preach a perennial truth, or the *logos* as the early Greek philosopher Heraclitus would call it. That truth is simply this: stripped of all our creature comforts and left to our own cerebral devices, humanity discriminates and stratifies itself, eventually strutting down the red carpet to our own grandiose destruction, our beautiful deaths. We are, at our core, murderous bigots.

Across temporal and geographical divides, some, more than others, are keenly aware of this possibly imagined, possibly real disposition. A few have attempted to reach out to the rest – to warn perhaps or maybe to just draw attention to this leviathan within us. One such attempt transformed a little known World War II veteran by the name of William Golding into a literary sensation following the release of his first novel, *Lord of the Flies*. Golding's 1954 work narrates the descent into dystopia of a group of young boys who are stranded on an uninhabited island. In Golding's imagining, boys will not be boys but barbarians who discriminate, stratify and hunt each other like game in pursuit of power.

Prophet Muhammad understood the ubiquity of bigotry all too well. He suffered it in his hometown Mecca at the hands of his own flesh and blood, Abu Lahab, in the early days of Islam. It was reported that Abu Lahab once threw the entrails of a sacrificed camel over his paternal nephew who was praying at the Ka'aba. Yet this aggression was mild compared to the savagery that befell the subalterns and the pariahs who had converted to Islam in pagan-majority Mecca. Take, for instance, the African slave Bilal ibn Rabah, who was dragged roughshod around the streets of Mecca. Bilal then had his limbs stretched and was made to endure the weight of a hefty boulder on his chest. While Bilal survived his ordeal to become Islam's first *muezzin*, the betrothed pair of Sumayya bint Khayyat and Yasir ibn Amar were not as fortunate. As 'immigrants' with no familial affiliation in Mecca, the two Muslim converts did not enjoy the benefits of tribal protection. Sumayya's poor standing was worsened by the fact that she was a former slave. Seeing that the couple were vulnerable, Meccan tribal leader Abu Jahl and his men tortured the two poor souls before ending their lives.

The horror. The horror. Traumatised are those who have to live through the pain of seeing their closest friends and allies brutalised. Given Muhammad's emphatic temperament and humane character, it is not difficult to imagine him honouring the memory of Sumayyah and Yasir while delivering his now famous lines during his last sermon at Mount Arafah: 'An Arab has no superiority over a non-Arab, nor does a non-Arab have any superiority over an Arab, a white has no superiority over a black, nor does a black have any superiority over a white, except by *taqwa*'. Uttered way back in the seventh century, these lines pre-empt what modern intellectuals of colour today define as racism. Seen in this light, Muhammad was, indeed, prophetic. Yet any exegete worth his salt would say that the politics of translation necessitates a lengthy treatise on what the Prophet meant by *taqwa*. Conventional wisdom would equate it to 'piety'. But what really connotes 'piety' and how is it to be judged? This is a crucial question. The danger with mistranslating *taqwa* here is that a message that is meant to be inclusive can ironically be distorted to justify a sense of superiority. This is the idea that men of taqwa are to tower above the rest, and their words have to be taken as sacrosanct. Throughout the annals of Islamic civilisation, we have seen this scourge of moral superiority rear its ugly head through the acts of *takfir*, the practice of excommunication, declaring other Muslims as apostates or simply infidels, committed by the Kharijites during the formative phase of Islam, the Wahhabis, the Talibans and the jihadists of the so-called 'Islamic State'. In one form or another, members of these groups have deemed themselves exemplary men of *taqwa*, decrying those outside their fold to be lesser beings.

At least, one can take consolation in the fact that we now stand at a critical juncture of our intellectual development where bigotry can be 'called out'. Thanks to the likes of Frantz Fanon, ethnic minorities can say: 'Hey, that's racist'. Salute to Edward Said, whose scholarship has helped Muslims articulate: 'Mate, that's Islamophobic'. The same can be said of patriarchy and homophobia. The mainstreaming of identity politics in academia and civil society has made it easier to pinpoint instances of discrimination. This is all good, except that the situation in certain parts of the world is not that straightforward.

In the Malay Archipelago, for example, race matters, with many believing it to matter above everything else. Despite our privileged position on identity politics as opposed to our predecessors, modern man's blind spot with bigotry today is our fascination with essentialism that is seemingly natural, a sophisticated form of bigotry that cannot be 'called out'. That demon is racialism. Yet for the Muslims in this part of the world, this is not their most chilling bogeyman. A far more powerful and far more malicious *djinn* ravages this sprawl of tropical islands. They fear He whose terror does not discriminate. The Shi'as, the Ahmadiyahs, the Sufis and even members of the majority Sunnis have faced his wrath. He goes by *takfir* but he is also legion, for he is many.

The Malay Archipelago is known for its lush greenery. The array of flora and fauna that thrive here is so expansive that the prophet Adam himself might have taken more time than usual to learn their names way back in prehistory. The archipelago's richness of species also encompasses its human denizens. In this part of the tropics, there are Malays, Chinese and Indians. But scratch the surface and you will unveil another layer of ethnicity amidst these overarching ones. Indeed, the Malays can be further divided into the Kelantanese, Javanese, Boyanese, Bugis and Batak, to name a few. The Chinese, meanwhile, can be sub-divided into clans and dialect groups. Then there are Chinese folks who identify themselves as the Peranakans or Straits Chinese. The Indians comprise Tamils, Ceylonese and the more recent North Indian migrants. One must not forget the Arabs and Eurasians who also live here. Considering that the region is home to a wealth of ethnic groups, and multitude of names, could Adam have fumbled here too? This flourishing of life does make the adjective 'Malay' in Malay Archipelago sound a tad misleading. Yet three of the four countries that make up the archipelago are insistent on retaining Malayness as its core national character. The constitutions of Singapore and Malaysia specify that the Malays are *bumiputera*, or 'sons of the soil'. Officially recognised as the region's indigenes, the Malays are therefore deserving of special rights. Brunei, probably the most traditionalist of the archipelago countries, entrenches this credo further by way of its national philosophy specified as

'*Melayu, Islam, Beraja*', which translates as 'Malay, Islam, Monarchy'. What of Indonesia? Refreshingly, it is the only country in the archipelago whose constitution is not centred on Malayness, though this has not always been the case. Once upon a time, Indonesia too was officiated along the lines of Malay-centricity by way of its *pribumi* protocol. *Pribumi* is the Indonesian equivalent of *bumiputera*. For a cosmopolitan region such as this, the push to favour one ethnic group over others is sure to spell trouble. Why then its appeal?

The *bumiputera* protocol is often defended by invoking colonialism. This has to do with the way the protocol can be seen as chastising wave after wave of colonialism that had assailed the region. Colonialism in maritime Southeast Asia began with the Portuguese invasion of Malacca in 1511. Over the next few centuries, Portuguese rule made way to British colonisation that had subsumed contemporary Malaysia and Singapore into the fold of the British Empire, as well as Dutch conquest of most parts of present day Indonesia to form the Dutch East Indies. During World War II, a new master in the guise of imperial Japan subjugated the archipelago. Allied with Hitler's Germany, the East Asian nation occupied most parts of the region, overthrowing both the British and Dutch. However, Japan's explosive defeat in 1945 saw the archipelago returned to their respective former masters. This was not to last, as independence was finally gained by Indonesia in 1949 and Malaya in 1957.

For a people who believed they were subjugated by foreign powers over centuries, the *bumiputera* protocol can be seen as righting a historical wrong; it is the recognition of their sufferings, and the emboldening of a more pristine past. After all, before Europe's successive incursions, the archipelago was home to a series of thriving Malay kingdoms, most notably in Malacca but also in Samudera Pasai (present day Aceh) and Mataram (central Java). More popularly, the *bumiputera* protocol has been defended on egalitarian grounds. In the postcolonial states of the archipelago, Malay political elites point to economic indicators that show the majority Malays to be fiscally weaker than the region's largest ethnic minority, the Chinese. In trying to balance the playing field, they responded in the only way they know how – that is, to institutionalise a pro-Malay economic programme.

Thus, Malaysia launched the New Economic Policy in 1970, which remains in force today in more or less the same form. In neighbouring Singapore, the nation's minority Malays – about 13 per cent of the population – are entitled to education subsidies, an affirmative action policy that continues still. Meanwhile, Indonesia saw *pribumis* benefit from economic policies under its second president, General Suharto in the 1970s. Calling them '*golongan ekonomi lemah*' or 'economically weak group', Suharto made available loans and special tendering rights and privileges for *pribumi* businessmen and traders.

At face value, the allure of the *bumiputera* protocol lies in its noble aims. Yet, is not the road to hell laden with good intentions? For those vying to defend the protocol as anti-colonial, it is probably erstwhile to note the origins of the terms *bumiputera* and *pribumi*. As Sharon Siddique and Leo Suryadinata astutely observe:

> This division into 'racial' categories, irrespective of their relative sizes, is an important feature of colonial society. Our own perspective brings into clearer focus the division of these ethnic groups into another, more fundamental, dichotomy: indigenous versus non-indigenous communities. The indigenous/non-indigenous dichotomy was fostered by the colonial powers in two ways: first, by their encouragement of immigration, or at least, the importation of immigrant labour; second, through their policies which encouraged both immigrants and natives to view themselves as collective communities.

Put another way, the *bumiputera* protocol is a continuation of the colonial idea of 'divide and rule'. That which once aided colonial hegemony can now be seen as prodding neo-colonial dominion. This has never been clearer than in Malaysia, where the lines are blurred between the affirmative action slant of the *bumiputera* protocol and the political concept of *ketuanan Melayu*, or Malay supremacy.

Political observers have noted how the nation's pro-*bumiputera* New Economic Policy has evolved over the years, away from its benign beginnings to benefit only a select group of Malays, thus giving rise to charges of cronyism for the ruling elites. This selectiveness is especially stark considering that the constitutional definition of *bumiputera* in Malaysia also includes the non-Malay indigenous communities such as the Dayaks and Ibans of the eastern states of Sabah and Sarawak. Alas, the idea that the *bumiputera* policy is egalitarian is nothing short of bogus. But Malaysia's neo-colonialising *bumiputera* impulse is not confined to the economic sphere; it has also bastardised the nation's intellectual growth. Here, it is ironic that none other than the great anti-colonial thinker Syed Hussein Alatas has been rendered an unwitting aide. The Malaysian translation of Alatas' 1977 seminal work The Myth of the Lazy Native into Bahasa has failed to capture the nuances of race relations as opposed to the Indonesian version. In the Malaysian incarnation, meaning is twisted to promote ideas of *ketuanan Melayu*. It portrays the ethnic Chinese as badly behaved and utilitarian in their ways where the original text has no such connotations. Something vile has been committed unto a great work, a violation done not from without but within. This is not just rape; it is incest.

Much has been written about Malaysia and its narrow conception of race. But I want to focus on the allure of racialism, its relation with power, and the ways in which the idea of race can be subtly engineered towards the attainment of insidious ends without people even realising it. In the field of critical race studies, scholarship about racialism is rather limited – something that cultural theorists desperately need to correct. Someone who has written on the subject is Michael MacDonald, an international relations scholar at Williams College, Massachusetts, who makes the following incisive distinction:

> Racism is necessarily invidious. Racialism, on the other hand, maintains that races are different and are sites of political identity and participation. As a version of culturalism, racialism locates individuals in races, makes races into foundations of political identities, and regards racial identities as the stuff of politics.

MacDonald was writing about apartheid in South Africa, which he describes as 'racist and racialist' – an observation that also holds true for Malaysia. After all, in toggling between affirmative action and *ketuanan Melayu*, the nation's pro-*bumiputera* protocol is both. It must also be noted here that racialism is not 'institutionalised racism', a concept that was popularised by American black activists, Stokely Carmichael and Charles V. Hamilton in their 1968 book *Black Power*. In essence, institutionalised racism feeds on the idea that certain races are inferior, whereas racialism gets its strength from the assumption that differences between races are natural – and there is nothing insidious about it.

There is one nation in the archipelago that has perfected the art of racialism: Singapore, the only Chinese-majority state in a Malay-Muslim backyard. I am of that city-state. Now, mine is a nation that prides itself as the most successful example of multiculturalism in the world today. Yet its inclusivity is truthfully limited to racial categories. Singapore has a fetish for things to be in their place. Like Adam, Singaporeans are prone to naming, or to be exact, an addiction to categorising. Unlike Adam, Singaporeans possess a vocabulary limited to four alphabets, CIMO, an acronym that stands for Chinese, Indian, Malay and Others. Singapore officialises the Other as a one-size-fits-all category for a bevy of minority races. An integral part of citizenry, race appears in identity cards and job application forms. Public housing, including rental accommodation, is subjected to racial quotas. Non-Singaporeans who did not grow up with this baggage are not exempt. An American friend of South Asian descent looking to rent was asked her race, told the rent of her potential neighbours, and even asked if her marriage was arranged. In one fell swoop, she was Othered.

Above all, social policies in Singapore are crafted on the basis of race-centric data, with the Malays consistently showing up as the least rich (household income), the least clever (education results), and the least healthy (obesity indicators). It is no surprise then that social aid funding is mostly dispensed through ethnic-based self-help groups. Needless to say, the Malays, being the most problematic on all sets of data, have the most number of such groups to 'help' them. So much so that this has given birth to another Singapore acronym – the MMOs, or Malay Muslim Organisations.

Racialism runs deep in the Singapore psyche. It is the de facto reality that grips the most conservative, as well as the most progressive, of Singaporeans. Every year, students and teachers celebrate racial harmony day by donning traditional costumes and staging cultural performances. They believe this to be the epitome of inclusivism. Others disagree. Instead, well-intentioned activists and artists speak and write of how minority races are oppressed. Their efforts 'call out' racism, but totally miss out on the workings of racialism. In an ironical twist of events, the more instances of racism are called out, the deeper racialism gets entrenched. In a Catch-22 situation, oppression of the Malays necessitates helping the Malays. The very viability of 'the Malays' as a racial category, as an imagined community, remains. Racialism also produces a newfangled form of piety, the worship of 'little boxes'. In this multicultural city-state, Buddhists, Christians, Muslims, Hindus and atheists are linked by their overbearing impulse to reduce complex human identities to neat categories, ritualised as racialism through social policies.

Unlike racism, racialism is hard to spot. In fact, racialism normalises, even makes it desirable, for people to see race as the principal lens for making sense of the world. It ensnares even the most open-minded. It manufactures consent in upholding racial hierarchies. But the practice of racialism extends beyond the archipelago. MacDonald showed it to be prevalent in South Africa. The irreverent television comedian Jon Stewart shows that it is equally pertinent and prevalent in America. In a recent episode of *The Daily Show*, 'Race/Off', Stewart has this to say about the unrest that broke out in Ferguson, during August 2014, following the fatal shooting of an unarmed black male by the police: 'Race is there and it is a constant. You're tired of hearing about it. Imagine how fucking exhausting it is living it'. Stewart is addressing a very real fear about racialism: the idea that it advocates a 'post-race' ideology. Such fears stem from the view that the world can never be colour-blind. Rightly so, race should never be discounted as an identity marker. True to Stewart's words, it is a constant. Yet it is a grave misunderstanding to think that racialist critiques are directed at dismantling racial identity. Its aim is much more nuanced – that is, the deconstruction of the idea that race is the primary identity marker, the fundamental constant. By that same token, racialist critiques also open us up to the idea of a fragmented self. Human beings are schizophrenic and contradictory, but this is not always a bad thing. It means that no one person can be defined solely by the colour of his or her skin. Schizophrenia also allows us to be adaptable and gives us access to different aspects of our identity that can be mobilised in different circumstances. Seen this way, schizophrenia is cosmopolitan itself.

Can we be optimistic that the world can tread the path of non-racialism? Perhaps Indonesia, often referred to as the world's most populous Muslim nation, offers some hope. In a highly racialised region, Indonesia is a welcome exception. Like Malaysia, it used to subscribe to a pro-Malay protocol in its economic and political support of *pribumis*. Over time, the protocol changed drastically following the stepping down of its authoritarian leader Suharto in 1998. In this post-Suharto period known as the *reformasi*, or reformation, Indonesia's racialism grew fainter and fainter. The decline began some four months after Suharto's resignation, when Indonesia's interim president B.J. Habibie issued a decree banning the government from using *pribumi* in official documents as a step to removing all forms of discrimination. Later in 2000, the nation's first democratically elected leader Abdurrahman Wahid lifted the ban on the public celebration of Chinese traditions, with his successor Megawati Sukarnoputri following up by declaring Chinese New Year a public holiday. Yet the most notable achievement, as pointed out by the political scientist Jacques Bertrand, was a 2001 amendment to the Indonesian constitution that removed the requirement for the nation's president to be 'indigenous'. As it stands now, anyone can be president as long as that person is an Indonesian citizen. If a moral can be derived from this story, it is that the racialised parts of our being, like Indonesia, need a jolt of *reformasi*.

But Indonesia is not immune from the beast of *takfir*. While it has an exemplary record of staving off the ill-effects of Malayness, it has achieved less in terms of Islamic identity. Like racialism, *takfir* glosses over the complexities of human identity. Unlike racialism, it thrives on cannibalism. When it reared its ugly head, the majority Sunnis began casting the evil eye towards their less-than-Muslim cousins.

In 2012, the *takfiris* raided and burnt homes of Shi'ites in the East Java village of Sampang, an attack that saw two Shi'ites killed and hundreds displaced. The world's first 'Anti-Shi'a Alliance' convention was held in the scenic city of Bandung on 20 April 2014. The convention saw the participation of local officials such as West Java's governor Ahmad Heryawan and Ahmad Cholil Ridwan, who heads the nation's highest Islamic authority, the Indonesia Council of Ulema (MUI). Worryingly, the convention ended with the adoption of a manifesto calling for sectarian purging. The spread of *takfir* in Indonesia also saw the prosecution of the minority sect of the Ahmadiyah, who have suffered attacks similar to the Shia. Homes were destroyed in 2013 in the West Java village of Tasikmalaya, while three Ahmadiyah followers were bludgeoned to death in another village, Cikeusik. With the latter incident, the Indonesian court responded by jailing an Ahmadiyah member for six months for defending himself against attackers. The Human Rights Watch described the sentencing as 'appalling'. Other instances abound; you only have to consult Google to discover them.

In Malaysia, the desire of government officials for a pristine Malay identity has now expanded into the Islamic sphere. So now a good Muslim is a Sunni Malay who follows the Shafi'i *madhab*, or school of Islamic jurisprudence. In this parochial *takfir* cosmology, the Shias can only be deviants. In March 2014, Islamic authorities arrested 114 Shia individuals in the state of Perak for intending to commemorate the birthday of Zainab, the daughter of Islam's fourth caliph, Ali. This was just the latest in a series of arrests of Shias enabled by the nation's internal security act (ISA), where a person can be detained without trial for an initial period of 60 days and subsequently up to two years. In 2010, 200 Shias were detained under the ISA for commemorating the *Ashura*, the tenth day of the Islamic month of Muharram. On this day the Shia mourn the martyrdom of Husayn, the grandson of Prophet Muhammad, at the Battle of Karbala. The situation has become so worrisome that the Malaysian Prime Minister, Najib Razak, felt the need to reiterate the need for Muslim unity!

There is no way one can make sense of this senselessness. The *takfiri* operates on the assumption of a binary code – good Muslim, bad Muslim, where we 'the good' are defined by sectarian belief. Read this way, *takfir* works in a similar manner to racism and racialism, fuelled by essentialism. Both racialism and *takfir* impart essential traits to a 'community', and thus establish a power hierarchy in a society as one community is thought to be possessing better traits than others. These multifarious tales of power in the Archipelago are full of paradox. The case elsewhere may not be all that different.

GOVERNING
BOSNIA-HERZEGOVINA

Sejad Mekic

The Bosnian war has left an indelible mark on Bosnia-Herzegovina. The atrocities and brutal ethnic cleansing, committed between April 1992 and December 1995, shattered assumptions of a secure and peaceful Europe that had endured since World War Two. Bosnia has rarely been in the headlines since, except for the trials of war criminals at the International Criminal Court at The Hague. The conflict slipped back into the subconscious of the European mind, and the plight of the Bosnians seemed once again of little consequence. Then in 2014 riots and mass unrest against the political class threw Bosnia back onto the front pages. Commentators asked if the people of Bosnia had begun the process of shaking off the chains of ethnic and religious divisions and were re-taking control of their own destiny.

The protests began on 4 February 2014 in the northern city of Tuzla. Peaceful at first they turned violent the following day when hundreds of demonstrators, mostly former employees of several big companies, such as Dita, Polihem, Guming and Konjuh, clashed with police near the Tuzla cantonal government building. At least 600 protesters tried to storm the government building, accusing the authorities of turning a blind eye to the collapse of many state firms following their privatisation. Local media reported some of the protesters threw eggs, flares and stones at the windows of the building and set tyres on fire, blocking traffic in the city centre. Police eventually forced demonstrators back and cordoned off the building, but not before twenty-two people, including seventeen police officers, were injured and twenty-four arrested. The next day the number of protesters swelled to 6,000. Schools throughout Tuzla were closed and residents of buildings yelled insults and threw buckets of water at police passing by in full riot gear. After a long day of protest, the outraged demonstrators broke the last line of police defence and around a hundred young protesters stormed into the

Cantonal building. They threw furniture and papers out of the windows, before setting fire to the whole building. Protesters demanded the release of those arrested the day before, including the 'informal' leader and organiser of the demonstrations, Aldin Siranović. A group of approximately 8,000 people started moving towards the municipal building and were met by tear gas. A pitched battle ensued, and after the police were forced back, protesters also set the municipal building on fire.

Unrest of some kind was inevitable but the extent to which the protests quickly spread and the degree to which the occupation and burning of government buildings became a central feature of the protests turned out to be beyond anyone's expectations. By 6 February protests had spread to various cities across Bosnia-Herzegovina, including Bihać, Sanski Most, Cazin, Mostar, Doboj, Zenica, Kakanj, Visoko and, the capital Sarajevo. However, something surprising happened on the afternoon of 7 February, well-illustrated in photographs taken at the time. A unit of special police of the Tuzla canton lowered their shields and took off their helmets, which caused a wave of enthusiasm from the crowd. Both the regular and the judicial police followed suit in front of the Court and the Prosecution buildings respectively.

A different story unfolded elsewhere. In Sarajevo, tear-gas and smoke blanketed the entire city. Police opened fire with rubber bullets on several thousand protesters who had set fire to the headquarters of the capital's cantonal government. Water cannons were used to disperse protesters who were trying to enter the presidency building. Dense smoke caused by the burning of several police cars near the building of the Presidency of Bosnia-Herzegovina billowed into the sky. Various state buildings were in flames. On the same day 200 protestors in the city of Zenica forced their way through a police cordon and set fire to a local government building and surrounding cars. The protesters shouted 'Thieves!', 'We want resignation!', and asked the police to side with them. The entire government of the Zenica-Doboj Canton promised they would resign. Although the Prime Minister of the Zenica-Doboj canton, Munib Husejnagić, did step down, most canton officials subsequently clung to their posts.

The riots petered out, although peaceful demonstrations continued throughout the days that followed. Without exception, protesters all over the country blamed local officials for allowing several privatised state firms to collapse between 2000 and 2008, leaving many workers unemployed and their families destitute. The protesters also demanded compensation for healthcare and pensions payments they had lost. On the morning of 9 February, people began clearing the streets of garbage and debris and by mid-April the anger had left the streets.

To understand the recent troubles which disturbed the country's diverse communities we need not only to consider the Bosnian war but also the long history of revolts and unrests in the region. Balkan history is replete with uprisings and riots. This is especially true for the territories of today's Serbia, Bosnia-Herzegovina and Kosova.

The first major uprising took place in 1594 in the Banat region, now in modern Serbia, against the Ottoman Empire. The rebellion, led by Teodor Nestorović, the then Bishop of Vršac, had the character of a holy war. The Serb rebels carried flags with the image of Saint Sava. On the other hand, Sinan Pasha, who led the Ottoman army, ordered the green flag of the Prophet Muhammad to be brought from Damascus to counter the Serbian flag. The uprising was crushed by the Ottomans. Fearing Ottoman retaliation, most of the Serbs from the Banat region fled to Transylvania leaving the region deserted. The Ottoman authorities, who needed population in this fertile land, promised clemency to all who returned. Various sources suggest the Serb population did return home and were granted a general amnesty.

Another revolt against the Ottomans was led by a Serbian officer, Koča Anđelković, between 1788 and 1793. What came to be known as the 'First Serbian Uprising', symbolising the struggle for a national identity and destiny, took place between 1804 and 1813. The Serbs were initially fighting to restore their local privileges within the Ottoman system but following 1807 the 'revolutionaries' demanded to be placed under the protection of the Habsburg, Russian and French empires respectively, thus becoming a new and important political factor in the eyes of the Great Powers during the Napoleonic wars in Europe. The period between 1815 and 1817 saw a second phase of the national revolt of the Serbs against the Ottoman Empire. Now the goal was securing total independence from the

Sublime Porte. By this time, as many historians point out, wider European events had helped the Serbian cause – political and diplomatic means were adopted in negotiations between the Ruler of Serbia and the Ottomans within the prevailing political framework of nineteenth century Europe.

The Serbian uprising, combining patriarchal peasant democracy with modern national goals, attracted thousands of volunteers among the Serbs from across the Balkans, including Bulgaria and Bosnia-Herzegovina. The Herzegovina Uprising of 1875–77 was led by ethnic Serbs against the Ottoman Empire from where it spread into Bosnia. It is one of the most significant rebellions against the Ottoman rule in Bosnia-Herzegovina. The uprising was precipitated by the harsh attitude of *beys* and *aghas* of the Ottoman province of Bosnia. The recurrent uprisings and conflicts in the Balkans, led to the Congress of Berlin, convened in 1878, which gave Montenegro and Serbia independence and territorial expansion, while Bosnia and Herzegovina, though remaining nominally under Turkish sovereignty, became governed by Austria-Hungary. The Bosnian political parties established under the Austrian occupation, and those which later grew out of them in Royal Yugoslavia between the wars, were religious and ethnic in their allegiance, a tendency that re-emerged after the collapse of Communism in 1990.

In the years prior to the Second World War, there was a regular dialogue between parties and a willingness, particularly in the leading Muslim party, Yugoslav Muslim Organisation (JMO), to form coalitions and seek accommodation among competing points of view. The developing quarrel between the Croats of Croatia and the Serbs of Serbia, which only began after the formation of Yugoslavia in 1918, spilled over to infect Bosnian Serbs and Croats. Generally, however, Bosnians were less agitated by ethnic issues than their neighbours. It is important to realise this as it undermines the contemporary claim that the war in Bosnia was merely a continuation of centuries of religious or ethnic hatred. Indeed, over centuries, Bosnians had gone beyond tolerance to embrace synthetic, eclectic religious norms, with each religious group often borrowing customs and rituals from its rivals. Tragically, nationalism changed all that, and the area became the scene of systematic persecution, ethnic cleansing and mass slaughter. The four-year war in Bosnia and Hercegovina displaced around two million people and resulted in the deaths of about 100,000; the worst conflict that Europe has seen since the Second World War.

Despite the conflicts and uprisings, three major faiths of Bosnia, Islam, Catholicism and Serbian Orthodox, managed to coexist in relative peace during the Ottoman period. Although religion was the norm that defined ethnic communities of the Ottoman Bosnia and kept them separate, it did not create a culture of intolerance. Rather than suppressing one another, the region's ethnic and religious groups learned to cooperate and mediate their differences. As such, it was a useful negotiation tool that served as a buffer between East and West for most of its history. This is why, despite the tragedy that overwhelmed Bosnia-Herzegovina, prominent local theologians, such as Adnan Silajdzić, Marko Djurić and Mato Zovkić, who represent the country's three major religious communities, still believe that the region can find its way back to religious tolerance by separating religion from ethnicity and by establishing firm boundaries between church or mosque and state.

The post-war governance arrangement in Bosnia is one of the most complex in the world. The Bosnian government is a three-headed hydra, with a presidency that consists of representatives from three 'constituent peoples': Bosnian Muslims (Bosniaks), Croats and Serbs. The Dayton Peace Agreement, signed on 14 December 1995, divided the country into two mini-states: the Serb Republic and the Bosniak-Croat Federation. The two semi-autonomous entities are united under a parliament and three-member presidency. Despite the efforts to build up the powers of the central state, both entities are still highly autonomous, with separate political, police and financial structures. Similarly, a common education system is yet to be put in place, with schools still segregated by ethnicity and stocked with nationalist textbooks. As commentator Igor Štiks has observed, 'the political and administrative apparatus, consisting of one state, two entities, one district, ten cantons, some thirteen governments at all levels, 180 ministers of all kinds, 600 members of various parliaments, and a vast army of public servants, costs this impoverished country around 66 per cent of its entire budget'. For example, in 2010 alone five hundred million euros were spent on maintaining the country's bureaucracy. Employers within both entities are saddled with astonishingly high costs for social security, health care and other taxes — levies that require companies to pay around 68 per cent on top of worker's take-home wages. On the other hand, the so-called 'grey economy' has drained the treasury of tax revenue.

In spite of the current less-than-enticing political and economic situation, Bosnia managed to attract some international investment, mainly because foreign employers are exempt from various taxes for the initial five years of their investments. Arguably the most notable example of a foreign firm finding its way to post-war Bosnia is ArcelorMittal, the world's largest steelmaker, which employs around 3,000 people in the central town of Zenica. The German automobile upholstery manufacturer ASA Prevent, based on the outskirts of Sarajevo, which employs about 3,500 people, provides another example. Despite these economy-boosting examples it is beyond any doubt that the country's economy is in a state of decline and general recession. One simple but significant indication of this is the fact that the railroads have not been rebuilt since the war. Indeed, Bosnia-Herzegovina is one of the poorest countries in Europe. While prices for food, fuel and housing are fast approaching Western levels, the average monthly salary is a paltry 420 euros. The European Union has added to these financial woes by its December 2013 announcement that it would half its financial aid to the country because of lack of progress with reforms needed to join the Union.

Bosnia Herzegovina is way behind other former Yugoslav republics on the path to joining the EU. Croatia and Slovenia are already full members, while Montenegro, Serbia and Macedonia have begun serious accession talks. Bosnia-Herzegovina started high-level accession talks with the EU in mid-2012 but the complex institutional structure in the country has led to an almost permanent political stalemate because of inter-ethnic disputes.

The paralysis that defines the Bosnian government is well illustrated in the fact that after the general elections of 2010 it took over sixteen months for a state government to be formed, and it collapsed almost immediately. As a result, Parliamentary sessions are held only on rare occasions with the members mostly concerning themselves with calling for the expulsion of their political opponents.

The initial impetus for reform between 1996 and 2006 has all but completely ceased and since then the country has jerked from one constitutional crisis to the next. The international community, in the form of the Office of the High Representative (OHR), has directly intervened in the internal political process in Bosnia on a number of occasions. The OHR has made several attempts at constitutional reforms. It has drafted a constitution for Bosnia, imposed laws and disqualified election candidates, with the goal of supporting, supervising and eventually controlling the development of democratic governance in Bosnia - leading to the charge of authoritarianism. Bosnian politicians, on the other hand, simply lack the commitment to tackle the complex issue of constitutional reform. During the past decade, no major political decision or reform has been made without the involvement of the OHR, giving no incentive to Bosnian politicians to cooperate with each other. As a result, the politicians do not consider themselves accountable to the voters. When the internal political crisis reaches its peak, foreign powers enforce what they deem fit. Both politicians and citizens feel that no one is up to the challenge.

Democracy, as we know, cannot be enforced from the outside or above, it has to spring from the grassroots. Development of true democratic processes in which people place demands on their political representatives and hold them accountable for both successes and failures is a gradual process. It cannot be created instantly by the force of law. Conducting multi-party elections every two years, with a voter turnout barely topping 50 per cent, does not add up to democratic governance. It is not that the citizens of Bosnia and Herzegovina are undemocratic by nature or that because of the communist past they prefer authoritarian rule to democracy. The problem is that the local people have become too used to waiting for others to make the decisions and shape their internal political process from the outside. Instead of just blaming the international actors, the local population needs to look inside, at their political leaders and civil society, and find ways to 'unfreeze' the current obstacles standing in the country's way. It is not just a question of EU integration, but more importantly, accountable, responsive and democratic governance. Given the political impasse, it was inevitable that some kind of civil resistance, disobedience, online activism, open demonstrations and protests would take off.

A major cause of the unrest is the decades old insensitivity shown by all levels of Bosnian government to the social and economic destitution of citizens, particularly the youth and the 1992–95 war veterans. Encouraged by international overseers, the political class has embraced the mantra of neo-liberal economics. Shallow government privatisation schemes have dismantled flourishing industries in the cities of Tuzla and Zenica, sold them off for parts, and left thousands of workers jobless – many still owed thousands of euros in back-pay. For example, in the Tuzla region, between 2000 and 2008, four large former state-owned firms (Konljuh, DITA, Polihem and SODASO) were sold to private owners allegedly to make them profitable. The new owners promptly sold the assets, stopped paying workers, and filed for bankruptcy. The official unemployment rate has remained frozen for years at around 40 per cent, while youth unemployment is above 57 per cent. One in five citizens struggle to live below the poverty line. Pensions are miserly too; the sight of senior people digging through waste bins is a regular one in every part of the country. In contrast, the wages of elected officials have grown exponentially. In addition to the generous salaries they award themselves, office-holders are able to further supplement their earnings by claiming pay for membership in boards, commissions, consultative bodies and other quangos.

At no point have the international architects of peace in Bosnia-Herzegovina made any efforts to include ordinary citizens, students, workers or pensioners in the reforms which European and American diplomats insist the country requires. Instead, by engaging exclusively with members of the country's recalcitrant political establishment, they have cemented the oligarchs in their posts while the pleas and demands of ordinary citizens, students, workers and civil rights activists have been generally ignored.

However, the recent uprising, and the mood behind it, has the potential to reverse this impasse. The uprising that began in Tuzla was organised by the workers who protested against not only the closure of companies that employed them, but also the corrupt and shallow privatisation processes. Protestors from other cities made similar demands. Although the protests spread rapidly throughout the country, and involved similar groups, there is no evidence to suggest that they were centrally organised. But this does not mean they were spontaneous or without coherent demands. Two informal citizens' groups 'Revolt' and 'Udar', both based in the city of Tuzla, have been the most vocal supporters of the protests. Both associations have a strong social media presence and are highly active on

Facebook and Twitter, which are used to inform, invite and organise their supporters. The founder and leader of the 'Udar', Aldin Siranović, was named by some as the 'informal' leader and organiser of the Tuzla protests.

The fact that almost from day one the Tuzla protesters produced a 'Manifesto for New Bosnia and Herzegovina', containing 37 clear demands and points, indicates that the protests were pre-planned, seeking serious political and economic reforms. Among other things, the Tuzla Manifesto called for the reduction of politicians' salaries, budget changes, an independent anti-corruption committee, free health care and commitment to youth employment. It called on state-level politicians to resign and that nationalist and religious-based political parties should be banned. High on the agenda was the abolition of the cantons and the two entities, in order to reduce the enormous costs of public administration.

Those who took to the streets had given up hope of changing the government, or direction of society, through elections. This view has legitimacy as the multiple layers of government mean that paradoxically everybody is in power somewhere and nowhere simultaneously. Similarly, there are complex and fluid coalitions at the entity and state level that blur the line between government and opposition. The manipulative use of ethnic and national identities by those in office has also systematically undermined any trust in the political process. This is why resignations of government officials and canton ministers were high on the protestors' demands. As a result, prime minister of the Tuzla Canton, Munib Husejnagić, prime minister of the Zenica-Doboj Canton, Suad Zeljković, prime minister of the Sarajevo Canton, and Hamdija Lipovaća, prime minister of the Una-Sana Canton, all resigned during or shortly after the protests. Similarly, canton administrators in Sarajevo, Tuzla, Zenica, Bihac and other places stood down.

Arguably one of the most positive developments of protests has been the birth of direct democratic assemblies. The sudden emergence of these assemblies in large parts of Bosnia and Herzegovina has taken many by surprise. The first appeared in Tuzla where the protesters were most articulate and most organised from the start; later citizens' assemblies began to emerge in other cities such as Zenica, Mostar, and Sarajevo. There are ongoing efforts to coordinate and centralise the existing assemblies on the state level to develop and establish common national and not just local demands. A shared topic of discussion is the waves of privatisation and the salary levels of officials. Another common problem being addressed is the political and legal unaccountability of the political class.

Despite the long-existing ingredients for the recent unrest, all the major actors – the political class, the international community and established civil society – were all caught flat-footed and have been scrambling to react. Their knee-jerk tendency to react to these protests by sticking to long-established talking points further demonstrates how out-of-touch they are with the people in the street. The international response to the protests has been confused as well, displaying the gap between international actors and the reality on the ground. The EU and foreign ministers of European countries repeated the mantra that citizens should have the right to protest, but that they should remain peaceful.

On particular consequence of the protests was the serious damage to historically important documents belonging to the Ottoman era in a fire in the presidential office in Sarajevo. The loss only adds to the sad fact that the National Museum of Bosnia and Herzegovina has been closed since October 2012. Despite the existence of four separate levels of government, not one of them seems to consider the preservation of the country's cultural monuments a priority. Bosnia's National Museum, an institution that has survived three wars and has operated continuously for well over one hundred years, is on the brink of collapse not because of the recent protests but because of the current government's lack of concern for its historic value.

A few months after the protests, in May 2014, the citizens of Bosnia found themselves confronted with a test of another sort. Bosnia was hit by catastrophic floods triggering huge landslides. Some villages and towns were completely submerged with nothing but the rooftops emerging from the ground to testify that these places were once inhabited. The water also inundated minefields in Bosnia, dislodging the previously hidden explosive devices. Although the destruction and loss brought by the floods caused much pain and suffering across the country, the response of the citizens was overwhelming. Thousands joined the relief efforts by donating funds, collecting essentials, and distributing food, water and medicine to the affected people. Although the politicians mostly remained in their respective areas, rescue troops and rafting teams crossed the real and imagined borderlines, going from Bihać to Doboj and from Foča to Zenica, to help their fellow citizens, regardless of their ethnicity or political affiliation. Student and youth organisations in Bosnia also organised volunteers to assist with the clean-up. Hotel owners provided free accommodation for the displaced. Initiatives of private individuals also sprung up on social media; people throughout Bosnia-Herzegovina were offered shelter through Facebook to those who had lost their homes. Similarly, diaspora in Europe and abroad immediately responded with contributions. Convoys of humanitarian assistance collected by Bosnians, Serbs and Croats living abroad crossed the borders to reach affected areas. The solidarity that emerged from the flood disaster was uplifting; an example of unity, solidarity and humanity, which still prevails in the country.

The citizens' assemblies played an important part in the 12 October 2014 General elections. In the Bosniak-Croat Federation, the Social Democrats, who have dominated Bosnian politics in recent years, lost heavily to the The Party of Democratic Action, founded in May 1990 by Alija Izetbegovic. Moreover, a new party, the Democratic Front, also garnered considerable support from the urban middle class. In Republika Srpska, the 2014 elections confirmed that Milorad Dodik, the president of the Serb Republic who is determined to split Bosnia into two, is no longer an untouchable oligarch with his party, the SNSD, losing a significant number of seats in the National Assembly of the Republika Srpska.

Although the elections may usher some positive change, it is the census of 2013, the full results of which are yet to be revealed, that will have a major political impact. It will reveal the changes in Bosnia's ethnic distribution and the extent to which once multi-ethnic cities and towns have been divided. The census is a product of considerable political negotiations – the leading political parties disagreed whether to include those living in the diaspora, and whether to ask questions about ethnicity and faith. Finally, an agreement was reached to include the two questions concerning identity as optional, giving citizens a right to self-identify, to not disclose, or to indicate any other affiliation which they prefer. A trial census in October 2012 indicated that 35 percent of the sample, mainly youth, classified their ethnicity as 'Bosnian and/or Herzegovinian' – indicating that a significant percentage of the population seem to put greater weight on being a citizen of the country, rather than their ethnicity.

The census has been highly politicised, and aggressive media campaigns have been launched to 'educate' citizens about the census, or rather their national identity. This has especially been the case with the Bosniak population, who identify themselves as 'Bosniak', 'Bosnian' or 'Muslim'. Croat political parties have also invited all Croats to be present in Bosnia during this time, in order to ensure higher numbers in the census. The issue of language has been nearly as contentious as that of ethnicity. Disclosing ethnic and religious identity is optional in the census, but giving one's mother tongue is not. Although all Bosnian citizens speak the same language, the name of the language they speak is a matter of dispute. Most consider 'Bosnian', 'Serbian', and 'Croatian' as three separate languages, thus selecting one of them in the census automatically indicate the person's ethnic identity, regardless of whether they answered the 'optional' questions.

Some hope that the census results will narrow the space for political manipulation. But the results are also likely to revive debates of ethnic cleansing throughout Bosnia, especially when the 1991 data is compared with the current number of Bosniaks in the heavily Serbian part of Bosnia, or the number of Serbs living in Sarajevo, the mainly Bosniak capital.

Whatever the political impact of the census, one thing is clear. A viable future for Bosnia can only be assured by reaffirming its historic principle of religious tolerance. There is evidence to suggest that this is possible. None of the demands emanating from the 2014 protests were based on nationality, religion, or any other division expressed in Dayton. All the anger was directed towards a vicious cabal of political oligarchs who, as Jasmin Mujanović asserts, kept using 'ethno-nationalist rhetoric to obscure the plunder of the country's public coffers'. It was dissatisfaction with this venal economic and political system that pushed diverse Bosnian groups to unite in protest. By coming out onto the streets, the citizens of Bosnia-Herzegovina have shown that they are willing and able to act in a unified way, rather than passively suffer under a self-serving and divisive elite. So don't write off Bosnia-Herzegovina as a dysfunctional country – just yet.

FATHER, MY FATHER

Hussain Ahmed

On the morning of 16 December 2014, most Pakistanis woke to a damning reminder of the chequered record of the one institution that many call 'Father'. That day is the anniversary of the loss of Pakistan's eastern wing in 1971. Victory Day in Bangladesh is, in contrast, a day of sadness in much of Pakistan; more so in recent years following allegations that the national army was complicit in human rights abuses against its Bengali citizens. But forever more, 16 December will now be remembered for another atrocity: an act of indescribable inhumanity against the children of the nation's soldiers. This was the deliberate, targeted, calculated, and cold-blooded murder of more than 130 children attending Peshawar's Army Public School. The mornings to follow were characterised by grief, remembrance, helplessness, and the anger brewed by such vulnerability.

16 December became the day when all Pakistanis wept uncontrollably together. Pakistan's soul had been stabbed.

Perhaps sensing the scale of the reaction, the Pakistani Taliban, while claiming responsibility for the attack, pretended to justify its massacre—as if any defence is possible—in retaliation for military 'operations' in North Waziristan and the killing of Taliban militants in government custody. Reports emerged that Pakistani intelligence was privy to a suspected attack on the school. According to the leading national English-language daily Dawn the government had prior knowledge that the killers had entered Peshawar three days ahead of the attack. The tragedy still occurred.

Following three days of mourning, the nation's fractious political and military leadership united in a show of strength and produced a checklist of actions, announced on national television by Prime Minister Nawaz Sharif. But what Sharif had to say amounts to yet another victory for the politics of force. Military courts, where the rights of the accused are curtailed, will now be used for terrorism cases. The death penalty has also been reinstated. Pakistan has settled on retribution as its response to the Army Public School attack. It was perhaps the most convenient response too; because neither democratic nor military leaders want to provide answers that are rooted in history, domestic or foreign policy, or even the rotten state of public institutions, governance or justice.

Democratically-elected leaders, writers and commentators remain concerned, especially about the prospect of the return of military courts, a mainstay of many a military dictator. Journalist and TV anchor Talat Hussain said on Twitter: 'Army chief, on hearing the narrative from civilian leadership about past duality of approach, reportedly said: "Bury the past, now it is different".'

In the end, all trust was reposed in Father. Father's house had become a den of disunity. Order needed to be restored and it was he who could fix it best.

Up until the morning of 16 December, Pakistan had been convulsed by a political impasse between the Sharif government and a popular opposition party led by former cricketer Imran Khan, with the military watching somewhat nervously. Khan and hundreds of his supporters had camped outside Parliament for about four months demanding the resignation of the prime minister following revelations of irregularities in vote counting at the last general election. But weeks into what appeared to be a genuine protest led by a popular leader, something quite extraordinary happened. One of Khan's top aides quit his party, claiming before the nation's media that the sit-ins had the blessing and the backing of the military and its all-powerful spy agency, the Inter Services Intelligence (ISI). Had such a claim been made by anyone else, it might not have been believed. But Javed Hashmi, formerly Khan's senior vice president, owes his political career to the military. He rose to prominence during the dictatorship of General Ziaul Haq in the 1970s and 1980s. He later redeemed himself by challenging the legitimacy of General Pervez Musharraf's dictatorship, for which he was imprisoned.

The military was sufficiently rattled to issue statements on alternate days, either side of Hashmi's press conference, warning that it retained the ability to step in if the protests escalated. The first statement said:

While reaffirming support to democracy, the [Corps Commanders] conference reviewed with serious concern, the existing political crisis and the violent
turn it has taken, resulting in large scale injuries and loss of lives. Further use
of force will only aggravate the problem. It was once again reiterated that the
situation should be resolved politically without wasting any time and without
recourse to violent means. Army remains committed to playing its part in
ensuring security of the state and will never fall short of meeting national
aspirations.

The second statement came immediately after Hashmi's allegations:

Army is an apolitical institution and has expressed its unequivocal support for
democracy at numerous occasions. It is unfortunate that the Army is dragged
into such controversies. Integrity and unity of the Army is its strength which it
upholds with pride.

Father had spoken; he shall not be challenged.

In many respects, Pakistan's military remains the envy of its counterparts
around the world. In more developed societies, soldiering is often a poorly
paid or part-time profession; with large periods of boredom punctuated
by the horrors of war, post-traumatic stress, demobilisation and long
periods of civilian unemployment or working contractual jobs. In Pakistan,
however, there is no other profession that brings as much reverence, trust
and material gain as being a high-ranking army officer. In nearly seven
decades, Pakistan's military has become integral, seemingly indispensable,
to the state apparatus. At the slightest hint of trouble its omnipresence is
presented, through its many supporters among academics and opinion-
shapers, as part of a solution rather than it being a problem.

And this is no coincidence. Father's place in society has been carefully
crafted and constructed: he is simultaneously the ultimate patriarch, the
symbol of Pakistani masculinity, the most-*sadiq* (truthful) and most-*ameen*
(trustworthy) – traits traditionally used to describe Prophet Muhammad.
The Pakistan army's reliance on Islamic imagery is not unique in the
Muslim world; neither for its portrayal of righteousness nor for its
language of heroism and martyrdom. But a shared and often violent history
with India strengthens the Pakistani military's credentials as defender of
the faith. Without the army, goes the argument, the state won't survive.
Therefore as guardians of the state, the army must be permitted to act as

it deems fit so that both physical and ideological boundaries are protected. These dynamics give Father the status of the hegemon. He creates the rules of the game and his domination, though subtle, is absolute. The military's control over society, economy, and politics is structural, and it defends its hegemony through a combination of real and imagined power. This doesn't necessarily mean that the wheels of history will cease to move forward without the military; only that history will move forward at a pace that the military is comfortable with.

That Father has the right to act in ungainly ways is street knowledge; that his behaviour needs to be tolerated is street wisdom too. Father's power manifests itself in political, business and societal forms. Those who disobey Father — as attempted by media giants Jang Group / Geo Network — befall terrible consequences. Those not in Father's good books are ultimately squeezed out of the power spectrum.

So how exactly does this work?

'The military rarely creates monopolies, but it monopolises resources with its civilian partners. This is a good model of patronage, which encourages support from within society,' argues Ayesha Siddiqa, author of *Military Inc: Inside Pakistan's Military Economy*. The military's overwhelming presence in nearly all forms of society and activity is established through what Siddiqa calls 'milbus'. Milbus is a contraction of 'military' and 'business' and is shorthand for the military's internal economy. The true extent of milbus remains a mystery to civilian eyes, but its existence and far-reaching tentacles cannot be doubted. Indeed, in a country of parallel economies, the one run by the military is often more highly regarded than its civil counterpart because it comes with the perceived benefit of security and trust. Siddiqa dates the establishment of milbus to 1954 following the creation of the Fauji (soldier) Foundation, a philanthropic endowment for servicemen. This organisation was carved out of the money received from the British in lieu of a share of the 1942 Post War Services Reconstruction Fund. Unlike in India, which opted to distribute its share of the fund to war veterans, the Pakistani military realised that it could make money from this legacy. Over the years, Fauji Foundation has made crucial investments across both wings of what was then United Pakistan, and in industrial sectors that demonstrate high consumer demand, such as tobacco, sugar, textile and rice. In 1977, the air force followed the army's example, and set up the Shaheen Foundation. The navy was the last to join; its Bahria Foundation was launched in 1982. In 1972 the Army Welfare Trust (AWT) was created with an initial endowment of Rs 700,000, then equivalent to the price of a large house. The aim was partly to generate funds for the children of service men killed in action, war widows, and to provide for the rehabilitation of disabled soldiers. The AWT and the Fauji and other foundations and associated ventures have allowed the military to emerge as the nation's largest landowner, in both rural and urban sectors. The creation of Bangladesh from what was East Pakistan punctured the growth of milbus — Pakistan's elected Prime Minister Zulfikar Ali Bhutto's programme of nationalising public and private enterprises meant that the military found itself in unfamiliar, subservient waters and reduced profits. But in 1977, Bhutto was toppled in a coup by the very general he had handpicked to run the forces. The military returned, having learnt its lesson not to hand absolute control of governance — and by extension, the growth of milbus — to civilian leaders ever again.

Since that time, milbus has been a consistent indeed expanding presence. There is little if any civil accountability. Moreover, the military has time and again sought constitutional protection to safeguard its status. Among other things, the army is in effective charge of the (in principle, government-run) Ministry of Defence, which deals with national security, military finances and development. It is during this period that the military began expanding its network of schools originally built for the children of its officers, such as in Peshawar and elsewhere across the country. But military accounts being classified information, its commercial deals and those of its subsidiaries escape attention. With one or two minor exceptions, neither elected government nor indeed any media organisation has ever been able to lift the lid.

But there are exceptions, and they have helped to underscore the scale of Pakistan's military incursion into the state. One of the army's biggest, most aggressive and perhaps most profitable moves have been in the services sector. In 1978, for example, the National Logistics Cell (NLC) was set-up. This was a branch of the army ostensibly created to help speed up the process of docking and unloading cargo at Karachi's harbour. At the time, the argument put forward was that the country was at risk of wheat shortage because of 'civilian inefficiencies' in handling cargo. Civilian personnel, the military claimed, were costing the government 'US$14.3 million in demurrage to foreign shippers'. But the NLC has stuck around ever since. More than that, it has grown. Indeed, Siddiqa argues that the NLC compromised the development of the nation's railway network by in effect 'hijacking' its share of cargo transport. The NLC is the principle vehicle now through which cargo, such as supplies to the US military, are sent.

After the NLC's runaway success, there has been no stopping the men in uniforms from growing their commercial empire. Today, few sectors have been left untouched. The shadow of the rifle butt stalks everything from banking, finance and insurance, to travel, education, IT and energy. Indeed, far from challenging the army's gathering influence, civil leaders have chosen the opposite course. By 1988, when General Zia died in a plane crash, the military's entrenchment in the political economy of the county was absolute. Even though successive democratic governments have tried to curtail this, most realised that compromise was better than conflict.

In fact, civilian leaders were more than willing to team up with the military for development projects. In the province of Punjab, for example, chief minister Shahbaz Sharif has worked with both the NLC and its sister concern, the Frontier Works Organisation (FWO), in developing the province's road infrastructure. Even as the provincial chief executive, it seems that Sharif believes that this is better suited to road building than specialist private companies.

There is one area, however, where the military has copied more or less straight from the civilian playbook. Pakistan is famously a land of landowners, or *vaderas* as the nation's famous feudal landowning families are known colloquially. But while traditional feudal landholding has contracted over the years, mostly because of inheritance laws, the military has taken its place to become the most powerful *vaderas* of the land. Most of its land deals remain hidden, but occasionally we get a glimpse of what goes on inside the barracks. The case of Anjuman Mazareen Punjab (Association of the Landless Peasants of Punjab) is a good example. This organisation represented landless peasants settled on military property, in villages across some 170 kilometres of land. Their tenancy dates back since before Partition in 1947 — so long ago, in fact, that the constitution allows them to claim ownership rights. However, these tenants were forced to organise because the military was insisting that they hand over fertile agricultural land in the heart of Pakistan's most populous province to them. Many of the association's leaders and activists went to prison for resisting. Since a large segment of landless peasants is Christian, many a mosque pulpit was commandeered in the cause of their eviction. Loudspeakers were used to instigate ordinary and high-caste Muslim villagers to report 'suspicious activity'. Activists who worked with the association argue that the military's desire to expand its land ownership is also partly about wanting to work with global agribusiness. The tenants were a mere hindrance in their way.

One could argue that it isn't possible for a standing army to have such pervasive influence in the economy and society without help and facilitation from the civil sector. And one would be right. Some of Father's business are either jointly owned or fronted by influential civilian businessmen.

One such influential civilian businessman with extensive links to the army is Malik Riaz. In the mega-city that is Karachi, for example, Riaz's land development company, Bahria Town, is constructing a skyscraper on prime seafront land. As it happens, this land is owned by the military, which means Riaz needs to work with them in order to pursue his development projects. That in turn means that both sides must benefit from the partnership. In practical terms Riaz's company has to pay the army's land-owning wing, the Defence Housing Authority, for access to services, facilities and so on. In fact, Riaz's association with the military began in 1995, when he invested in a paint factory set up by the (naval endowment) Bahria Foundation that was to manufacture paint for use in naval ships. He then partnered again with the Bahria Foundation for the construction of two housing schemes, in Lahore and in Rawalpindi. As per the initial contract, Bahria Foundation would receive ten per cent of shares and 25 per cent of the housing plots. In 2000, the Bahria Foundation transferred its shareholding to Riaz.

Riaz also acts as the go-between between the military and other civilian heavyweights. Consider his investment in the Sindh Festival, a showpiece cultural event fronted by the otherwise little known Bilawal Bhutto-Zardari, the latest scion of Pakistan's Bhutto political dynasty. His parents are the former president Asif Zardari and the assassinated former Prime Minister Benazir Bhutto. While provincial machinery was no doubt used to execute operations during the festival, Riaz's Bahria Town advertisements were widely shown during the province-wide event.

Asif Zardari's government was the first democratically-elected one to complete five years in office in Pakistani history (2008–13). This was partly because Zardari, no stranger himself to military prisons, was pragmatic enough to agree that he could do business with the military, irrespective of the trust deficit that existed between the two in the past, and that this relationship could be mutually beneficial. That the military is now able to accept Zardari as a business partner tells its own story of civil-military accommodation.

In recent decades, Pakistan has evolved a loud, at times raucous and fiercely independent media sector. No elected politician is immune from its investigative reach, no public figure can hope to escape its satirical gaze. But when it comes to the military, all the old rules are still in place. When covering anything to do with the forces, reporters are still required to behave with appropriate deference, just as they were in the days of the old military dictatorships. A soldier's image of piety and righteousness must never be questioned. If it is, then Father's rage is guaranteed.

Recently, when one of the nation's most powerful media groups chose to challenge that presumption, the result was blowback, from which the group has still to recover. The Jang group is perhaps the largest media group in Pakistan. Its flagship Urdu daily, *Jang* (meaning war), is complemented with an English daily *The News*, several local and regional evening papers in both languages, consumer magazines, and a host of news and entertainment TV channels. In terms of market share, its flagship TV news channel, Geo, arguably has the largest mass media audience in the TV news sector.

On 19 April 2014, one of Geo's high profile political interviewers was attacked by gunmen in Karachi. The journalist, Hamid Mir, is understood to have left instructions with his employers that if an attempt was made on his life they were to broadcast his claim that the attack was the work of Pakistan's spy agency, ISI. Senior ISI officers were unhappy about Mir's unrelenting questioning of their policies. The channel complied, in a show of solidarity with a colleague, but also, in what it believed to be a cause of strengthening democratic principles. In doing so, the media group believed, wrongly, that the sympathies of its viewers would be with their injured colleague, and that citizens would be able to see for themselves what Pakistani journalists are up against when they speak out against the military.

This did not happen.

Viewers of Geo TV and those of rival channels, too, voted with their remote control off-buttons at what they saw as an attack on a sacred institution. It didn't matter that one of Pakistan's bravest sons could have been killed. What mattered more was that the army, guarantor of national security, and now provider of food, energy, roads, education and so much more, was being maligned. At the same time cable TV operators moved to block Geo transmissions, including in military-controlled areas. Worse, reporters and camera operators belonging to Geo and other parts of its network began to be physically attacked. Jang/Geo vans were stoned and access was denied to them for routine political events. The TV journalist, Sana Mirza, was hit by bottles and stones when broadcasting live from an Imran Khan Opposition protest in Lahore.

This is where Father's more favoured sons and their friends in the media stepped in. They sought to reassure him and remind him that, while Geo was an errant child, he could rely on others to do his bidding. And that they would start by taking down Geo through their broadcasts and newspapers. The principal charge laid at Geo's door was that, by linking the ISI to the attack on Mir, the channel had behaved in an unpatriotic way. Another way of interpreting this is that Geo and its owners had in effect risked national security. This charge was broadcast relentlessly across Pakistan's media, including from Geo's rival, ARY News. Little attempt was made to balance the coverage with opposing views. Since ARY is watched by audiences all over the world, its coverage of the Mir incident was brought to the attention of the UK broadcast regulatory body Ofcom, which concluded that ARY's coverage had indeed been biased.

But the charge of lacking patriotism was not the worst. Geo was also accused by its critics of blasphemy — a charge that carries the death penalty. It was also accused of being friends with India (which is almost as bad), accepting funds from foreign donors (nearly as bad), and trying to shame the military at every given opportunity. Most mass media groups rely heavily on public sector advertising. This started to drop, resulting in Geo staff salaries being delayed for months on end. Some of Geo's key staff was poached too, by a new media organisation that had emerged, suddenly, offering much more generous pay scales. In one fell swoop, not only was the Jang/Geo Network critically damaged, but the democratic principles that it stood for were also being discredited. An attack on one media group thus turned into an attack on whatever procedural democracy Pakistan has managed thus far to build.

The 'peoples' reaction to TV journalist Hamid Mir's shooting, and the zeal to rush and defend the nation's defenders raises another aspect of the military's all-pervasive nature.

Pakistan is sometimes described as an 'insecurity state'. This is a reference to the tendency of commentators, at home and abroad, to measure its self-worth in relation to the real or perceived threat posed by India. It is also to a large degree a theocratic state, and, officially, Pakistan is an Islamic republic. Since the days of General Ziaul Haq, the military has slowly but deliberately positioned itself as defender of faith. That means to criticise the generals is in fact to criticise Islam. And we all know what that entails.

At a time when milbus was in its expansionist phase, General Zia was on a mission to 'Islamise' Pakistan. He largely succeeded. Over time, a Saudi-inspired bent on theology has become central to the project of hyper Pakistani nationalism. Since the period of General Zia, the army has been on a mission to make the country more pious. Jihad has become the cornerstone of Pakistan's foreign policy. It is also the barometer used in its assessment of foreigners, too. The largest education facilities created by the state — again, by the military, its Saudi associates, and domestic clients — are those of the madrassah network. The ordinary foot soldier enters the army infused with ideals of piety and patriotism. By drawing on Islam for inspiration in its curriculum, the army provides the best of both the material world and the Hereafter to those who join it. As Shuja Nawaz argues in Crossed Swords, the crop at the helm of affairs within the army now is the generation that grew up during General Zia's reign. Its ideological prism remains the same xenophobic one despite some cosmetic changes, and its tentacles have spread far and wide. Put another way, the Pakistani state now has new teachers and defenders of xenophobic norms and values that were set in the decade of the 1980s. These propagators exist both within the army and without, and they include both serving and ex-service men and women.

As a global phenomenon, Islam is under both evolution and attack. In more secure societies, for example, debates are taking place on Islamic reforms, on gender equality, on reformulating the Sharia. But in Pakistan such deliberations are inconceivable. Indeed, any perceived questioning of the Saudi-inspired theology would be punishable, irrespective of the reality that it might be happening elsewhere.

Pakistan and its army's response to Islam's global evolution is to barricade itself from the outside world, by reinforcing the status quo, through force if necessary, and with little or no regard for democratic principles. Father retains a monopoly over all instruments of coercion and He keeps a strict vigil on what is being taught or said on almost every platform. Not many question his gaze, because Father can do no wrong. And especially not now, not after the Peshawar school massacre.

Were a moment in Pakistan's history to be captured today, it would read (among other things) as a story of military dominance, colluding elite, naked profiteering, a blissfully ignorant young middle-class, and a more frustrated working class. This moment goes beyond the post-colonial legacy in Pakistan; it is a reality that has been carved indigenously, and terrifyingly, through a willing acquiescence of the citizenry.

THE WISDOM OF SYRIA'S WAITING GAME

Foreign Policy Under the Assads

Bente Scheller

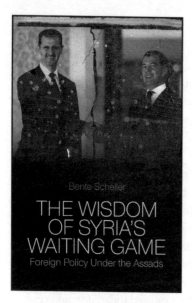

ISBN: 9781849042864
£30.00 / Hardback / 244pp

Syrian foreign policy, always opaque, has become an even greater puzzle during the Syrian revolt. Irrespective of the regime's international isolation in the wake of its violent response to domestic protest, it has paid lip-service to international peace plans while unperturbedly crushing the rebellion. The rare televised appearances of President Assad have shown a leader detached from reality. Has he—in his own words—'gone crazy'? In this book long-time Syria analyst and former diplomat Bente Scheller contends that Bashar Assad's deadly waiting game is following its own logic: whatever difficulties the Syrian regime has faced, its previous experience has been that it can simply sit out the current crisis.

The difference this time is that Syria faces a double crisis—internal and external. While Hafez Assad, renowned as an astute politician, adapted to new challenges, his son, Bashar, seems to have no alternative plan of action.

Scheller's timely book analyses Syrian foreign policy after the global upheavals of 1989, which was at the time a glorious new beginning for the regime. She shows how Bashar Assad, by ignoring change both inside Syria and in the region, has sacrificed his father's focus on national security in favour of a policy of regime survival and offers a candid analysis of the successes and shortcomings of Syrian foreign policy in recent years.

'Bente Scheller has written a timely and sober analysis of Syrian foreign policy. Anyone interested in understanding why the Assads have lasted for over 40 years and why their missteps led to the revolt of 2011 should read this book.' — Joshua M. Landis, Director, Center for Middle East Studies, University of Oklahoma, and author of SyriaComment.com

WWW.HURSTPUBLISHERS.COM/BOOK/THE-WISDOM-OF-SYRIAS-WAITING-GAME

41 GREAT RUSSELL ST, LONDON WC1B 3
WWW.HURSTPUBLISHERS.COM
WWW.FBOOK.COM/HURSTPUBLISHERS
020 7255 2201

AN ACTIVIST SPEAKS

Najah Kadhim

A few years ago I got involved in a deep discussion with a Salafi man. We started talking about the Qur'an. I pointed out that the sacred text celebrates diversity and pluralism in over 200 verses and encourages Muslims to think and reflect. We can interpret the Qur'an in a contemporary way to promote knowledge, democracy and the evolution of civic societies in the Muslim lands. He replied that democracy was a Western innovation that had no place in Islam; and, in any case, there was only one God, one Qur'an and therefore only one correct and pure Islam. There was no place in Islam for thought as this led to a deviation from the true practice of Islam. Islam, he suggested, should be practiced in the same way the Salaf, the first three generations of Muslims. As our argument proceeded, he started to quote Sheikh Muhammad Abd al-Wahhab, the eighteenth-century founder of the Wahhabi movement. He pointed out that, according to Sheikh Abd al-Wahhab, *kuffur* (disbelief) and *fikr* (thought) are the same because the two words in Arabic are made up of the same three letters: Fa'a, Kaf and Ra'a. Our discussion became a little heated when I discovered his intense hatred for the Shia. The argument ended with him denouncing me as an apostate and an enemy of Islam. And me asking him: was the Qur'an revealed to the Prophet, Muhammad ibn 'Abd Allah or Muhammad ibn 'Abd al-Wahab?

I have been an activist most of my life. As the Chair and Director of International Forum for Islamic Dialogue (IFID), for the past fifteen years, I have travelled extensively around the Muslim world. IFID is a non-governmental organisation that aims to develop a modern understanding of contemporary Muslim issues through dialogue. Our goal is to create independent and prosperous Muslim societies led by visionary and ethical leaders. The biggest hurdle we face in our work is the conservative ideologies of Salafism and Wahhabism. It is well near impossible to engage with any kind of dialogue with our Salafi brothers and sisters – if they are kind enough not to murder me; they are nevertheless ready to denounce me as a member of a dangerous and deviant thinking group.

Even with the so-called moderates, the dialogue reaches a quick impasse. A couple of years ago, I got involved in a conversation with a middle ranking leader of the Muslim Brotherhood regarding society and democracy. Our conversation took place in the post-Arab Spring period, prior to the 2012 elections in Egypt, which saw Mohammed Morsi and the Muslim Brotherhood come to power. The general assumption throughout the Arab world was that the Brotherhood had matured politically and learned to play the democratic game. They were supposed to be 'pragmatic'. My hypothetical question to him was simple: what would happen if a Muslim society did not end up electing a political Islamic party? The *ummah*, he shot back, would always elect its own Muslim vanguards to run their affairs, as the *ummah* rejects secularism. That was the end of our conversation. It was hardly worth pointing out that it was civil society activists and secularists, and not Islamists of the Muslim Brotherhood, or their Salafi collaborators, who initiated and led the Arab Spring of 2011.

There is little doubt that the governance experiments of Islamists across the Arab world have been catastrophic. In Egypt, as has been well documented, the regime of the Muslim Brotherhood was marred by infighting over the new constitution, corruption, and attempts at running the state to the exclusion of all others. The Muslim Brotherhood, in collaboration with the Salafis, introduced a closed-minded style of governance where their standard puritanical approach was applied in social spheres, in education and preaching. If politics is defined as the art of the possible by some, for the Salafists and the Muslim Brotherhood it is simply the art of managing puritanical affairs and the destiny of man. Regardless of the wishes of a sizable opposition, the Morsi government went ahead with the formulation of a dominant role for Sharia in the new constitution, which treated the minorities – including women, Copts (who account for about 10 per cent of Egypt's population) and Shias – as second class citizens. The Salafists created an environment where the citizens worried, even inside their own homes, whether they were abiding by Sharia. Moreover, the Morsi government had absolutely no idea how to handle the economy, which was close to collapse when the government was overthrown.

In Iraq, Islamists, both Shia and Sunni, have failed miserably in building the foundations for a democratic State, or independent political institutions. There is centralised power and plenty of it but no institutions that can harmonise the political process and provide a real foundation for the political community. The disintegration and incompetence of the Iraqi army in dealing with the Islamic State of Iraq and the Levant (ISIL) in June 2014 in Mosul is a prime example of the political failures in the country. Corruption is rife amongst all variety of Islamists – Sunni or Shia. The 2013 Transparency International's Corruption Perception Index ranked Iraq as the sixth most corrupt nation in the world in a top ten list that includes Somalia, North Korea and South Sudan.

In Libya, Islamist militias are running riot. The democratically elected government has no mandate in certain parts of the lawless country. The situation has become so chaotic that Arab commentators now talk of the potential 'Somalisation of Libya'. The failures in Sudan and Iran, in terms of state management or human rights violations have been well debated. Add the case of Gaza, with its own experiment of Islamist governance, and you have a complete political map of chaos, paradoxes and contradictions.

Tunisia is often cited as a success story. It has been able to build a consensus on the constitution and managing pluralism. It is paving the way for a social contract between the state and society. Nevertheless, all this has only happened because the secularist opposition parties who managed to remove the word 'Sharia' from the constitution have kept the Islamists of the Ennahda party in check.

The harsh reality is that Islamists and Salafists have turned the Arab World into a wasteland. Their rigid and non-flexible agenda, and puritanical outlook, leaves no room for dialogue, let alone negotiations of any kind. The fact is that they are intensely exclusive, intolerant, and operate with a one-dimensional mentality that goes against the very basic tenets of an inclusive democratic rule that encompasses pluralism and diversity. Whether moderate, radical, or violent, the basic message advocated by all Islamists is rooted in Salafism. It is predicated on division and jihadism, even if Jihad is limited to mental onslaughts. The psychotic obsession with ideological purity (similar to the eugenic theories used by the Nazis) and the 'true' representation of God's will is readily rationalised as the need for obsessive control and demonisation and exclusion of all others. In their view, the Shi'ites are Rafidahs or rejectionists, as they call them, and should therefore either be treated as non-Muslims (the 'moderate' view) or killed as apostates (the extremist view). However, it is not just the Shia who are the target of their wrath. Sufis too should be dealt with harshly as a result of their 'distorted ideologies'. Jews and Christians, although labelled in the Qur'an as 'People of the Book', are classified as *kuffar* or infidels and deserve 'the exit' or to be beheaded according to one violent Salafist. I have heard these views and words again and again in my travels in the Middle East. The very idea of a moderate Islamist, as far as I am concerned, is an oxymoron.

When not denigrating, or indeed eradicating, all those who they consider *kuffar*, the Salafis turn on Sunni Muslims. Those not following the Hanbali School of jurisprudence are declared 'bad Muslims'. During the 1990s Algerian civil war, the Groupe Islamique Armé (GIA), carried out a violent campaign of massacres against Sunni civilians justified by fatwas issued by radical Imams, such as Abu Qatada, who was then a member of the Al-Qaeda fatwa committee. To some extent, ISIS are simply carrying on where GIA left off.

Both the 'moderate' and extremist Salafis believe in the fundamental role of Sharia in governing the lives of people. Sharia law, in its medieval form and outlook, would become the basis for enforcing 'puritanical Islam'. Its ancient and fossilised rulings would be interpreted only by *fuqaha* (jurists) or religious scholars. Therefore, only the *fuqaha* would be the source of power to interpret 'Allah's rule' on earth. The absolute in dogma is thus transformed into the absolutism of political policy to enforce what is considered truth or right, and what would be considered false or wrong. This is then transformed into the absolutism of the social aspects of government, as clearly envisioned by jihadi Salafis such as Osama bin Laden, Abu Musab al Zarqawi, and Abu Bakr al Baghdadi, the 'Caliph' of the 'Islamic state'.

It seems that the Salafis have learned nothing from almost four decades of the Wilayat al-Faqih system of Iran – where all human behaviour is regulated by the dictates of a Supreme Ruler and a Guardianship Council. The Muslim Brotherhood have established a similar al-Murshed al-A'am (General Guide) set-up. The citizens are referred to as *raayia*, the Arabic word meaning shepherded. Therefore, the people are by definition sheep who need to be shepherded by a Wilayat al-Faqih or a Murshed al-A'am! The Islamists look at the individual with suspicion and regard him or her as incapable of doing anything without the guidance of those who are qualified to interpret religion. Notice how the 'Islamic State' has put up posters in Rifah and other towns they have captured telling the citizens how to pray, perform ablution, dress and brush their teeth. The aim is not just total intellectual tutelage, but also how to exist as a human being – every aspect of life, however minute, has to be governed by the dictates of 'Sharia', which simply means the dictates of those with religious power.

The Sharia peddled by the Islamists has no notion of citizenship, human rights, freedom or the dignity of man. It is intrinsically tied to *aqidah*, belief or faith. The mantra of the Islamist, of any particular ilk or persuasion, is correct *aqidah*. This is why 'Guardians of Faith' and 'Morality Police' are needed – so everyone can have the right belief and do the right things according to this belief. In their nature and practice, these enforcement groups are no different from the Spanish Inquisition that dominated Europe from the late fifteenth to the early nineteenth century.

What the Islamists mean by Sharia was brought home to me in the summer of 2004. I was in Nigeria attending a conference on 'Democracy and Sharia'. I recall the late Sudanese thinker, Mohammad Hajj Hammed, showing me one of the documents that the Nigerian Muslims were using in the North of the country as guidance. The document contained what can only be described as pretty obnoxious rules about slavery, treatment of women, and included the word for an ancient currency – in use over 900 years ago in the Middle East – in which business transactions were to be undertaken. This old interpretation of men long dead was seen as immutable. I wondered how this 'guidance' could possibly be of any use in Northern Nigeria in the twenty first century. A few years later, Boko Haram provided me with an unambiguous answer.

It is commonly believed that the Islamists, the Wahhabis, the Deobandis and others of the Salafi bent, are a minority. But it seems to me that they would rapidly become the majority. From Egypt to the Sudan, Morocco to Iran, the most common Muslim I encounter carries some sort of Salafi or Wahhabi gene. A 2012 survey in Jordan suggests that 61 per cent of the population prefers a political system similar to the one in Saudi Arabia with only 17 per cent preferring the Turkish model. Another survey in Jordan showed that 62 per cent of respondents demanded a system of government ruled by Islamists, with no elections. In Egypt, a 2011 Pew survey revealed that 88 per cent of respondents believed in the death penalty for apostasy, and 80 per cent supported stoning for adultery. In a region saturated with mosques, where schools, hospitals and basic amenities are conspicuously lacking, citizens yearn for more mosques – which are being constructed in increasing numbers.

Islamists of all shades have embedded their ultra-puritan religiosity in every sphere of life. A significant proportion of the population of the Arab world believes that Sheikhs and Ayatollahs have the answers to all our problems – despite the overwhelming evidence to the contrary. In a region steeped in religion, the average citizen thinks that more religion is the answer. And the answers we need have already been given by our religious scholars. Religious scholars themselves perpetuate this myth as I discovered during a recent conversation with an influential Islamist who is both an established jurist and a 'leading light' in a political party. How are we to define the 'abode of Islam' in a globalised worlds, I asked the learned Sheikh. He instantly replied that this problem has already been dealt with by an influential Mawlana, two hundred years ago; and proceeded to quote chapter and verse. 'O Sheikh', I retorted, 'what is your opinion about equality in citizenship that corresponds with our time, the twenty-first century, and the rule of democracy? Can the concept of citizenship in the modern world actually be defined by an ancient division of the world in black and white?' He dismissed me with a wave of his hand.

Religion has always played a major part in the social and psychological makeup of the individual and society in the Arab world. Perhaps that is why religious reforms are so difficult in the Middle East, a region that has witnessed the birth of all three major religions. Europe, where religion was imported, had a much easier task. But it is obvious to me that no progress of any kind, or positive development of any type, can take place in the Middle East without radical reforms in Islam.

The term Salafi was coined by Mohammad Rashid Rida (1865–1935), who is regarded as a great reformer and a symbol of the 'Arab Awakening' of the early twentieth century. Rashid Rida's political philosophy of the 'Islamic state' influenced most of the twentieth century reformers and Islamist thinkers. He believed that the technical skills needed for the renewal of Muslim affairs should emerge from deep Islamic morals. As long as you comprehend Islamic rules 'correctly' you should be able to succeed in the here and the Hereafter. Rashid Rida formula led to the wide-spread belief that as long as the Arabs are religiously pious, regardless of the circumstances on the ground, they would be able to solve all their problems – a magic template, which provides for every aspect of life, is available to true believers. It has now become the fundamental precept of all shades of Islamists. This is where Muslim Brotherhood's slogans such as 'Islam is the solution' and 'The Qur'an is our constitution', a contradiction and legal puzzle in itself, come from. Notice how quickly and easily these slogans, which reduce all complexity into a reductive ideology and emerged from a 'moderate' movement, were embraced by extremists such as the Taliban and ISIS.

The mentality that correct belief solves all problems is deeply entrenched in the Arab world. The Arab Spring was able to dismantle the political barrier of fear, but the intellectual, cultural and social barriers of fear remain firmly in place. Arab intellectuals are still not able to express their ideas freely, loudly and publicly for fear of being labelled as heretic by Islamists, or Salafists, or traditional religious institutions. Researchers will not touch 'hard' cultural issues in an evaluative manner, as the expanding environment of suppressive taboos is a de facto barrier. Authoritarianism is embedded deep in the mind and the personality of individuals and society. Despotism of thought is prevalent in the Arab world. In his celebrated book, Tabai al-Istibdad wa-Masari al-Isti'bad ('The Nature of Despotism'), the Syrian intellectual and pan-Islamic activist, Abd al-Rahman al-Kawakibi (1855–1902), argued that the demise of the Arab world was due to the oppressive rule of the Ottoman Empire. 'Oppression manipulates facts in people's minds', he wrote, 'leading people to believe that whoever seeks truth is sinful, that whoever abandons his rights is obedient, that the one who cries out against oppression is mischievous'. The oppression of the Ottomans has now been replaced by the oppression of the Islamists. Al-Kawakibi's words are as true in a post-Arab Spring Middle East as they were in the nineteenth century.

The humane aspect of the Qur'an, its emphasis on diversity and pluralism, and tolerance towards the other, have all been lost – thanks to the Islamist's ideological and political approach to the faith of Islam. One of the most beautiful attributes of Allah, Ada'ala, or Justice, has been squandered at the altar of an abstract legalistic approach. In the Arab mind, Islam is equal to *fiqh* (jurisprudence) and *fiqh* is equal to Islam like a crude mathematical equation. The goal of Islam is reduced to establishing a despotic ideological state rather than creating a universal moral order.

How can one engage in meaningful dialogue with such closed minds that defy all logic? As an activist I think there is an urgent need, beyond all other needs, to broaden the deeply entrenched mental makeup of Arab societies from authoritarianism in all things political, social and cultural towards an inclusivity, diversity, pluralism and openness. Only open minds can produce open society and open government allowing the flow of ideas that create positive change.

A number of questions need answers. Was Islam revealed in order to determine the politics of a certain historical community? Or was it revealed essentially as a universal message that addresses the moral and social malaise of humanity? How do we liberate our societies from the influence of the religious scholars – the *fuqaha*? How do we create social institutions, rooted in Islamic sources, with teeth to act as checks and balances to prevent corruption, suppression and oppression, protect the rights of citizens and promote the transparency of government? Clearly, the concepts of freedom and rights have no meaning if there are no institutions to safeguard them; and these institutions should be effective in protecting the moral code and working for social justice, which is the objective of the Qur'an.

The only real antidote to Salafist thought of all kind is viable answers to these questions. The alternative, the spread and dominance of Salafi ideology, does not bear thinking about. It is not just Shias they will kill.

THE POWER OF WORD

Boyd Tonkin

During my sixth-form years, I studied Ancient Greek for the first and last time. It played no part in my A-level curriculum. My school, a suburban academic hothouse that liked to show off the breadth and balance of its teaching at the same time as it delivered those all-important grades, insisted that senior pupils should taste a subject that had no direct relation to the pursuit of qualifications and certificates. Nonetheless, this high-minded gesture towards the value of a purely liberal education was – in my case, at least – not quite all it seemed.

The headmaster himself took our Greek class. Like many high-achieving teachers of his generation, he was a promising scholar who had risen, or fallen, into administration. A recreational return to the world of Euripides, Plato and Herodotus transported him back, for an hour or two, to a blessed place remote from problem pupils, wayward staff, building plans and pushy parents. So, on the morning of our lessons, he would stride back to his study from the morning assembly with a spring in his step. Our band of volunteer classicists would be sitting outside. 'Come along, my Grecians,' he would almost sing, as we followed him into the inner sanctum for a mind-expanding dip into antiquity.

I never learned all that much of the language. After all, I knew I need not try too hard. No tests or exams lay at the end of our ancient way: that was the point. Yet we did work from a book that consisted of easy-access extracts from canonical works, mostly drama and history – with a little light philosophy. In sips rather than drafts, I tasted the Athenian source at its point of origin rather than having to rely on dilutions in a modern bottle. Via scattered fragments, I heard Sophocles' Antigone speak defiance on behalf of her dishonoured brother against Creon and his almighty state. I tried as well to decipher riddling Socrates when – according to Plato –

the condemned subversive teased and jested with authority in the hours before his hemlock-speeded death.

Our textbook also made room for a few selections from the Greek of the New Testament. Even then, I understood that the 'Koine' of the four Gospels and the Acts of the Apostles was considered no match in subtlety or elegance for the tongue of the pagan playwrights and sages. A workaday lingua franca of ports and markets across the eastern Roman Empire, it allowed the peoples of the Mediterranean to talk and to trade. No classicist – as opposed to theologian – rated Koine Greek very highly as a vehicle for literary expression.

Yet the Gospel had its moments. And one of them lodged, indelibly, in my memory. For around 1,900 years, no one has been quite sure how to interpret the opening sentence of the Gospel of St John: the most mystical, intellectual and elusive of the quartet of texts that emerged from decades of scholarly winnowing to make up the approved New Testament. *En archē ēn ho Lógos, kai ho Lógos ēn pros ton Theón, kai Theós ēn ho Lógos*: 'In the beginning was the Word, and the Word was with God, and the word was God.' So runs the King James Version of 1611. Other, less orthodox translations maintain that 'the Word was a god'. That rogue indefinite article undermines the doctrine of the Trinity, of three persons in one deity: the monotheistic back-stop installed by the Church fathers to defend their fresh faith against the default polytheism of the cultures through which it spread, with their altars, shrines, groves and temples that housed a god for every large and small thing.

I knew nothing of Christology then, and know very little more these days. All the same, I did grasp through the Greek that, at the root of this religion, lay the power of the Word. And not only the Christian creed that St Paul began to fashion out of the reform Judaism of Palestine in the early first century. The Logos drives monotheism. For the Abrahamic faiths, the sacred scripture – with its energising junction of storytelling and exposition, fable and doctrine – served as a kind of rocket-fuel. The holy text not only gathers the faithful around the Word but turbo-charges resistance, expansion or conversion.

Written around six centuries before the Gospel of St John, the Book of Exodus reports that Moses brought the Law to the Israelites from the swirling clouds of Mount Sinai: 'And the Lord said unto Moses, Come up to me into the mount, and be there: and I will give thee tables of stone, and a law, and commandments which I have written; that thou mayest teach them.' (Exodus 24.12; King James Version). After another half-millennium, in the early seventh century, the Qur'an would reinforce the primacy of the sacred text. 'Recite! Your Lord is most bountiful. He taught with the pen. He taught man what he knew not' (96.1). Or, as 2:2 proclaims: 'This is the Book in which there is no doubt, containing guidance for those who are mindful of God'.

In the beginning, the Word was a fount of authority - but also a spring of dissent and ambiguity. God, or a god? The Word, the story, the argument: Logos can embrace all three. Above all, the Word empowers its expositors and interpreters. Its idioms and dialects can enrich students in every way, tangible and intangible. Our merry sessions of sixth-form Greek served an ulterior purpose. The headmaster could endorse university applications and write other references. The better he knew you, the clearer you might stand out from the crowd. For concrete as well as abstract reasons, I had no cause to regret my mornings as a trainee 'Grecian' confronted with the deepest enigmas of the Word.

II

For all their quarrels with one another and among themselves, the People of the Book paid a common homage to the majesty of Logos. Scripture, often as gnomic and ambivalent as the first words of St John, required interpretation from scholars and sages, rabbis, priests and imams. The Word generated authority – and challenges to authority – across all the lands where Abrahamic belief took root. Within monotheistic faith, it solidifies hierarchy, but equally it dissolves hierarchy. The Word can be turned against the forces that have seized it.

Far back at the fountain-head of Abrahamic faith, parts of the Talmudic tradition celebrate not only the value of argument between man and man, but between man and God. Bewilderment, bemusement, even anger at God accompany the birth of belief in an undivided deity. For all three faiths, God's inscrutable demand that Abraham should sacrifice his son Isaac stands as the primal mystery – and burden – of the disembodied Word. Isaac's last-minute reprieve ('Lay not thine hand upon the lad') may, for the anthropologists, commemorate the ancient transition from human to animal sacrifice. For ordinary believers, and ordinary doubters, it more often represents the head-splitting strangeness of all divinity.

Later in the Hebrew manuscripts that came to be known as the Old Testament, the Book of Job reinforces the idea of a single God as an unreadable, even sadistic taskmaster. In his answer 'out of the whirlwind' to the just Job's ever-growing litany of afflictions, God mandates merely blind trust, infinite patience and worshipful awe in the face of his tetchy majesty: 'Shall he that contendeth with the Almighty instruct him?' (Job 40.2). The Lord does not account for himself. Rather, he rewards Job with 'twice as much as he had before' (Job 42.10).

From the beginning, the divine Word gives rise to resistance. For the ageing Sigmund Freud, no longer a diagnostician of individual but of cultural maladies, humanity never quite knew how to receive the gift of monotheistic belief. The words of the scriptures, at once peremptory and unfathomable, both asked for too much and said too little. According to a positively antique Jewish joke, the divine wisdom of the entire Torah – the five books of Moses – can be summed up in four words: 'Because I say so!' God disposed, and man shuffled, grumbled and rebelled. For Freud in his revisionist essay 'Moses and Monotheism' (1939), human beings never truly reconciled themselves to a form of faith that so sternly cut against the grain of the ancient, populous pantheons. He posits the idea that the Israelites showed their gratitude to Moses – whom Freud sees as an Egyptian – by murdering him. Yet the invisible God that the prophet brought down from Sinai would in time propel the secular Word as it developed in philosophy, literature and science. Deity dematerialised, from idol into text, and with this shift came a world-changing 'advance in intellectuality'.

Today, the Israeli novelist Amos Oz has little time for the formal observances of supernatural faith. He still puts his trust in the supreme dialectical value of dispute with and even against the voice of heaven. Co-written with his historian daughter Fania Oz-Salzberger, Oz's book *Jews and Words* (2014) voices his own credo. 'We have no use for the synagogue,' Oz told me. 'We believe that Judaism is a civilisation based mostly on language.' Oz cites his favourite tale of 'reverent irreverence' among the rabbis of the Talmud: the story of Akhnai's Oven. 'Two saintly rabbis argue about interpreting the law in their capacity as judges. And they cannot reach a verdict. They will die arguing, but finally God has mercy on them. A voice is heard from above, saying 'Rabbi Eliezer is right. Rabbi Yehoshua is wrong. Go to sleep'. And then the loser, Rabbi Yehoshua, turns his eyes upward and says, 'Please keep out of it. You have given the Torah to human beings. Buzz off! Buzz off!"

Ever since Abraham wrangled with God over the fate of Sodom like 'a shrewd second-hand car dealer', Jewish dialectic has dared to scold the Almighty. But can purely verbal believers such as Oz pick and choose: the jokes, the heroes and heroines, the tall tales, but none of the theological Word? He argues: 'People will hurl at us that Judaism is a package deal: take it or leave it. It's not a package deal. It's a heritage. And a heritage is something you can play with. You can decide which part of the heritage you allocate to your living room, and which part goes to the attic or to the basement. This is the legitimate right of every heir. And I regard myself as a legitimate heir of the Jewish civilisation. I can relegate some of the heritage to the attic.' Buzz off, God, indeed.

From another Abrahamic faith, the Turkish novelist Elif Shafak has explained to me that, for her, the embroideries and embellishments of the Word in Sufi traditions of Islam can disperse power beyond its official interpreters. Against or outside patriarchal authority, 'I realised that women who have been denied any power in other spheres of life can find a means of existence in this little world of superstitions, of folk-tales, of storytelling… They are the queen in that sphere'. For Shafak, the living Word of Sufism – a matter of the spirit rather than the letter – liberates the writer to absorb and harmonise many different stories. 'This is something that perhaps I derive from Sufism. Because I think the human being is a microcosm: all the conflicts present outside are also present inside him… Art has the capacity constantly to deconstruct its own truths. That's again why I think there's a link between Sufism and literature. For me, both of them are about transcending the self, the boundaries given by birth.'

III

The scriptural text constrains, but it can also emancipate. As if in response to some human instinct for intellectual ju-jitsu, rebels, reformers and revisers both within and against religious tradition turn the power of the divine Word back on itself – and sometimes leave it flattened on the floor. Yet heresy requires orthodoxy. Revolt requires order. Dissent requires doctrine. In the Christian West as well, what Greek drama would have called antagonistic process of challenge, riposte and redefinition drove change. One kind of order modified, subverted, refreshed but did not simply demolish another. Post-medieval movements of enquiry and Enlightenment drew strength from the established institutions of belief. Both Renaissance and Reformation enlisted the power of the Word to subdue or transform the authority of state and church. New words, and new laws, sprang from old words and old laws.

As with many cultural revolutions, Renaissance and Reformation alike presented themselves as a return to the origin. For Renaissance scholars, poring over classical manuscripts in the princely libraries of Italy, the authority to be revived lay in the canonical texts of Greece and Rome. To a political prophet such as Machiavelli, as for the English revolutionaries of the Civil Wars, the radiant future lay far in the past. Republican Rome, as idealised in the works of Cicero or Livy, should guide the statesman in search of a better tomorrow.

For sixteenth-century Protestant reformers in the wake of Martin Luther and John Calvin, the corrupt accretions of the Roman church had settled in a crust around the Word of God. Liberation would arrive when the mass of Catholic commentary had been stripped down and cleaned away. Within Europe, the printing press had since the 1450s had amplified the power of the subversive word. One memorable dramatisation of the belief that the letterpress will re-make the world comes in Victor Hugo's novel *The Hunchback of Notre Dame* (1831). It was published a year after the 'July Revolution' in Paris, led by a squadron of journalists, artists and poets. The plot unfolds in 1482, not long after Gutenberg had recreated the Asian craft of moveable-type printing in Germany. At one point, Archdeacon Frollo looks up from a printed volume to the towers of the cathedral. 'Ceci tuera cela,' he muses: 'This will kill that'.

It never did – no more than it extinguished the synagogue or mosque. On the contrary: the Church – like embattled institutions ever since – harnessed the power of new media to fight back against subversive or reformist ideas. Martin Luther probably never physically nailed his '95 theses' against ecclesiastical abuses to the church door in Wittenberg in 1517. He did offer them politely to the Archbishop of Mainz. However, by

January 1518 they had been printed – and spread like bushfire across Europe. Very soon, however, the partisans of Rome struck back in kind. An epoch-defining war of words began.

Polemic moved quickly in the early Reformation. Merchants, scholars and envoys carried books and pamphlets along the trade routes that knit Europe's cities together. One literary gambit trumped another in an escalating battle of ideas. In 1520, Luther had launched a salvo of calls for church reform. In 1521, Henry VIII of England – or so it said on the title page – responded with the orthodox *Defence of the Seven Sacraments* (ghosted by his thinker-in-chief, Thomas More). In gratitude, Pope Leo X granted the English monarch the title of Fidei Defensor, defender of the faith. Look at the face of any UK coin (still marked 'F.D') for a glimpse of how much doctrinal tracts mattered to the state.

From the age of Reformation through the age of Revolution, the power of the printed word as a solvent of dogma became an article of faith for both radicals and reactionaries in Europe and then the Americas. Because it was so fervently believed, it might have grown more real. And nobody believed in it more steadfastly than the Holy Office in Rome, which drew up and enforced the Catholic Church's 'Index Librorum Prohibitorum' between 1559 and 1966.

From Kepler and Galileo through Voltaire and Hume to Sartre and Simone de Beauvoir, the banned works on the Index add up to a gazetteer for 400 years of Enlightenment. Paradoxically, the attentions of the Index confirmed a belief in the secular Western book as ground-breaking dynamite. In every age, the censor's proscription salutes the power of its target. Authority does not ban what it does not fear. Conversely, persecution can spread the Word faster and louder than indifferent acceptance. Galileo's trials in 1616 and 1633 echoed around the literate world, and hastened the triumph of the new – or rather, the revived – heliocentric cosmology. Rome did learn its lesson. By the 1860s, the Index chose to overlook Charles Darwin's *Origin of Species* (1859). That neglect (or smart decision) has exempted the Catholic Church from having to take part in the evolution wars over the past 150 years.

Words burnt frequently across the late-medieval and early-modern world, as struggles between and within rival monotheisms took their cue from holy books and their state-sanctioned interpreters. The people who

created, imported or preached the revolutionary Word burnt too – from
the Protestant radical William Tyndale, whose English translations of the
Bible underpin the later King James Version, at Antwerp in 1536; to the
free-thinking scientist Giordano Bruno at Rome in 1600. Meanwhile, the
so-called 'Reconquest' of Spain and Portugal by Catholic monarchs
sent much of the Muslim culture of Iberia literally up in smoke. At a book-
burning in Granada in 1499, a reported 5,000 volumes in Arabic – both
sacred and secular – were consigned to the flames.

IV

Yet, even at this front-line in the holy wars, another concept of the power
of the Word made itself heard. In Granada, some Christian clerics pleaded
for the library of the Emirs to be saved from the pyre. Theology aside, they
knew that the Islamic kingdoms of Spain had hosted the Muslim and Jewish
scholars who, via Arabic, both transmitted the scientific and medical
learning of the ancient world to Europe and enriched it with new research
along the way. For some minds, the idea that the true power of the Word lay
in addition and accretion rather than a mortal struggle against enemies had
already germinated.

Slowly, it became possible to think that someone else's Word and way of
thought might deepen rather than threaten your own. By 1580, Michel de
Montaigne – a sceptical Catholic of partly Jewish descent – could look out
across landscapes ravaged by the Wars of Religion in France and think
sympathetically about the 'Cannibals' of the newly-explored Americas as
people with stories and customs worthy of respect. To Montaigne, 'I find
that there is nothing barbarous and savage in this nation, by anything that I
can gather, excepting, that everyone gives the title of barbarism to
everything that is not in use in his own country.' The idea of plural realities
corrects the delusion that, on our home turf, 'there is always the perfect
religion, there the perfect government, there the most exact and
accomplished usage of all things.'

At roughly the same moment, in Mughal India, the Muslim emperor
Akbar gathered scribes and sages from all the faiths he knew – Hinduism,
Islam, Christianity, Judaism, Buddhism, Zoroastrianism, Jainism – in an
ornate audience hall at Fatehpur Sikri outside Agra. The Emperor asked

them to debate the differences between their creeds, and to find their similarities. If the venue is correct (and no one knows for sure), you may still stand among those carved columns and ponder the birth of a syncretic Word that gains its power by amendment and comparison rather than competition, conquest and erasure.

Historians warn against trying to romanticise, or modernise, the acts and motives of pre-modern rulers. Akbar no doubt wanted the assorted clerics to argue among themselves, not with him. All the same, that multi-faith durbar at Fatehpur Sikri does feel, as with Montaigne's pluralism, like a breakthrough of sorts. Shortly before a new age of rational investigation opened in Europe, Akbar had hinted that one could call a truce among the warring Words.

Open-minded curiosity about the traditions and convictions of others of course pre-dated the Renaissance in Europe. In the Islamic world, Ibn Battuta had on his travels in the fourteenth century from Spain to India pioneered the art and science of cross-cultural analogy The outlines of a new relationship between the Word and power begin to emerge. In place of the agonistic struggles of the age of faith-driven conquest, a more dialectical style comes to the fore. Writing of Shakespeare, himself (as *The Tempest* proves) a student of Montaigne, John Keats praised the 'negative capability' that can hold complexity and contradiction in a stable suspension without any 'irritable reaching' after certainty. For Montaigne himself, the European encounter with the Americas had not given the incomers a licence to plunder but a chance to learn: 'Our world has just found another, and who can be sure that this will be the last of its brothers?'

In Europe, this opening-up to the power of another's Word took place in fits and starts. Militant Protestants still looked for conquest rather than conciliation on the battlefield of interpretation. Both a theological and political revolutionary, John Milton may have defended freedom of expression during the English civil wars in his tract *Areopagitica* (1644). But he did so in the belief that his preferred Logos would undoubtedly prevail: 'Whoever saw Truth put to the worse, in a free and open encounter?' Besides, Milton's tolerance of dissent built fences of its own. In common with much of the Protestant tradition, he tended to treat Islam as a misguided but interesting deviation from proper monotheism while saving his real ire for Roman Catholic superstition and ritualism. Milton served

Oliver Cromwell, who formally readmitted Jews to England in 1656, but he did not extend tolerance to Catholics because he thought them potential traitors to the state. Some Words stayed beyond the pale.

V

Even when science and Enlightenment took over from proselytising Christianity as the keynote of European advancement, the Word retained its drive towards dominion. One strand of rational enquiry did choose to compare rather than to conquer. In the eighteenth century, the *philosophes* in France picked up Montaigne's pluralistic thread to contrast their own native cultures- often unfavourably – with conditions elsewhere. Satirical reproofs to the status quo may come from outer space, in Voltaire's Micromegas, from Persia, in Montesquieu's Lettres Persanes – or even across the Channel, when the young Voltaire (in Letters on the English) used the idealised example of a commercial, decentralised, multi-faith state under the rule of law as a stick with which to goad absolutist France.

Yet Enlightenment could just as easily mean the quest for a master-narrative to ingest or even eliminate other people's Word. The historian Jonathan Israel has plotted the continuing tension between *Radical Enlightenment* (2002) as a project of individual and social self-analysis, and the forms of instrumental knowledge that the combative states of the Age of Reason wished to employ. In the 1650s, the philosopher Baruch Spinoza's bid to reframe the power of the Word as a power of self-reflection and unlimited enquiry could still outrage the norms of a world that believed in a monolithic Truth. Expelled from the Jewish community of Amsterdam, Spinoza became the prototype of the modern blasphemer. Yet, in one crucial aspect, the cap does not fit. His Ethics, published in 1677, might have fed an underground river of dissenting speculation that did much to nurture a metaphysics and morality beyond organised religion. But Spinoza doubted human doubt as much as he eroded religious dogma. No positivist creed can be adduced from his work, and its conflation of the idea of a depersonalised God with nature and reason – in short, with the Word.

Other scientific path-breakers proved equally resistant to the rational Word as a secular religion. If Charles Darwin's narrative of evolution proceeded in part from his private loss of faith, it never resolved into a manifesto for materialism. The power of this Word lies in unending, self-revising curiosity – a winding path of tests, variations and adaptations to match its own narrative of natural selection. His peroration to the Origin of Species speaks of the nobility of change and complexity in nature rather than the satisfaction of a fixed system: 'There is grandeur in this view of life,' so that 'whilst this planet has gone cycling on according to the fixed law of gravity, from so simple a beginning endless forms most beautiful and most wonderful have been, and are being, evolved'.

The power of infinite curiosity, of Keats' Shakespearean 'negative capability', proved harder to sustain than the idea of an exclusive creed. Soon after the Origin appeared in 1859, the anti-ecclesiastical militant Thomas Henry Huxley – 'Darwin's bulldog' – had, although he coined the consciously open-minded term 'agnostic', begun to reframe the defence of evolution in terms of knock-down bouts with bishops. Needless to say, the church hierarchy was happy to oblige. Word against Word, with polemic the means and victory the end, remained the default setting of the European mind. Matthew Arnold, another homeless refugee from the breakdown of belief, wrote in 'Dover Beach' of his desolation as the 'sea of faith' ebbed to leave merely 'ignorant armies that clash by night'.

Frequently, those ignorant armies took their Word as a unitary law. In colonial India, Thomas Babington Macaulay fused Protestantism and Enlightenment into a forced march towards modernisation that would swing reason like a scimitar against traditional belief. In his *Minute on Education* (1835), Macaulay envisaged the breeding of 'a class who may be interpreters between us and the millions whom we govern – a class of persons Indian in blood and colour, but English in tastes, in opinions, in morals and in intellect.' He objected in particular to the government-funded teaching of Arabic and Sanskrit classics, and the printing of texts in those languages, given 'the intrinsic superiority of the Western literature'. For Macaulay the model moderniser, echoing Milton, 'We do not even stand neuter in the contest between truth and falsehood. We are not content to leave the natives to the influence of their own hereditary prejudices.'

Elsewhere, the words that encouraged social revolution had no more qualms about the exercise of power. For Karl Marx in his *Theses on Feuerbach*, written in the spring of 1845 but first published in 1924, 'the philosophers have only interpreted the world in various ways; the point is to change it'. As if – as the thinker who found Hegel 'standing on his head' and turned him the right way up well knew – interpretation were not itself an agent of change. Marx was no Marxist (he said so himself), but he did usher in the age of manifestos and so helped the secular Word adopt its own version of the missionary position.

Still, a paradox lies at the heart of the Marxist and sociological belief in the force of revolutionary discourse. It can only bring about what was already destined to happen. From the *Manifesto of the Communist Party*, co-written with Friedrich Engels in 1848, to the three volumes of *Capital* (1887, 1885, 1894), Marx became an archetype of the writer whose books might alter the course of events. Yet most of his work tells another story. Although admirers of his Hegelian '1844 manuscripts' might dispute the idea, the overall effect of Marxist materialism was to downgrade the firepower of beliefs as fuel for history's march. For radical thinkers today, the notion that the economic 'base' determines the cultural 'superstructure' counts as 'vulgar Marxism'. But the vulgar version took hold, for better or worse. Class conflict would, especially as re-imagined by Lenin as a licence for vanguard-party elitism, trump the battle of ideas.

For the wider radical movement, books remained icons, totems and talismans. They worked conversions and propelled the struggle. No one can survey the career of Leo Tolstoy, say, and not acknowledge that the novelist's global renown lent his works a missionary force that touched hearts – and altered the course of events. Not only in Tsarist Russia, either: you might argue that, via the impact of his tracts about non-violent revolution on MK Gandhi and other anti-imperialists in India, the Count even helped to bring down the Raj.

Other novels have moved mountains, at least in the popular imagination. None did so to more spectacular effect than Harriet Beecher Stowe's Uncle Tom's Cabin. After 1852, its sentimental melodrama became a battering-ram for the anti-slavery cause in America's Civil War. The remark attributed to President Abraham Lincoln on meeting Stowe in 1862 – 'So this is the little lady who started this great war' – is most likely apocryphal. Nonetheless, it captures what countless contemporaries thought. The British prime minister Lord Palmerston, that original gunboat-despatching liberal imperialist, said that 'I have not read a novel for thirty years; but I have read that book three times, not only for the story, but for the statesmanship of it.'

This mass-market Word could aspire not merely to influence over an elite but to 'statesmanship'. Yet the Marxists, along with other sociological determinists, had cast doubt on the text as a tool of transformation. If vast epoch-making forces of class, economy and state drove world-shaking events, did it matter what treatises or stories advocated? That puzzle haunted writers who stood on the fringe, or in the thick, of nationalist as well as socialist upheavals. 'Did that play of mine send out/ Certain men the English shot?' WB Yeats asked in his poem 'The Man and the Echo', referring to the Easter Rising in Dublin in 1916. He left the question unanswered. Lenin, strategist first and thinker second, brutally cut through this knot by fashioning the close-knit party as a machine that could jump-start historical change. Read Sayyid Qutb, or scrutinise the tactics of the Muslim Brotherhood across the Middle East, and it is hard not to conclude that this Leninist Islam has absorbed from the Europe of a century ago both the power – and the paradox – of the militant, transforming Word.

VI

Creeds rise and fall, mutate and mix. The hunger for a killer book of revelation – or revolution – persists. As I write, the comedian Russell Brand's scattergun treatise *Revolution* (2014) rides high in the British bestseller charts. Brand may stand at the farcical fag-end of a long tradition of empowering words. Still, his acclaim confirms that it can still emit a glow. As late as the 1960s, the antediluvian dogma of Mao Zedong's *Little Red Book* played its part in impoverishing lives and lowering horizons in the world's most populous nation. Advancement there, however unequal its outcomes, meant tearing up the book.

As the ideology-scourged twentieth century waned, many of the creative writers whose own words carried most weight did just that. As they surveyed the killing-fields of their time, literary figures tended to measure an ever-wider gap between their words and any form of scriptural orthodoxy. When George Orwell denounced the 'smelly little ideologies contending for our souls' in an essay on Charles Dickens in 1939, and in *Nineteen Eighty-Four* dissected the totalitarian abuse of language, memory and history, he spoke for a generation that elevated solitary truth against collective faith. As he wrote in 1943 in a polemic on 'Literature and the Left', 'there is no knowing just how much the Socialist movement has lost by alienating the literary intelligentsia. But it has alienated them, partly by confusing tracts with literature, and partly by having no room in it for a humanistic culture.' Orwell regrets that writers who sought to take a radical stand 'were first regarded with patronage and suspicion and then, when it was found that they would not or could not turn themselves into gramophone records, they were thrown out on their ears. Most of them retreated into individualism.' Seven decades later, they still do.

By the 1940s, an all-weather advocate such as George Bernard Shaw – zealously proselytising for causes from socialism to eugenics to vegetarianism – had begun to look like a historical throwback. Although post-war thinkers such as Jean-Paul Sartre would wrestle to align individual choice with class solidarity, the murderous 'grand narratives' of the twentieth century West tended to sever truth from power. Almost three-quarters of a century after WB Yeats had danced around the edge of a revolution, another Irish poet would scan the chasm that divided speech from force. Seamus Heaney not only stood at a conscious angle to overt commitment, for all the eloquence of his meditations on the Irish past. He made his intimate detachment – so near, and yet so far from the punch and counter-punch of history – the subject of much of his best verse.

In 'The Flight-Path', for example, the poet looks back from the relative stability of the 1990s to the height of the Troubles in 1979. He recalls a meeting en route from Dublin to Belfast with an angry Republican – by implication, an IRA supporter if not an actual guerrilla – who demands: 'When, for fuck's sake, are you going to write/ Something for us?' The poet replies: 'If I do write something,/ Whatever it is, I'll be writing for myself.' With Heaney, however, one stratum of irony overlays another. A few lines later, having invoked the 'dirty protest' of IRA inmates at Long Kesh jail, the poet sees the red eyes of the enraged militant 'Drilling their way through the rhymes and images/ Where I too walked behind the righteous Virgil'. 'I too', because Heaney has also just alluded to Dante, an earlier disciple of the Roman poet. As Heaney understands, his beloved Virgil wrote as the flag-waving bard of Roman imperialism under the poet's patron, the first Emperor Augustus. In his lecture 'What is a

Classic?', which Heaney knew, TS Eliot approvingly connects Virgil's Aeneid – the epic of Rome's foundation – at once to the birth of the 'classical' tradition in Western literature and to the idea of empire. Speaking in 1944, with the Third Reich's own appropriation of the classical-imperial Word still in power over much of Europe, Eliot dubs the Roman imperium and the Latin language 'an empire and a language with a unique destiny in relation to ourselves'. Willing disciple of Virgil and Dante, Heaney, the man of unsullied words, can no more dodge power in its entirety than he can step away from his own shadow.

VII

Given the bad faith, moral coercion and outright intimidation that have part-nered the demand for creative minds to serve some 'struggle' or other, Heaney's refusal to enlist becomes exemplary. Neither, in his case or others', does it impede a willingness to commemorate historic injustice and salute the memory of its victims. In the modern literature of conflict, naming the dead becomes an act of restoration that returns to the Word its primal, almost magical authority. Yeats himself knew this when, in 'Easter 1916', he chanted the names of the Irish revolutionaries whose cause he could support only in the most doubt-encumbered way: 'I write it out in a verse –/ MacDonagh and MacBride/ And Connolly and Pearse/ Now and in time to be,/ Wherever green is worn,/ Are changed, changed utterly:/ A terrible beauty is born.'

The Word may remember the dead, inscribe their sacrifice, and give a voice to the voiceless even if it seeks no role in the state or any other mode of power. In the twentieth century movements of liberation, expressive language performs a key function in resistance if not in active revolution. From Frantz Fanon and Simone de Beauvoir to Edward Said and Ngugi wa Thiong'o, empowering the oppressed has taken on a distinctly literary hue. Read any emancipatory landmark of the past half century or so, and the critical analysis of a hegemonic literature or ideology will often give it crucial leverage. Germaine Greer's *The Female Eunuch* (1970) in large part an exercise in counter-patriarchal LitCrit, is just one case in point. One might dub this (as post-colonial theorists have) the Caliban strategy, after Shakespeare's enslaved 'monster' in *The Tempest*: 'You taught me language,' he tells the invading Prospero, 'and my profit on't/ Is, I know how to curse. The red plague rid you/ For learning me your language!'

Post-colonial or anti-patriarchal, the Calibans of the unshackled Word write back to power in its own approved tongue. For an age that – zealotry aside – has lost much of its belief in positive authority, the language of resistance has a special charm and potency. It lends the Word all the glamour of critique without any of the stain that comes with the exercise of power. Before the abortive 'Arab Spring', as tyrants tottered across the Middle East, the Muslim Brotherhood could in its neo-Leninist fashion gain traction by stating on every occasion that 'Islam is the solution'. Meanwhile, the secular Egyptian novelist Alaa Al-Aswany had in his newspaper columns struck back at religious populism with his own motto: 'Democracy is the solution'. Such words of resistance, although they may stiffen the sinews of opposition, can also deal in sentimental uplift rather than furnish a true alternative to the powers-that-be.

Back in Europe's own tyrannical backyard, one standard-bearer of resistance via the Word never lost a sense of scepticism about literary combat. In 1980, in the depths of his country's neo-Stalinist midwinter, the Czech dissident Vaclav Havel theorised 'The Power of the Powerless' in an influential essay. In the wake of the Soviet invasion that crushed the 'Prague Spring' of 1968, the playwright already had experience of clandestine organisations, of campaigns and open letters, protest manifestos and prison sentences. He had helped to write and launch the pro-democratic 'Charter 77' and denounced his nation's state of fearful paralysis in a defiant letter to President Husak. Yet 'The Power of the Powerless' insists that literary activism will not thaw this frozen society, but 'living in truth': the daily practice of honesty and integrity in thinking, writing and personal conduct. Havel's quietism does not issue in passivity. Instead, the true word spoken, written and above all performed will bring a 'repressed alternative' to fruition. This 'parallel polis' can in time defeat the actual one.

Even in October 1989, on the cusp of world-historical change, Havel warned against the hubris of those who wished for the Word to re-write reality. Accepting the annual Peace Prize at the Frankfurt Book Fair, he said that 'it always pays to be suspicious of words... The same word can be humble at one moment and arrogant the next. And a humble word can be transformed easily... into an arrogant one'. On the brink of a revolution that he had helped to create, Havel set the words of humility against those of mastery. Soon, in an irony worthy of his own surreal and paradoxical plays, the writer who shied away from authority not only became his nation's President in January 1990 but, repeatedly re-elected, held that post until 2003. For all his inevitable blunders, no professional wordsmith has done better in high office.

It could be that his wariness about the almighty Word rendered Havel all the more effective as an artist of the state. His truthful text was above all defensive rather than imperial. His words seek not to conquer but to cherish and conserve. They challenge the missionary position, in language and culture, that has spread darkness as well as light. Merchants of the word always enjoy stories that hail their muscle and majesty. 'This will kill that!', as Hugo's book-brandishing cleric insists. Perhaps, as Havel hints, too many books – sacred and secular alike – have set out to change the world, and have done so all too successfully.

VIII

The Word may now shine brighter as a shield than as a sword. In the weary aftermath of modern wars of faith, it needs more power-challenging defenders and fewer power-hungry zealots. The defensive Word can take many contemporary forms. Prison and persecution can lend a text value in a context remote from its creation. In the 1970s, political detainees in apartheid South Africa read and re-read the so-called 'Robben Island Bible': in reality, a copy of the *Complete Works of Shakespeare* smuggled into the South African prison by a prisoner, Sonny Venkatrathnam. In this racist Calvinist theocracy, the Word of God retained a peculiar authority. Or of the gods: Venkatrathnam had covered his Shakespeare edition with pictures of Indian deities so that he could pass it off as a sacred Hindu scripture. Inside the island fortress, inmates would debate the plays with passion and even add a signature to sections that meant the most to them. One prisoner marked the lines from Julius Caesar in which Caesar says, 'Cowards die many times before their deaths/ The valiant never taste of death but once'. Nelson Mandela signed these words on 16 December 1977.

In the face of tyranny or menace, the unfettered Word becomes something to cherish more than something to impose. In his third-person memoir *Joseph Anton* (2013), Salman Rushdie tells the story of his transition after the Iranian fatwa of February 1989 from an assertive combatant in the culture wars to a fugitive under sentence of death who had to depend on champions, advocates and safeguarders. Not all emerged unscathed: the Japanese translator of The Satanic Verses was assassinated; Rushdie's Italian translator and Norwegian publisher both suffered grave injuries in fatwa-driven attacks. Above all, Joseph Anton gives homage to the guardians of the Word under siege. As Rushdie explained when we discussed the memoir, 'Many people had stood up for me vocally, with great courage and principle, and I wanted to give back what I could.' Rushdie in this mode no longer sounds like an experimenter or transgressor, but a celebrant of 'people who love me'. 'One of the things I'm most happy about,' he said, 'is to have had the chance to talk about how much people helped me.'

Under suspicion, under attack, under threat of banning or burning, the Word inspires not a lust for conquest but a protective tenderness. Heinrich Heine famously said that: 'where they burn books, they will in the end burn people too.' True enough, but how many of those who cite Heine know that his maxim first referred to burnings of the Qur'an by the Spanish Inquisition, and appeared in his 1821 tragedy, Almansor? In a modern paroxysm of military book-annihilation, Serbian artillery began in August 1992 to bombard and set ablaze the buildings of the National and University Library of Sarajevo, with its 1.5 million volumes and 150,000 rare books and manuscripts housed in the neo-Moorish old town hall. Most of the collections perished; other city libraries were also shelled to ashes. The Oriental Institute lost many priceless Jewish and Islamic manuscripts. Yet some people in Sarajevo, of different backgrounds, put their lives at risk to save the Word. Dr Mustafa Jahic and his colleagues – including a nightwatchman from Congo – managed to carry 10,000 books and manuscripts, under sniper fire, from the library of the Gazi Husrev Beg mosque.

Only two years ago, a parallel story unfolded in Timbuktu. As early as the 1320s, the Malian ruler Mansa Musa I converted the madrassa of Sankore into a fully-fledged university. Thanks to Sankore and other institutions, Timbuktu accumulated its renowned treasure-trove of manuscripts, perhaps 700,000 in all. They covered the range of arts and sciences known to the late-medieval world. In January 2013, during Mali's civil war, the retreating fundamentalist rebels of Ansar Dine reportedly put to the torch both the Ahmad Baba institute and a separate warehouse as they fled Timbuktu. Yet, after the rebels evacuated the city, it emerged that most manuscripts had survived the puritan hatred of the rebels.

Led by Abdel Kader Haidara, director of the Mamma Haidara Library, representatives of Timbuktu's thirty-two family libraries had secretly and at grave risk transported more than 350,000 items to Bamako. The Word had escaped beyond the reach of bombs, flames and dogmas. For art historian Julie Chaizemartin, writing as a recent exhibition devoted to the 'Timbuktu Renaissance' opened in Brussels, their mission constitutes 'one of the biggest cultural rescue operations ever in the context of an exacerbated political-ideological war'.

IX

In the long run, sheer apathy may menace the power of the Word more than censors, burners, banners and warriors both sacred and profane. Deep in the vast indifference of the internet all our texts can be stored but scorned, filed and forgotten. As early as the 1940s, a quarter-century before progress in computing wove the first strands of the Web, Jorge-Luis Borges had already contemplated the melancholy of the infinite Word in his story 'The Library of Babel'. Borges's Library, which becomes the whole universe, consists of a hive of hexagonal galleries that contain not merely every book that exists but every book that could conceivably exist. 'When it was proclaimed that the Library contained all books, the first impression was one of extravagant happiness. All men felt themselves to be the masters of an intact and secret treasure. There was no personal or world problem whose eloquent solution did not exist in some hexagon.' However, as each human being searches vainly for the personal volume of 'Vindication' that will justify 'the acts of every man in the universe', disenchantment follows. 'As was natural, this inordinate hope was followed by an excessive depression. The certitude that some shelf in some hexagon held precious books and that these precious books were inaccessible, seemed almost intolerable.' Borges' unbounded archive of the Word promises salvation but delivers only bewilderment.

At present, many people fear that the Word on the net will function as a hot, sharp tool of persuasion – in one common narrative, as the ignition-key of 'radicalisation' that via bellicose sermons and treatises sends young jihadis off to distant wars. Whatever the motivation in each case, the image of the charismatic online recruiting-sergeant may belong more to our past than to our future – to Victor Hugo's 'This will kill that!' dream, or nightmare, of rival words in combat to the death. More widely, the universal archive of the Web – and now the Cloud – may threaten not turbulence so much as a stunned calm, with every human word on file but few of them in mind. In that case, the words that we cherish – that we take to heart – will be those that live longest and strongest. The pursuit of resilience may count for more than the yearning for revolution.

Published in 1953, Ray Bradbury's dystopian novel *Fahrenheit 451* imagines state-directed 'firemen' with orders to incinerate every book. It belongs to the same disillusioned moment as George Orwell's *Nineteen Eighty-Four* – to whose ideas it owes a clear debt. In the West, if not further afield, the legacy of totalitarian ideology had tarnished every all-embracing vision of human betterment. Culture in this mood becomes a matter of desperate, last-gasp survival against inflammatory power. In Bradbury's story, a secret cell of dedicated readers commits the entire text of beloved classics to memory. This is his science-fiction reprise of the ancient arts of remembering and recitation that preserved the Homeric epics in Greek-speaking lands for centuries before the first recorded manuscripts or, in the Islamic tradition, honours the 'hafiz' – the guardian – who has memorised every verse of the Qur'an. Human minds, and the bodies that bear them, incorporate and incarnate the power of the Word.

Montag, Bradbury's reformed 'fireman', meets Plato's *Republic*, and Swift's *Gulliver's Travels*, and the *Book of Ecclesiastes* – all in human form. 'Here we all are, Montag,' the memory-rebel Granger tells him. 'Aristophanes and Mahatma Gandhi and Gautama Buddha and Confucius and Thomas Love Peacock and Thomas Jefferson and Mr. Lincoln, if you please. We are also Matthew, Mark, Luke, and John.' For Granger, 'all we want to do is keep the knowledge we think we will need, intact and safe. We're not out to incite or anger anyone yet. For if we are destroyed, the knowledge is dead, perhaps for good.'

For St John, in the beginning was the Word – and in the end as well, since it may soon have need of dedicated guardians against online oblivion as much as purist violence. In the future, taking the Word to heart –

rather than carrying it to any front-line — may prove the most robust source of its ineffaceable power. Those heterodox interpreters of the Gospel that I learned about as a teenage 'Grecian' in the headmaster's study had a case. Perhaps the Word was 'a god' rather than the single almighty force that forever demands blood and fire from its adherents. If so, we should hope, or write, or pray, to ensure that it will be a god of peace and not a god of battles.

This essay makes use of some material from interviews originally conducted for *The Independent*, whose support is gratefully acknowledged.

ARTS AND LETTERS

FATHER AND DAUGHTER

Laksmi Pamuntjak

Although she was only twelve, Amba knew a thing or two about being faithful. Her own mother was faithful, waking before sun up every morning and, talc-dappled and fresh-faced, serving her husband's first coffee of the day. She kept her house sober and fragrant even though times hadn't always been easy. She was the smile that sent her three girls away to school every morning.

Amba was told that her mother, when she was growing up, was considered the most accomplished girl in her village. She was multi-talented, did well in school and was exceptionally pleasing to the eye. Her parents had done all they could to safeguard her purity, for a flower so fair was so much more than a child — she was a duty. Her soulful face and dulcet voice had also made her one of her hometown's favourite *pesindens* — female singers — of the local shadow puppet troupe. In fact, so fond was she of singing that she learned many more old Javanese lyrics, and more *keroncong* melodies in Dutch or Indonesian-Malay, than she was ever taught at school.

The story of Amba's mother's encounter with the great performer Srimulat, the beautiful lead artiste of the Rose Flower Keroncong Orchestra, was the stuff of family legend, titillating not so much for how close she had been to being lured away by Srimulat and her troupe, than for the fact that she wasn't. Whenever her daughters asked her the reason why, their mother had only one answer: 'Where was I to go? And what was I to run from?' Her parents, despite their strictness, had doted on her, and her loveliness was, to them, a source of pride. They had promised her a good match, a man who would show her the lasting joys of marriage. Who knows, they had murmured, maybe they would find her someone like Srimulat's husband, a man so gentle, so loving, he who would speak to her soul. A man who would encourage her to sing and watch performances for the rest of her life, for by then she would be a respectable adult woman.

Amba's mother had accepted Amba's father's proposal three months later. And to him she had remained faithful. Only in the last ten months, after sixteen years of marriage, of tending to the needs of her family and of never earning her own money, had she been supplying local desserts to Rusmini's *warung*, the most popular local roadside eatery in town, a small but important way of having an income of her own.

The fact that it had taken her this long to effect such a little change to family tradition, was itself a form of loyalty — to the idea that any man worth his salt could, and should, single-handedly look after the well-being of his entire family.

Yes, Amba's mother had certainly been faithful, and Amba had loved her in the way most daughters loved their mothers: as tutor, role model, caretaker, someone who taught her to do things like cook, clean, sew, and look after her sisters. But some days she didn't think of her mother at all. It was her father who taught her how to feel.

*****

When Amba was eight, she suddenly discovered there was another way to see her father. He was her father, but he could also be her friend. At first, the revelation was startling. But Amba soon saw why it had made sense. Hadn't he given her half of the blood that coursed through her veins, hadn't he given her part of her bones, her tissues, her cat's eyes? Didn't that make them soulmates, wedded to each other for as long as they lived? It made absolute sense that he would want to share with her things that really mattered to him. Things that were honest and true. Some of the literature she had read had taught her that there comes a time when a man stops talking to his wife and starts looking for other objects he can possess. And because of this a man needs the ear of someone he can absolutely trust. It was her father's luck that that person was she.

Besides, she knew certain things about herself that made her particularly well-suited to the task. She had a ready wit about her, yet she always used her judgment before throwing a barb on anyone's path. This made her feel powerful. She also knew that something in her sharp, knowing eyes, and in her fecund imagination that had a way of running riot, spoke to her father, to the inner things he often felt, but which were not proper for him to admit. She was a child before her time, and indeed that lovely anomaly, a self-willed bird.

Later, when he had to account for why he had loved Amba more than his other daughters, he said it was because of something she asked him one day, after she'd just turned eleven. It was as if he'd forgotten his first daughter in the joy of siring twins, and twins too beautiful at that, but on this day she bewitched him anew.

*****

This is what happened on the day Sudarminto fell in love with his eldest daughter.

He was returning a few books to the shelf in his little study. He had a few loose sheets of paper in his hand, and when he thought nobody was watching, he bent down to shove them back into a cardboard box on the bottom shelf, like a dirty secret. But Amba was behind him all along, sitting on the living room chair with a textbook on her lap.

'What makes Centhini so important?'

Sudarminto swung around.

'I mean, Centhini is a woman, a servant no less…'

'Have you read the book?'

'Just some parts.'

Sudarminto paused. He thought about what he should say if Amba had indeed read the whole *Book of Centhini*, and, worse, the parts that she was not supposed to. He could already see how this long, languorous day he had set aside for himself, a day after his own heart, would now have to descend into a strained disquisition on sex and debauchery, and then a moralising discourse on sex and morality, religion and redemption—stuff he himself had always wrestled with, finding no easy answers. For it was no secret that certain parts of *Centhini*, Book 9 in particular, were startlingly lubricious, while somehow managing to remain cool and cheeky, and they were decidedly inappropriate for a child.

Sudarminto looked at his daughter. He was almost certain that she had indeed read the book in question — the girl was a book freak, as other teachers had told him. Despite all the texts he had on explaining the unexplainable to children, he hadn't prepared himself for this unexplainable.

It came as a surprise to him, then, when his eleven-year-old daughter decided to save her father the embarrassment, saying, 'I think I know the answer. Centhini is a servant, a low caste, an outsider, someone who's paid not to have her own opinion, and because of that she can't possibly give advice to or pass judgments on others. And that is a wonderful thing.'

So relieved was Sudarminto that he forgot those very words had once come from his own mouth. Amba had recited them verbatim. For Amba, nothing about that moment pleased her more than realising that, with intellect, she had staked her claim over her father.

*****

It was no secret that Amba's father, a school principal, had loved such old Javanese texts as *Wedhatama* and the *Book of Centhini*. He loved the *Centhini* in particular. He believed that this had endeared him to his wife-to-be, Nuniek, for she had performed parts of it as a teenager and knew most of the songs by heart. He loved this work so much because he was, first and foremost, a teacher, someone whose chief duty was to educate children and ripen their souls, and there was no greater cause for magnified love than the need to hide parts of it, those parts too inflammatory for young minds, from the subjects of his vocation. He learned to select which passages from *Centhini* were appropriate to read to his students, which parts should be replaced with milder songs from the *Wedhatama*. Meanwhile, the book's grand design still fell into clean segments and he never had trouble following them.

The Book of Centhini isn't only one of Indonesia's oldest manuscripts. It is also an encyclopedia of life filled with poetry, song and prophecies. What's more, it is named after a maid. Yes, a maid — the maid companion of the Lady Tambangraras, to be precise. A coddler, a liberator, a clown and sage rolled into one, but a maid all the same: a woman low on the pecking order, but one who held all the wisdom of the world. Sudarminto always thought it a rather gorgeous idea that a woman of such a lowly description could rise so in respectability, but try telling this to thirty sniffly schoolchildren in a crammed classroom, most of whom were so poor they had not the faintest idea what having a maid even felt like. So he waited patiently for that moment, when one of them would ask, 'Why Centhini, why the maid? Why is the book not named after Centhini's mistress or her mistress' husband, whom the book is mostly about?'

At such a moment in the narrative, Sudarminto had learnt to skirt the brink of the allowable; he would recite a livelier poem and scan his students' faces, one by one, to test for signs of appreciation. Out of such experiments came those rare moments when all childish voices were suspended and it seemed the world softened to a hush. Once, in such a time, a young girl had broken the silence by asking what it meant: If you make water thirst, water will thirst for you.

Then Sudarminto would recite another poem to them. Each time this happened, he could barely remember having been so happy. It was like falling in love with versions of the same woman. He would go home, light as air, marinated in a sense of rightness about what he was meant to do in life, and when he went to bed he was impatient for the morning sun.

Other men might have dreamed of winning a lottery, buying hectares of land and building grand houses; they might have hunted the strongest, most elusive prey and married off sons and daughters. But all Sudarminto wanted to do was to write down years of secret dreams.

In bed at night he would listen to the radio — to familiar *macapatan* songs, or to Pak Besut's famous talk show, or to the music accompanying a shadow puppet performance that he reluctantly abandoned halfway for the kindness of sleep. But often sleep eluded him altogether. He would lay still for what seemed like an eternity, listening to the noises of the night and his wife's soft breathing next to him. Then, as if in an opium-induced trance, his thoughts would travel with Prince Jayengraga on his sexual escapades. Sometimes he had difficulties dampening his gasping breath and the next morning his spine would hurt from being pressed too hard against the bed frame.

Whatever his guilty night pleasures, the next morning he would wash them off with dawn prayer, in much the same way Jayengraga would rush to the mosque after a wild night with a seducer. Sudarminto would call to mind particular lines, and sometimes quote them loudly:

'Behold the fire of hell/Burning all of your sins/And the ridicule of all ingrates/For while faith's flags live on/Divine revelation has turned into ash/And while the soul is a labyrinth of smoke/The universe of the body is but wood/Sin like sperm falls of a sudden/The fire dies within me/ Leaving only a spirit that rules.'

All the while, young Amba was watching and taking notes. She instinctively realised her father secretly admired the randy prince. There was nothing sexier, she later learned, than a man who dared design his own destiny, and who made no apologies for chasing pleasure. (That the prince happened to be handsome and virile was a bonus.) Even at the age of eleven, she understood how this sort of bravado, this confidence in life might have appealed to her father, who could hardly be considered in charge of, let alone the architect of, his own fate.

*****

Despite his little secrets, Amba's father too had been faithful. Not once did he ever betray the love of his wife, or the trust of his daughters. For he had an even larger kingdom to rule than his wife's, and a bigger example to set. Being a teacher made life in so many ways easier for him, for it gave him respectability and trust. But it also made life difficult because it meant that he had the wisdom of many books, and was as such permitted no error of judgment. To the town folk, knowledge and wisdom were not things he had to teach or train himself in; they were supposed to have come to him like a mandate from heaven. Knowledge was supposed to be part of him. Moreover, he was both a teacher and a member of the aristocracy — his father, a school principal, was also a *priyayi*, a man drawn straight from the administrative layers of the royal court of Yogyakarta — and this gave him a rather special status in town.

Although Amba's father called himself a Muslim, he was not a descendent of a religious person. Most Javanese are only partly Muslim, meaning they were also faithful to local traditions older than the fourteenth century, the time when traders from other parts of the world began to spread the Islamic faith. Like most Javanese, Amba's father held onto traces of Buddhism, Hinduism and animism as if they were glorious sequins of the past.

Sudarminto felt he was first and foremost part of Kadipura. The small town was located on the foot of the Merapi Mountain, not far from the Central Javanese city of Klaten. It only took twenty minutes on bicycle to reach the main road. The town's paddy fields, which supplied rice for the neighbouring towns, possessed a sturdy irrigation system. Through the centre of town stretched a shopping street and rows of solid stone houses, interspersed by colonial buildings left by the Dutch. The old missionary school, once the pride of the town, was suddenly no more; it had been replaced by new schools and staffed by new teachers who seemed to have sprung out from nowhere. These included the so-called 'instant' teachers brought in to match the alarmingly fast- growing number of students.

Sudarminto was not among them. He was proud to call himself a 'true teacher.' And he was the truest among the true. How could he not be? His father was a school principal, so was his grandfather. He also knew how to distinguish the instant from the true at a glance, and he knew how to surround himself with his own kind.

But Kadipura had changed all too swiftly: its town hall, its mosques and its schools suddenly found themselves overcrowded and it had taken Sudarminto some time to notice that the true teachers were being fast outnumbered by the instant ones, quite a few from the neighbouring towns. In time, like everybody else, they too became split into two camps. One called the other 'That PNI person' or 'That PKI person,' 'That Nationalist' or 'That Communist.' The rest, who weren't quite sure where they were in the ideological divide, stayed silent.

Sudarminto was a moderate man. He smoked in moderation, liked his coffee triple-sugared, and couldn't stand even the merest hint of garlic or chilli in his food. He had no visible hobbies other than those he felt compelled in showing off every now and then — gardening, mainly, something soothing and entirely non-polemical. He never understood how to be in the middle, how to avoid tension. Perhaps he was too mild-mannered. Of his dark secrets only he and Amba knew, and this complicity made Amba love her father more deeply, more fiercely, even though he didn't know it. But he sensed that he was living and labouring on an escalating crossfire.

Amba didn't make matters easier.

*****

One afternoon in late 1956, Amba went looking for her father in his study. As she later remembered it, the air was hot and thick despite the settling of dusk, and all around was the familiar mix of incense, burnt grass, oil and fermented prawn. She could hear the sound of footsteps and soft patter in the kitchen. Soon on the table there would be fried soybean cakes, a relish of grated coconut and spices and mixed blanched vegetables served with steamed white rice and prawn crackers. And few pieces of fried chicken, if Amba's mother was feeling generous.

Amba was clearly upset. Before her father could ask her what was wrong, she told him that her religion teacher just reprimanded her for not reading the Qur'an.

'Is that true?'

'Well, I don't mind learning the Qur'an but I find Arabic letters hard to pronounce,' Amba said, 'Mr Baedowi said everyone has to be able to read the Qur'an properly, for that is the sign of faith. He told me I shouldn't become like those Kadipurans who love their *macapatan* but are strangers to their religion.'

'I guess your teacher is right, Amba.'

But deep down Sudarminto was just as upset as his daughter. This man named Baedowi was a newcomer in Kadipura. Sudarminto heard he was never seen attending any *tablikh*. Nor was he ever invited to preside over sermons in private houses, as was increasingly the norm in those days. Was it possible that he was a free agent, a religious teacher unattached to a boarding school? For he didn't seem one of those loud and combative *kyais* from the Nahdlatul Ulama, with loyal disciples and followers. Why had Sudarminto not attended to his recruitment into the school more carefully? Now this simpleton was teaching his children.

Yes, Kadipura was changing. The world Sudarminto knew had begun to slip away. He wanted to tell his daughter that whoever wrote his beloved Book of *Wedhatama* was *wruh sakdurunging winarah*, a seer, a prophet, because he had seen the coming of a new age. He wanted to say to his daughter, 'And that age, my tiny love, is the one we live in today: one which bandies religion about as pure show and passes damning verdicts on people.'

But Kadipura was made up of silences. Not the silences of things lacking, but rather the silences behind things. And Sudarminto understood these silences more than anybody else. He was part of this world, he had helped make it. Flawed architecture and lack of money might have contributed to the gaps in the walls and windows that didn't close, but what the walls and the windows concealed ran deeper than blood. Although people discussed troubles as calmly as they could, or avoided discussing them altogether, he soon learned that his absence from the mosque during Friday prayers had been a hot topic for some time. Some had been blunt: Be careful, there will come a time when the distance you deliberately kept from God will cause you to fall and perish. There will come a time when these Commie bastards will come to your house in the night, and cut your throat and the throats of your wife and children. Then you will regret not having been closer to the Plumbon men of faith.

And it was the silence that accompanied these words, in the straight-faced greetings of his neighbours, in the seemingly respectful nods of his students' parents, which to him was the greatest silence of all. It was deep and wide as the Serayu River. It was heavy as the gravestone of his grandfather.

*****

For Sudarminto, things had been different back when the girls were born, Amba in 1944, the twins two years later. In those days, most people had thought like him. They certainly didn't lose sleep over this shapeless, faceless God of the preachers and zealots. For how could they, when life kept changing with such speed and force — the Second World War, the fall of the Netherlands Indies, the arrival and then the defeat of the Japanese, the renewed battle for independence, the Dutch aggression, the battle against pre-occupation, rebellions by the scores...

Sudarminto had lived through all of this with a certain calm, a certain confidence, made possible by his quiet submission to old wisdoms passed down through generations. For centuries the Javanese had lived with a poetic prophecy that hinted at the coming of foreign rule. The *ulemmas* might scream their lungs out about Allah striking down these foreign enemies, but even before they came, the Javanese had always known they were coming: 'The Javanese would be ruled by whites for three centuries and by yellow

dwarfs for the life span of a maize plant prior to the return of the Just King.'
God might be all things to all people but, as far as the Javanese were
concerned, they were united by one faith: that the foreigners would
eventually be banished from their land. And banished they were, as surely as
the ages that came and went, ushering change, ushering new beginnings.

But neither God nor any subversive poem from old Javanese texts nor
prophecies of the most profound sagacity had prepared Sudarminto for
being the father to three daughters. Even though he taught for a living,
what he taught his own daughters was different to what he taught other
people's children. No theory. No science. No platitudes. Just folk tales.
And tales from the *wayang*, drawn from the great Indian epics, which
flowed through their lives and the lives of the people around them.

Blessedly, his daughters seemed to know what he expected of them and
proceeded to teach themselves how to breathe meaning to their names.
They understood instinctively that telling is always retelling, casting the
old anew.

Yet Sudarminto was also slightly afraid of them, those girls. Especially of
his eldest daughter, who, despite herself, had the qualities of a princess:
hard-headed, self-absorbed, self-entitled. He found her utterly
mesmerising.

*****

'Pak, in the Centhini, Ki Amongrogo and his wife are said to meet with
their family after their death. How is that possible? How do the dead
communicate with the living?'

'Hmm. Do you believe in spirits?'

Amba didn't answer right away.

'Well, do you?'

She didn't say it but of course she did. Every day at least one of her
friends at school would talk of one sighting or another. A dead
grandmother, who materialised at dinner and told stories of her life. Or a
special corner of a house was 'our dead brother's corner,' where the mood
of the dead brother set the tone of the day. Friendly spirits could keep a
boy out of harm's way, or reveal the fiend that murdered a family not so
long ago.

Amba lowered her gaze.

Something swelled in Sudarminto. He began speaking in the way she knew and loved so well.

'Amba, know that in the world I know, the dead do not sleep; they existed in the same sphere as human beings. Remember that while reincarnation may be the pillar of Hinduism and Buddhism, it is not known in Islam. Yet we, in Java, live with both. We are Javanese because we are both...'

Amba was deaf to anything else, completely entranced by her father's voice.

*****

Meanwhile, beyond the two of them, outside the vicissitudes of their family, the times were changing. Something larger was taking hold.

It had begun the previous year, 1955, the year of the first General Elections for the new Republic of Indonesia. There was something acid and shrewd in the air. It was as if blood had been spilled long before anybody stepped in it. At work, among his fellow teachers, politics had become more and more unbearable for Sudarminto. He often came home subdued and tired, for there was no space for moderates like him.

There were so many party emblems to choose from that people had difficulty remembering which was which, what each signified, what was good what was bad. But still they chose, as though the highest truth. Families and neighbours started to avoid, rebuke or repel each other, just because they didn't share the same political beliefs or choose the same party.

Voices became coarser, throats lined with broken glass. People started to lock their doors.

Through it all, Amba watched how her father, who had prided himself on running a pretty simple ship, couldn't quite convince his wife to vote for the Nationalist Party. He'd warned her of the dangers of fragmentation, saying it was one thing to dream up a nation and quite another to live it. Independence has its costs.

*****

One day, a few weeks before the General Elections, Amba's father found his wife coming home a few hours late, the vegetables almost wilted in the shopping basket.

Even Amba could see that Nuniek looked different. Her face was glowing. She didn't even apologise for being late.

'You remember our old neighbour in Kertosono?' she asked, before he had a chance to admonish her. 'The one whose aunt just died of lung disease?'

'Hartoyo, you mean?'

'Yes, that's it. Well, I just saw him speak at the town hall. He was really impressive. Talked a lot about women and their struggle. At the end of his speech, everyone applauded.'

Sudarminto looked a little rattled.

'Well, he's always been a smooth talker. And of course he was talking about women because the place was surrounded by Gerwani.' Gerwani was the shortened name for the Indonesian Women's Movement, and it was closely linked to the party of this neighbour who had so impressed his wife, the Indonesian Communist Party, a new party which had surprisingly come fourth in the elections, having gained a lot of traction in a short period.

'Still. He seemed to know what people wanted,' Nuniek said.

'As our dear president Bung Karno said, what our country really needs is unity,' Sudarminto countered.

'Well, Bung Karno is a revolutionary, so of course he would say that. But where is the revolutionary fervour in the Nationalist Party? To unite is well and good, but tell me, where is the revolution?'

Sudarminto's face instantly changed.

'It is astounding,' he said, 'how easily impressed you are by the power of cheap rhetoric. That Hartoyo isn't even the best of them. But did you really listen to his speech?'

Amba watched her mother retreat. She knew that you had to feel your way through a marriage, not unlike politics. Just when you thought your relationship with your husband was firmly in place, the tables began, ever so swiftly and unfathomably, to turn. But as she went to the kitchen and laid down her sad and shrivelled veggies, it was plain that she was annoyed at her husband.

'Precious little good had the principle of unity done to the Nationalist Party,' she whispered to Amba conspiratorially. 'For didn't it, just the other day, split into two parties? One had for its symbol a chicken feather pen, the other a shovel. Now how idiotic is that.'

Some weeks ago Amba's father had had the walls of the house pasted with the image of a bull's head inside a triangle. Then the same scenario played out so many times Amba lost count: her father insisting to her mother, 'We have to choose correctly. The bull's head means the Nationalist Party and that means Sukarno,' and Nuniek responding, 'How about the hammer and sickle? How about the Communist Party?'

At which point Sudarminto's pedantry would border on caricature: his eyes would roll, his brows arch in mock astonishment: 'My dear, just look at these two things — the hammer and the sickle. The hammer, granted, is the tool of the labourers. Fine. Now look at this sickle. What's wrong with this picture? We're talking the working class, aren't we? We're voting for them, yes? Because they are the true revolutionaries we've been dying to have, yes? So why are we looking at a sickle? Is it not a fact that with a sickle the peasants can only cut grass, or a small branch? Shouldn't we be looking instead at the shovel, a tool that is capable of so much more? So, even the symbolism of the Communist Party is suspect. Now ask yourself, should we be voting for a party that cannot even get its emblem right?'

Later, Amba would learn that politics is not about getting it right. It's about getting it wrong rightly.

Then she would remember how fond her father was of saying that all the islands of their country were like a thousand little foundlings with their mouths turned towards their mother, which he called The Big Nipples, who had to endlessly provide. She remembered him saying, 'Ten years after our country gained independence, in the chaos that was the 1955 General Election, those thousand foundlings had fused into four fat suckling sons. They were the Big Four. They were the chosen ones. The Giant Nipples then spoke to the first son, the Indonesian Nationalist Party, known as PNI, and to the second son, Masyumi, or the Council of Indonesian Muslim Associations, and to the third son, the Islamic Party Nahdlatul Ulama, shortened to NU, saying, 'Go over to the right hand side of the table.' To the fourth son, the Indonesian Communist Party, commonly referred to as PKI, she said, 'You, stay where you are on the left hand side of the table.' Then the father, President Sukarno, said proudly, 'We are all one family sitting at one big dinner table.'

'But the truth was, the table never seemed big enough for those four suckling sons. Besides, it was not in them, those different, greedy children, to get along. Most certainly not with that kind of mother: too various, too sprawling, too soft and porous in her constitution.

'So when the fourth suckling, the Indonesian Communist Party, rose spectacularly, claiming a membership of three million in less than a year, his three siblings cried foul: 'How can our brother be more important than we are? It's impossible."

And yet Amba understood that anything was possible, in the tuck and tumble of those hungry, grasping mouths all sucking on The Giant Nipples, the mother who was simply an idea. An idea that was starting to shrivel away.

FIVE NOTES ON ROOTLESSNESS

Andre Naffis-Sahely

Tu enim Caesar civitatem dare potes hominibus, verbis non potes

Caesar, you can grant citizenship to men, but not to words.

Marcus Pomponius Marcellus

Borderlands

Both my parents come from borderlands. My mother was born in Modane: a small sleepy French town in Haute-Savoie, now the final stop on the TGV before it heads through the Mont Blanc tunnel and spills into the Valle d'Aosta across the Italian frontier. After years of roaming from job to job, restoring churches and installing electrical lines, my grandfather found work clearing stretches of forest with dynamite to cut a path for the roads leading up to the tunnel. When the construction of the tunnel was completed in the mid-1960s, he moved his young family back to Venice. Although he never lived in Germany, nor expressed any desire to do so, my grandfather was very fond of his Teutonic neighbours. Unlike his compatriots, he did not view them as stern or overly fussy. He valued their determinacy, earnestness, and above all, their interiority. He considered Italians emotionally incontinent and found their flamboyancy neither charming nor amusing. There was Ghibelline blood in his veins. Had he been born during the twelfth and thirteenth centuries, I've little doubt he would have taken up arms against the Papists. My father, on the other hand, was born in Bandar-e-Pahlavi, on the southern Iranian shore of the Caspian Sea, now known as Bandar-e-Anzali. His maternal great-grandparents were of Russian stock and had once owned vast holdings on the northern shore of the Caspian, where they had set up as sturgeon farmers. They had been lured to Iran in the late nineteenth century by the Qajar Shahs, who enticed by the profitability of caviar, paid them handsomely for their expertise. Before losing most of his property on the Russian side of the border to Stalin's Red Armies in 1917, my great-grandfather had had the prescience to move his family and some of his valuables south. Definitively exiled to Iran, my great-grandfather continued to fly the white flag of the Romanovs from his rooftop. Every time a delegation of Iranian officials would pay him a call and politely request he lower the outdated flag, he would fire a few rounds of buckshot at them, eventually leading them to give up their quest. He was over 100 when he died, but still fond of the slim cigars he had smoked since the age of sixteen. The only memento of this Russian past is a handful of roubles bearing the portrait of Peter the Great. These roubles are still in my father's possession, pressed between the pages of old volumes of Persian poetry.

Adaptations

My father was the only one of his siblings who elected to move to Europe instead of America. He had decided to study architecture and landed in Italy in 1963, first spending a year in Perugia, followed by one in Rome, finally settling in Venice. He quickly integrated, easily mastering the local dialect. Although very dark-skinned, he took so effortlessly to Italian customs and mannerisms that Venetians usually mistook him for a Sicilian. My father studied under Carlo Scarpa and roomed with Homayoun Ershadi, now one of Abbas Kiarostami's favourite leading men. My father told me how Scarpa had once grown frustrated with Ershadi in class one day and snapped: 'you'll never make much of an architect, but as you're not bad looking, why not try your luck as an actor?' In between classes, my father attended left-wing demonstrations and took part in sit-ins at the Iranian consulate, activities that would later land him a few months in prison on his return to Iran. From what I have pieced together of my father's stories, he and Ershadi had a good time. Back then, foreigners weren't undesired, but exotic. As for my mother, she was six years old when her father relocated back to Venice, and had grown up speaking French. While her older sister worked on cruise ships that took her all over the Mediterranean, my mother instead worked in beach resorts on the Venetian littoral, coming into contact with various foreigners and developing a deep-seated interest in other cultures, particularly their books. My mother still cherishes fond memories of her literature teacher at secondary school, an Italian Jew who had survived the Nazi death camps and lived to impart her passion for words to an entire generation of people, many of whom later became partial to the ideas of the Lega Nord, a xenophobic separatist movement. When my parents met, my mother was twenty-seven, while my father was forty. I was born roughly a year after their relationship began, in 1985. My father insisted I was to be given an Italian name and baptised into the Catholic Church, although I have never to this day heard him speak of God with anything other than derision or contempt. His rationale was that it would facilitate my own integration. It did not.

Origins

I was conceived in the United Arab Emirates, where my parents had gone to establish a branch of the architecture firm that employed them in Venice. When she discovered she was pregnant, my mother, eager to raise her child in Italy, asked my father to return to Europe. I was born in Venice some months later. It would be eight years before I saw the Emirates. In the early 1990s, my father accepted a job offer in Abu Dhabi and moved us out there not long after he had set himself up. I became fluent in English in a matter of months. The ease with which I mastered that language – and others – was neither peculiar nor singular. I saw many of my coevals adapt just as easily. I simply did so at an age which Cicero noted was optimal for such absorption. I thus became proficient in four, adding English, French and later Arabic to my repertoire. Keeping them in running order has been a daily task, sometimes a chore, like polishing your shoes. The country I began to acquaint myself with was an open construction site: cranes rising their necks out of pits as far as the eye could see. The Emirati desert was flat, and the wide highways that cut through it unfenced. Bewildered camels would often stop in the middle of those roads, interrupting their continuous chewing to stare at the honking cars. The roads were later fenced off and the camels disappeared. Most of the people who lived in Abu Dhabi were foreigners, and the majority of them from the Indian subcontinent. The Emiratis kept themselves apart from this macaronic miasma that oil wealth had ushered. I attended schools where I came into contact with Arabs,

Europeans, North and South Americans, and Indians, and forged friendships with all of them, at least in so far as I could. Each community lived in its own bubble-like ghetto. Socialising in the United Arab Emirates was thus like hopping from one island of strangers to another; and sometimes you overstayed your welcome. My Emirati friends were few. Friendships with expatriate children were actively discouraged. The Emirati attitude was simultaneously one of generous compromise and apartheid. Their state, built and largely run by foreigners, is designed to cater only to them. So long as they can afford them, every other nationality can enjoy institutions of the same quality, but theirs belong to the private sector. Even then, the Emirates struck me as being almost as young as I was. It wasn't far from the truth. After initial explorations began in the 1950s, it didn't take long for those efforts to bear their black fruit, destroying a nomadic way of life that had persisted for centuries.

History

When Sheikh Shakhbut, who ruled Abu Dhabi from 1928 to 1966, was asked by the British political agent Charlie Lamb how he might like to employ the fabulous wealth now at his disposal, having been presented with a list of options, Shakhbut replied that he thought his country was beautiful just as it was. It didn't take long for Shakhbut to be unseated in a bloodless coup staged by Zayed, his younger brother, whom the British favoured. By this time, Harold Wilson's government had committed itself to withdrawing from its last protectorates east of Suez. Zayed shrewdly flexed his fiefdom's economic muscles and stitched a network of alliances between the once-warring emirates, installing himself as head of a federal monarchy, in not too dissimilar a manner to the one that Bismark had employed a century earlier. The United Arab Emirates, as we now know it, officially came into being on 2 December 1971. Aware of his people's inadequacies to face what would be required of them in the coming years, Zayed opened his doors to immigrants. Each nationality was allotted a caste and status. What the Hindus achieved over centuries, Zayed did almost instantaneously. He just followed the blueprints. Indians became construction workers, taxi drivers and servants; East Asians were assigned nursing, secretarial and retail.

Europeans filled managerial posts while Emiratis were assigned ceremonial roles that hardly required their presence.

Belonging

Emirati citizenship is granted by royal edict. Thus, while I consider the United Arab Emirates my home, I know I can never belong there. Foreigners cannot own property in the Emirates and mixed marriages between Emiratis and foreigners are frowned on. When he worked for the current king's eldest son, my father met a Palestinian whose father had come to the Emirates in 1959 and set up a dairy farm in Ras al-Khaimah. His children had grown up there and had had families of their own. Three generations of that family and forty years later, the old man died, still a non-citizen. Once I turned eighteen, my father could no longer sponsor me under his visa and I was forced to leave. I have gone back twice in ten years. In order to secure a leave to remain, I would need to find gainful employment and therefore find myself unable to keep writing full-time. Shortly before my last visit, *The New York Times* broke a story which revealed that, in the manner of Medici princes, Sheik Mohamed bin Zayed al-Nahyan, the Crown Prince of Abu Dhabi, was raising an army of mercenaries whom the royal family could rely on should their non-citizens choose to rebel. Many of these men, who were brought into the country under the guise of construction workers, have been routinely employed to suppress uprisings and protect oil and diamond interests in the so-called third world. Forced to acknowledge the country I spent such a large part of my life in would rather employ mercenaries than extend the warm hand of citizenship, I opt for homelessness.

ANOTHER EID

Salim Nafar

Gaza is a city at breaking point. The economy has stalled and unemployment spreads its shadow over all the young people fruitlessly searching for any kind of work. Nor is the political climate any more hopeful. Every time one faction tries to turn the page, local, regional, and international interests unite against them to reinforce the status quo, and thus the siege separating us off from the world. Days pass, heavy as clouds in a polar winter but the madness that occupies our reality and imagination does not.

In this tense, charged climate the holy month of Ramadan arrives. We hope it will herald international efforts to ease our situation, if only for a short time, but this year it brings only renewed Israeli aggression. On the tenth day, as all Gaza is at home awaiting the Maghreb call to prayer which announces an end to the fast and a start to the feast, I hear a loud rumbling in the sky...Israeli warplanes. The ground shakes, windows shatter, walls come down and the smell of gunpowder fills our nostrils. Iftar is marked with Palestinian blood.

I jump up from my seat. Trying to work out what's going on so I can explain what's happened to my wife and kids, I turn on the television and fumble with the remote. The second I touch it I realise, to my horror, that this is war, or rather, Israeli aggression towards our already enfeebled city scarred by the wounds of past conflict. We barely touch our breakfast as a parade of the dead and wounded move across our screen not far from where we were sitting. I ask myself: Why war? Why now? What are its objectives? Questions to which there are no answers.

On the second day of the hostilities, I manage to make it out of the house to check on the state of the city, and that of my friends. We are not safe roaming the streets as warplanes pick off whom they please, not concerned whether their targets are children playing in the park or the elderly hugging their pillows in their sorrow-filled rooms. Everything in the city is a target, everything is under fire. At any moment, without warning, we may die, missiles surprising us from the land, sea and air.

The next day I went down town to my office on Wahda (Unity) Street in the heart of Gaza city. With the aid of a generator, I quickly worked on a few things on my computer, sent some poems and articles to newspapers, then went down to the street to hail a taxi knowing my children would be in a state of fear and confusion. Standing there, I suddenly noticed how menacingly empty the street was of people, the atmosphere bleak and uncertain. I waited a long time to find a car.

A few minutes after I walked in the front door my mobile phone started ringing. The caller was a friend from the office. He was trying to make sure I was okay: an F16 missile had just struck the spot where I'd been waiting for the cab. I inhaled deeply: Oh God! It's only destiny that shields you from death and gives you another chance at life. It is only by chance that life in Gaza can be lived another day. And the odds are not stacked in our favour.

After a week of savage and barbaric aggression that had no mercy for children, women, and the elderly – this aggression successfully distorted our senses and killed the smile on the lips of our children. This is one of the most important achievements of Israel's armed hostility.

On the evening of the seventh day of hostilities I was at the door of my building trying to discern the general feeling of the people. Exhausted from the lingering smell of gunpowder and the sighs of loss I went home, took off my shoes, changed my clothes and sat down in front of my laptop to follow the media coverage. After ten minutes, everything stopped. A missile from a reconnaissance drone rocked the foundations of our building. I shut down my computer and rushed to the other room where my wife, daughters and mother were huddled, fear etched into their faces. Just as I was trying to lighten the atmosphere and downplay the severity of the situation, another missile, this time from an F16 aeroplane struck and everything collapsed around me.

An earthquake shook the ground under our feet, tearing out the windows and our hearts from our chests. As the women's voices rose around me I found myself unable to speak, my pride hurt by my inability to comfort them. I could sense by their fear that they had been struck by shrapnel. It took me several minutes to reorient myself and calm down, surveying the shards of glass and curtains that now carpeted the room.

Our neighbour from the apartment opposite stumbled towards us, half-suffocated from smoke and fear, his home transformed into a pile of rubble, as had the buildings across the road and the cars in the street.

Fear masters us. The aggression continues. And so does my interminable insomnia, which started on the first day of this 'war' and keeps me awake, watching and monitoring, in an attempt to master the situation myself. One day, during the second week of the hostilities, I stayed up until morning scanning the radio waves because there was no electricity for the TV. I followed the news with my eyes fixed on the sky where missiles, rockets and flares fell like acid rain, unfurling its horror over the bedrooms of our children.

That night the shelling and killing stretched across all corners of the Gaza Strip, spilling Palestinian blood on the streets and homes of Shuja'iyyah and Beit Hanoun. Streams of people continued to arrive in the centre of the city from the north and east, even though there was no place for them. They sleep on the ground, pulling the sky over them as a cover. They have to take the ground as a bed, with only the sky for a cover or sit, hollow-eyed, on the pavement, as their children roam the streets.

The aggression continued and our days proceeded in loss, subjugation and sorrow. With the approach of Eid my children, seeking a sense of normality and calm like the rest of the children in the world, began asking: 'Baba, when are we going to buy new clothes? Isn't the holiday coming?' My chest tightened. Why shouldn't they ask these questions? They had a right to life. But the reality of this stricken and bereaved city forced me to be evasive. I tried to inject some hope into the proceedings, saying, 'Yes children, no matter how long this war lasts we will celebrate Eid and buy new clothes. Tomorrow will be a brighter day!'

But Lama, my quarrelsome and highly sensitive daughter, realised I was being insincere and told me so, crying out 'stop fooling us, Baba. I've seen Shuja'iyyah on TV, I've seen the destruction, the martyrs, the people sleeping on the pavements outside the clothes shops! Who will open their store after this? Eid? There will be no Eid!'

She is right. There can be no Eid this year. This is no time for joyful visitations, for family fun or tours of a ruined city.

Translated by Ghada Mourad and Tyson Patros

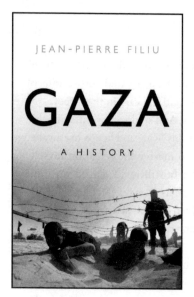

ISBN: 9781849044011
£25.00 / Hardback / 424pp

GAZA
A HISTORY
JEAN-PIERRE FILIU

Through its millennium–long existence, Gaza has often been bitterly disputed while simultaneously and paradoxically enduring prolonged neglect. Jean-Pierre Filiu's book is the first comprehensive history of Gaza in any language.

Squeezed between the Negev and Sinai deserts on the one hand and the Mediterranean Sea on the other, Gaza was contested by the Pharaohs, the Persians, the Greeks, the Romans, the Byzantines, the Arabs, the Fatimids, the Mamluks, the Crusaders and the Ottomans. Napoleon had to secure it in 1799 to launch his failed campaign on Palestine. In 1917, the British Empire fought for months to conquer Gaza, before establishing its mandate on Palestine.

In 1948, 200,000 Palestinians sought refuge in Gaza, a marginal area neither Israel nor Egypt wanted. Palestinian nationalism grew there, and Gaza has since found itself at the heart of Palestinian history. It is in Gaza that the fedayeen movement arose from the ruins of Arab nationalism. It is in Gaza that the 1967 Israeli occupation was repeatedly challenged, until the outbreak of the 1987 intifada. And it is in Gaza, in 2007, that the dream of Palestinian statehood appeared to have been shattered by the split between Fatah and Hamas. The endurance of Gaza and the Palestinians make the publication of this history both timely and significant.

'A magnificent piece of historical writing: clear in its exposition, careful in its use of a treasure-trove of new sources and judicious in its analysis of competing political claims to this small and troubled strip of land. It is difficult to see how it will ever be rivalled in terms of scope, intensity and sympathetic understanding.' — **Roger Owen, Emeritus Professor of Middle East History, Harvard University**

WWW.HURSTPUBLISHERS.COM/BOOK/GAZA

41 GREAT RUSSELL ST, LONDON WC1B 3P
WWW.HURSTPUBLISHERS.COM
WWW.FBOOK.COM/HURSTPUBLISHERS
020 7255 2201

BHOPAL

Avaes Mohammad

Let me tell you of a day when the earth stood still,
The birds stopped mid-flight and the sun felt a chill,
The planets daren't revolve, winds made tranquil,
The oceans even rose as her eyes did fill.

A day of human suffering of the likes unseen,
Aftermath that will remain, till the day of reckoning,
Innocent souls slain with the force of hurricane,
And a truth made sick by no want of questioning.

Now once upon a time ain't how this story goes
And the land of which we talk ain't as far as we're told
It's a recent event, not a story of old
Thirty years of injustice, still a case not closed.

Terrorists in our midst, hypothesis put to.
An act of evil somebody's, ain't too far from the truth.
But the villain we're dealin' with ain't Arab or Pashtun,
Ain't no bombs involved or towers times two.

See the terrors corporate so the motives quite clear
Ain't no honour involved, just a hungry profiteer
Let me cut to the chase and tell you all quite straight
Bhopal is the theme and we ain't leavin' till you hear.

On the third of December, nineteen eighty-four
Midnight struck the clock announcing death at the door
And like a thief in the night,
With indiscriminate sight,
A beast was unleashed from the white-mans' venture.

Now race ain't an issue so relax now your head
I ain't here to cause trouble, be intolerance lead
But the picture that I paint's from a next viewpoint,
Thousands of Indians maimed and the thousands dead.

So the phrase that I use, is to benefit you.
From the victims' standpoint is how we'll see this issue.
Lets recourse back from my sensitive trip
And deal with the matter which I set out to do.

A chemical factory's where the scene was set,
Union Carbide's how the placards were read.
A leak they could prevent
Safety measure's under spent,
Caused a poison cloud to be shot out and spread.

People dying still today,
And tomorrow, but anyway,
If the D-word's too much for you to even hear,
And you'd rather I chat about Santa and reindeer,
Then I hate to offend those sensitive ears
But you all can walk away, or confront your inner fears.

What I'm saying is all true
It's what money can do
But I can't just blame the green
Those people had a part too.

Those suits and those ties
And those smiles so wry
They're the cause of this cry
Yet you try to deny
That we breed terrorists in a deceitful guise,
Dignified handshakes with a fistful of lies.

So please let me know as it defies my belief,
How the value of a people seems dependent on their creed.
Yes genocide seems a worthy price to pay,
For a lot o' bit o' profit
And a westerners' delay.

REVIEWS

A THEOLOGY OF MORAL PROGRESS

Nader Hashemi

It is not easy being a Muslim in the West today. The year 2014, which roughly corresponds to 1436 in the Islamic calendar, will go down as an especially difficult time. Two sets of political developments have contributed to this state of affairs: the rise and expansion of the Islamic State of Iraq and Syria (ISIS), and the crushing of the Arab Spring revolutions.

The rise of ISIS has unleashed a tidal wave of Islamophobia not seen since 11 September 2001. The seizure of large parts of Iraq and Syria by this notorious militant movement, replete with the beheadings of foreign hostages, the enslavement and rape of women from minority communities, the mass execution of prisoners – all in the name of Islam, and with the apparent approbation of tens of thousands of Muslims who have flocked to the Middle East to help build a new Caliphate – has reinforced the worst Western stereotypes and prejudices about Islam and Muslims. The anti-Muslims floodgates have burst open. This time, however, the intellectual attacks are not only coming from the traditional centres of Islamophobia on the political right, but anti-Muslim bigotry has gone mainstream and is now being parroted by prominent voices on the liberal left. The one event that best captures this phenomenon was the recent debate between the comedian Bill Maher and the actor Ben Affleck.

Bill Maher has a long history of Muslim bigotry. On a previous episode of his widely watched show, *Real Time with Bill Maher*, he expressed alarm that the most popular name for babies in Britain was Muhammad. 'Am I a racist to feel alarmed by that?' Maher asked. 'Because I am [alarmed]. And it's not because of the race, it's because of the religion. I don't have to apologise, do I, for not wanting the Western world to be taken over by Islam in 300 years?'

His more recent outburst came in the context of the ISIS crisis, and was justified in the name of liberal values. With his usual arrogance and self-righteousness, Maher insinuated that ISIS was a reflection of Islam's essential nature, and that liberals should not be afraid of both affirming this and publicly condemning it. Islam is 'the only religion,' he claimed, 'that acts like the mafia, that will fucking kill you if you say the wrong thing, draw the wrong picture or write the wrong book.' When Ben Affleck pushed back against this characterisation, an intense debate ensued. The episode soon went viral and it has subsequently been viewed by more than two million people on YouTube. The clip has spawned a much larger debate on the relationship between Islam, liberalism, violence and Islamophobia.

Khaled Abou El Fadl, *Reasoning with God: Reclaiming Shariah in the Modern Age*, Roman and Littlefield, Lanham, Maryland, 2014.

The following day, CNN interviewed the prominent author and public intellectual Reza Aslan on the same subject. Another tense debate and terse exchange ensued. The two CNN hosts, Don Lemon and Alisyn Camerota, grew visibly frustrated and cantankerous when Aslan challenged their simplistic over-generalisations about the status of women in the Muslim world, with a set of nuanced arguments and empirical facts. The next day, the same CNN hosts invited the liberal television journalist and fellow CNN news host, Chris Cuomo, to comment on the debate. Cuomo took it a step further. He argued that Aslan had behaved like a typical Muslim militant, thus confirming and perpetuating the fears that many Americans had of Islam. Aslan's 'tone was very angry,' Cuomo claimed, 'so he wound up ... demonstrating what people are fearful about when they think of the faith in the first place, which is the hostility of it.' Then prominent left-liberal filmmaker, Michael Moore, leapt to Bill Maher's defence. There was no reaction from liberal intellectuals to Moore's strident defence of Maher's bigotry. Nor did Moore suffer any negative publicity, another reflection of the spread and mainstreaming of Islamophobia in the United States.

The second development that has contributed to a general sense of despair and frustration about the future of Muslim societies has been the defeat of the Arab Spring. Four years ago, beginning in Tunisia and spreading eastwards, a series of democratic revolts toppled three of the longest serving dictators in the Islamic world, and came close to overthrowing two more. These largely nonviolent protests shook the foundations of political authoritarianism throughout North Africa and the Middle East, while inspiring democratic forces to action around the world. There was widespread optimism at this time that the tide had finally turned, and a new democratic future had opened up for the Arab world. But this was not to be. The rollback and crushing of these democratic openings, most notably represented by the military coup in Egypt in July 2013, and the ongoing near genocidal onslaught of Bashir Asad against his own people, has been emotionally debilitating, and it has produced a deep sense of despondency amongst Muslim democrats. The old authoritarian and despotic order is back with a vengeance, buttressed by billions of dollars of Saudi and Emirati money, with the apparent approbation of the West, particularly the Obama Administration. John Kerry infamously described the military coup in Egypt as a case of 'restoring democracy,' while President Obama has steadfastly refused to support the Syrian revolutionaries – sarin gas, state-sanctioned war crimes and crimes against humanity notwithstanding – because he did not want to get entangled in somebody else's war of 'ancient sectarian differences'. To this picture one can add the ongoing colonisation of the West Bank, the recent Israeli attack on Gaza that killed over 2,000 Palestinians (including 500 children), the chaos in Libya, frequent bombings and massacres of civilians by Boko Haram and the Taliban, and the steady rollback of democracy in Turkey, once an inspiration and a model for its blend of religion and democracy, under the careful tutelage of Recep Tayyib Erdoğan. Tunisia stands alone as a bright democratic light in a sea of authoritarian darkness.

Given this wretched political context that characterises the contemporary Islamic world, and the accompanying deep sense of despair that hangs like a fog over Muslim societies today, the publication of Khaled Abou El Fadl's *Reasoning with God: Reclaiming Shariah in the Modern Age*, could not be more timely. Part memoir, part scholarly analysis, and part message to the bewildered, this book is precisely what is needed during these dark times to educate a non-Muslim audience on Islam's ethical potential, and to reinvigorate and inspire beleaguered Muslim intellectuals and activists who have been demoralised by recent events.

Khaled Abou El Fadl is the Omar and Azmeralda Alfi Distinguished Professor in Islamic Law at the UCLA School of Law, where he teaches International Human Rights and other subjects. He has served on the Board of Directors of Human Rights Watch, the US Commission for International Freedom and has won numerous awards, including The University of Oslo's Human Rights Award – Lisl and Leo Eitinger Prize. He is perhaps best known for *The Search for Beauty in Islam: A Conference of the Books* (2005), *The Great Theft: Wrestling Islam from the Extremists* (2007) and other books. *Reasoning with God*, which took ten years to write, is his eighth and most important book.

What gives Abou El Fadl's such a powerful and persuasive pen is his intimate knowledge of and affection for two intellectual and civilisational traditions: the Western and the Islamic. His Ivy League education and his formal training in Islamic jurisprudence in Egypt and Kuwait allows him to probe, critique and analyse both traditions at a profound level while making insightful cross-comparisons. He has thought long and hard about the challenges facing Muslim societies today, with a particular focus on how to reconcile tradition with modernity. While he has been invariably described as a shaykh, a law professor, a human rights scholar and a public intellectual, the label that best fits him is that of a Muslim ethicist, and this book could easily have been subtitled: a treatise on Islamic ethics.

He begins by noting that this has been a 'painfully personal book' to write. The social and political conditions that have led to the decline of Islamic civilisation and to the rise of Islamophobia are the source of his pain, but the problem is much deeper than this. With his characteristic intellectual honesty, a theme that permeates this book, he identifies a fundamental tension that adds to the intensity of his personal agony. One the one hand, he finds 'the Islamic faith to be a source of boundless wisdom and tranquility,' while also noting that 'it is difficult to deny that this same faith has become a source of anxiety and apprehension for many in the world today.' It is precisely this paradox that shapes this book, and it is one he seeks to reconcile.

Abou El Fadl focuses on God's covenant with Muslims: have Muslims upheld their end of the bargain? This is the leitmotif of the book. 'Per this covenant,' he writes, 'the role of Muslims in relation to the rest of the world is to bear witness on God's behalf, to call for the good and just, to resist what is evil and unjust.' By this reading, Muslims are obligated to pursue justice, and to embody the divine attributes of compassion and mercy, themes that are repeated in the Qur'an, the daily prayers and throughout Islamic jurisprudential theory. In this context, he asks his fellow Muslims to ponder the following question: how does your understanding of Islam 'contribute to goodness in the world?' Muslims must reflect upon this question and strive to answer it. If Muslims truly believe that Islam carries a universal message for humanity that is not limited by race, tribe or nation, 'the response given to the question of the moral quality of the contribution [to our world] must have some reasonable basis in fact to withstand scrutiny.'

Reasoning with God is divided into three parts. Part one, 'The Islamic Dream and the Chaos of the Modern Condition,' is largely descriptive in terms of laying out the myriad of problems that are tearing apart the moral fabric of contemporary Muslim societies. Part two, 'The Culture of Ugliness and the Plight of Modern Islam' focuses on examining the historical, political and ideological roots of the problems that are laid out in the first part of the book. Arguably, the most important chapter in this section is a play on words from Bernard Lewis' controversial post-9/11 bestseller: 'What Really Went Wrong.' Part three shares the subtitle of the book: 'Reclaiming the Shariah in the Modern Age.' It looks for solutions and explores possible avenues for developing an ethical and humanistic Islamic interpretation that is rooted in the Shariah, and is compatible with the demands of the modern age.

Abou El Fad begins the diagnosis of the crisis facing Muslim societies today with a gripping description of what he calls the 'Islamic nightmare.' We have reached a point in Islamic history, he observes, where 'criminal sociopaths pretend to be the guardians and ministers of the Islamic faith; one in which extremists assume the role of the spokesmen for the religion of moderation; one in which unspeakable acts of shameless ugliness are perpetuated on God's behalf and in His name; one in which the religion of compassion and mercy has become associated in people's minds with cruelty and oppression; and one in which many Muslims no longer recall the ethical norms that ought to guide their relationship to God and humanity.' He continues. 'Even more, it is a living nightmare in which apologetics passes for rigorous thought, in which the gift of intellect and human reason is declared to be the gateway to the Devil, in which the very idea of beauty and representations of beauty, such as music, are condemned as frivolous and corrupting, and perhaps most important of all…we have reached the point that in parts of the Muslim world, the more profound a person's ignorance about Islamic theology and law, the more expansive his bombastic demagoguery, and even the more "Islamically authentic" his wardrobe and outward appearance, the better the chances are that he will be recognised as a great leader and expert in Islam.' While this may sound polemical, it does not undercut Abou El Fadl's argument; it merely reflects the deep frustration the author feels with the state of the Islamic world today.

Personal anecdotes from within Muslim communities in the United States reinforce his argument that something has gone deeply wrong. Perhaps best among these is the story of an Islamic camp. One summer Abou El Fadl was asked to teach Islamic law at a summer youth retreat in California. While dinner was being prepared, someone suggested that soft Hawaiian music be played to pass the time. Unsure if this was Islamically permitted, Khaled's counsel was sought as the resident Islamic law expert. He replied that 'playing Hawaiian music might only be a sin because it is utterly boring, but other than that there [is] no problem with serving dinner to the elevator melodies of this music.' He thought nothing more of it until late in the evening when he was summoned to the mess hall. The camp elders were gathered with looks of consternation on their faces. They had been meeting for two hours to discuss this grave breach of Islamic norms. Abou El Fadl was informed that all forms of music were strictly forbidden in Islam, and he was asked to apologise for his transgression. If he refused he would have to leave the camp immediately.

Anyone who has spent time in a Muslim community in North America in past three decades can immediately relate to this story; variations of it are abundant and they highlight the rise of a toxic new interpretation of Islam that masquerades as authentic Islam. Abou El Fadl describes this development as the emergence of a 'culture of ugliness in modern Islam' that eschews notions of beauty and 'continues to be the single most important obstacle to articulating reasonable narratives of legitimate possibilities of Islam's contribution to human goodness'. The new 'Puritanical-Salafism', as he describes it, is a recent phenomenon in Muslim societies and it is directly related to the convergence of two corrosive developments: the legacy of colonialism and the spread of Wahhabism.

Both the colonial and postcolonial Muslim condition has left a detrimental legacy that Muslims are still struggling to overcome. Ideologically, Abou El Fadl argues, Muslims have become obsessed with trying to remedy a collective sense of powerlessness and political defeat by 'engaging in highly symbolic sensationalistic acts of power symbolism'. This has produced a 'doctrinal dynamic …of the theology of power in modern Islam'. The net result of this development is that 'the normative imperatives and intellectual subtleties of the Islamic moral tradition have not been treated with the analytical and critical rigor that the Islamic tradition rightly deserves but are rendered subservient to political expedience and symbolic displays of power.' Defining a religious identity against the West becomes the primary goal. 'Instead of Islam being a moral vision given to humanity', Abou El Fadl observes, 'it becomes constructed into a nationalistic cause that is often the antithesis of the West'. Muslims who work within this moral and intellectual paradigm are more anti-Western than they are pro-Islamic, he contends.

Abou El Fadl weaves a brilliant narrative that links these corrosive colonial and postcolonial effects to the emergence of an intellectual tradition of apologetics. He describes how this created a fertile ground for the spread of Wahhabi puritanism. The sequencing of these transformations and how they feed and reinforce each other are convincingly argued by the author. He observes that the challenges of modernity were met with 'pietistic fictions' about the completeness and perfection of Islam, as traditionally understood. There is nothing to be learned sociologically, philosophically and politically from the West, perhaps technologically there might be some useful borrowing, but that is all. This practice of Muslim apologetics 'proved to be like an addictive drug – it induced a pleasant state of oblivion alongside an artificial self-confidence, but the problems remained unchanged'. With time they became worse. The main effects are ideologically destructive. All of this has contributed to a 'sense of intellectual self-sufficiency that often descended into moral arrogance', Abou El Fadl observes. 'To the extent that apologetics were habit-forming, [they] produced a culture that eschewed self-critical and introspective insight, and embraced the projection of blame and a fantasy-like level of confidence and arrogance. Effectively, apologists got into the habit of paying homage to the presumed superiority of the Islamic tradition, but marginalised the Islamic intellectual heritage in everyday life'. This set the stage for the rise and spread within the Sunni Muslim world of puritanical Wahhabism.

While Abou El Fadl has written critically about Wahhabism in his previous works, in this book he draws upon original research with scholarly rigor and precision, to examine the roots and expansion of Wahhabi and Salafi intellectual currents. He convincingly argues that the Wahhabi interpretation of Islam, buttressed by Saudi petro dollars and a longstanding alliance with the United States and Europe, has contributed to the deep moral failures of Muslim societies, thus undermining the ethical potential of Islam's humanistic tradition. For anyone interested in the question of what went wrong with Muslim societies and how things could be set right again, these chapters are essential reading. And it is to this theme that the last part of the book is devoted.

It is not an exaggeration to say that given the extreme acts of ugliness that have taken place recently around the world, and which are justified in the name of Shariah, the word Shariah has become radioactive. Islamic law is widely viewed in the West as being as opprobrious as the dictates of Nazi law. It cannot be redeemed or reformed, and should not be promulgated anywhere. Abou El Fadl takes the exact view opposite view.

For Abou El Fadl, Shariah is not the problem, rather it stands as a major part of the solution. These final chapters of the book will be the most difficult for non-Muslims to absorb, given the current notoriety of Shariah. Abou El Fadl acknowledges this image problem, which is why he begins his book with an introduction to Shariah, and stringently clarifies the terms and concepts related to the Islamic legal tradition. The decline and corruption of Shariah, and how the tradition might be reconstituted to provide ethical and moral guidance for the rebirth of Islamic civilisation is carefully explained with a depth and nuance. Abou El Fadl's argues that the Shariah should receive the same consideration, treatment and respect as other legal traditions. It must certainly pain him deeply to see this tradition misunderstood, misapplied, abused and vilified by a whole host of groups from Orientalists and Islamophobes, to Wahhabis and mainstream Muslims. The task of reforming, renewing and recasting Islamic law for the contemporary age is the mainstay of this book.

From a Muslim perspective, this book was deeply soothing. It had the same effect that medicine does on a wasted human body. In this case, the malaise is not a physical illness related to human physiology, but the general Muslim political condition that is bracketed by the rise of ISIS and the deepening of political authoritarianism on the one side, and the proliferation of new levels of anti-Muslim bigotry and prejudice on the other. Its contribution to resolving our current existential crises cannot be overstated; and, as such, I would argue that *Reasoning with God* is indispensable reading for those who seek to understand how a healthy, flourishing and ethically rooted Islam can be re-created.

I am reminded of an argument made by the late Canadian scholar of comparative history and religion, Wilfred Cantwell Smith. Smith was concerned throughout his life with the future development of Muslim societies. He concluded his classic work, *Islam in Modern History*, first published over fifty years ago, by anticipating the destabilising effects of Muslim politics on global affairs. He wrote: 'the various intellectual and moral issues are today themselves internationalised. We would contend that a healthy, flourishing Islam is as important not only for the Muslims but for all the world today.' How prescient those words seem today.

THE COMPLEX SAMIHA AYVERDI

Aamer Hussein

I don't remember when I first read Samiha Ayverdi's name. Perhaps it was in a footnote in one of the numerous works of the noted German Sufi scholar Anne-Marie Schimmel, or in an article on pioneering Turkish women writers. What I did know, when I first came across a book by her in the early years of this century, was that she was a novelist and a chronicler of Istanbul in late Ottoman times, as well as a Sufi intellectual from a period when such figures weren't remotely fashionable in Ataturk's Turkey. She had barely been translated and was probably forgotten except by a handful of Western friends and local disciples.

Born in 1905, Ayverdi lived a life not dissimilar in its essentials to those of her Kemalist contemporaries, though their ideologies were often in opposition. She was an educated member of the elite, didn't wear a headscarf, and enjoyed all the privileges of a liberal, modern Turkish upper bourgeois milieu. She married young, divorced early, returned to her family home with her daughter, and published a number of books in various genres. At a fairly young age, she met Kenan Rifai, a Sufi teacher who changed the course of her life by bringing her back to what is now described as a moderate Islam, which she practised for the rest of her long life and saw as a defining element of a Turkish identity, as it brought together various ethnicities within the country. When Rifai died, she became the leader of his group of followers. Though like many Sufi teachers Rifai had often been accused of a syncretism that deviated from the norms of conservative religion by accepting other sects into its fold, his disciple prayed five times a day, and fasted during Ramadan. Ayverdi also established the celebration of Rumi's anniversary in Konya and would later reclaim public Islam as a potential force that transcended all borders and could unite diverse cultures in a common cause against a vaguely defined rank of enemies.

By late 2010, the time I read *Dost* (1999), Ayverdi's moving tribute to her mentor, which combined reminiscence, homespun philosophy, and religious reflection, public attitudes to the past of her homeland had begun to change in Erdogan's regime. I was on a plane, on my way to Istanbul, and Ayverdi's voice echoed some I had heard on my trip to Turkey the previous year, when I'd gone to launch a book called *Istanbul Through Asian Eyes* to which I had contributed. I had spoken to several young people, including a couple of my interpreters, whose perspectives differed radically from those of a previous generation I had met. These youths were intrigued by the Ottoman past, an Islamic heritage, and they seemed nostalgic for a time when Turkey was culturally linked to the lands that lay to its east. Often, a young Turkish friend would ask me to try to decipher an Ottoman inscription they couldn't read, or show us an amulet with a prayer on it. Ayverdi's works – or at least what I knew about them – were ripe for revival, and a visit to a bookshop proved that several of them were in print again.

Müderrisoglu Aysen, *A Woman Intellectual in Turkey in the 20th Century: Samiha Ayverdi*, Lambert Academic Publishing, Saarbrucken, Germany, 2014

Oddly, though, the only book I'd read before *Dost* was an odd little series of fragmented essays called *Let Us be Not Slaves but Masters*, which begins with a clarion call: 'Rulers of Islamic countries, leaders and thinkers of Islam, and all my brothers in Islam! This little booklet is written to propose that the 1,400th anniversary of the Hejirah be celebrated by an Islamic World that will have become united by then. It also dwells on some painful aspects of our lives as Muslims, and on certain problems common to all Islamic nations. We have now only three years before the anniversary arrives.'

I don't remember when I first found a copy of the book at SOAS library – probably in 2004, the year of my first visit to Istanbul – but it was certainly well after the events of 9/11, and its furious indictment of the West from a pan-Islamic perspective was reminiscent of many of the tirades we had heard from radical (and even not-so-radical) Muslims in recent years. Ayverdi, however, seemed to look back to a past that moved smoothly from the age of the Prophet through the glory days of Andalusia to a long period of Ottoman prosperity, calling all Muslims to unite for a common future.

In 2010, I reread the book along with *Dost* and in many ways they seemed to be written by two different hands. In the latter you heard the gentle mystic tones of the benign Sufi Schimmel appreciated, and Camille Helminski, the founder of Threshold Society, anthologised as a leading Sufi personage. The book was laced with the sort of platitudes and homilies that western readers of perennial philosophies, Khalil Gibran and Coleman Bark's versions of Rumi might find familiar. Ayverdi, however, was adamant about the fact that without Islam there was no Sufism: she might accept Western visitors such as Schimmel and Otto Spies into her fold, but they would remain, with honourable exceptions, outsiders. In the former, you were at times overwhelmed by the anger of a voice that more than once reminded you of Mohsin Hamid's eponymous 'reluctant fundamentalist' laughing when the twin towers fell. There was, though, no specific target for her ire except a generalised Europe which was the architect of the crusades, colonialism and Zionism; no tangible mention of wars or events of colonisation or decolonisation, and only an aleatory analysis of the consequences of Eastern or Western imperial conquests; her largely neo-Ottoman world view seemed to end in Iraq in the late 1950s. It was a visceral book, and powerful – if gratingly so to some of us – in its appeal to the disenfranchised and their feelings of cultural inferiority.

What was surprising, in the contexts of great changes in the world and in Turkey, was the book's date of publication: 1978, the same year as Edward Said produced *Orientalism*, his seminal study of cultural politics. That was two years after Islam was celebrated in Britain with a series of festivals inaugurated by Queen Elizabeth. In 1978 the Shah still ruled in Iran, Arabic was a fashionable language to learn, Afghanistan hadn't fallen to the Soviets, and Zulfikar Ali Bhutto, after restoring some sort of democracy to Pakistan, had been ousted in a bloodless coup and was awaiting his sentence: the world in general, and the Islamic world in particular, was a very different place. In 1979, when the book was translated into English and Arabic, Khomeini had risen to power, Afghanistan had fallen to the Soviets; in 1981, when it appeared in Urdu, Bhutto was dead, and the foundations of our new age were in place.

What had made the gentle, privileged mystic write a book so full of righteous wrath and choose to share it with readers beyond Turkey? What shaped her almost utopian yearning for an Islamic future predicated on the religion's glorious past? Was it nostalgia for the Ottoman age she had glimpsed in its decline, or despair with a world that seemed stable but was actually already rocking on its foundations? Did she see the situation of Turkey, which she felt had 'been slipping during the last decades from the line of sublime historical duty to Islam and sacrifice for Islam' after the decline of the Ottomans, as a template for the rest of the Muslim world? Did she reject the spurious modernisations of Turkey's near-neighbours, 'short-sighted, easy to deceive. And....often led astray by the deceitful words of Western politicians?' Ayverdi lived on until 1993 and one wonders how she felt when she saw her dreams of an Islamic Union explode all around her.

But in the era of Erdogan, and with the appearance on the international stage of writers such as Orhan Pamuk and Elif Shafak with their nuanced and syncretic approach to Turkey's past, a revived interest in Ayverdi's contribution is inevitable. Müderrisoglu Aysen's self-published monograph about her life and work, *A Woman Intellectual in Turkey in the 20th Century: Samiha Ayverdi*, attempts to re-establish the charismatic figure of this complex woman as a significant Turkish voice who bridges the gap between modernity and tradition, reform and religious faith.

Muderrisoglu, a historian, tells us that most writings and documentaries about Ayverdi have focused exclusively on her Sufi persona. Before extending the frame of her perspective to present us with a holistic portrait, she establishes Ayverdi's credentials as a moderate Muslim thinker who saw Wahabism as an aberration; she dismissed discussions of the veil as irrelevant to the real essence of Islam, seeing it as a multi-religious tradition rather than a Muslim rule; 'not as a distinctive sign that differentiates Muslim women from other women'. She followed her mentor in claiming that the proper implementation of Shariah would prevent exploitation between individuals and nations, but went on to say that a Sufi understanding of Shariah was necessary. As a teacher, she created a reflective space for middle-class Turks of all political ideologies who were in search of spiritual roots and values. In spite of her much-vaunted nationalism, she saw Turks not as an ethnic but a regional and cultural entity, so that her view of Turks included Kurds and other minorities. (The marker of this Turkish identity was Islam – other commentators have pointed out that Armenians and Jews often appear in sinister roles in her writings).

Muderrisoglu also glosses her subject's literary works – after a succession of fiction, there were memoirs and essays that recorded Ayverdi's memories of a Turkish century, and seem to be her abiding contribution to Turkish letters. However, the monograph's abiding interest is in its subject's understanding of Turkey's cultural past and her abiding sense of loss. Throughout her career Ayverdi criticised – though, it seems, cautiously – Turkey's abandonment of an Eastern past for a Western future, with the present as sacrifice. The monograph traces the development of reforms in Turkey from late Ottoman times to the age of Atuturk, and locates Ayverdi's discourse in each one of these periods as a radical critique of such reforms, though – like many commentators – the author is quick to point out that Ayverdi was not averse to modernity per se, only to its destructive elements. As early as 1948, she depicted, in an early novel, two kinds of reformers: the kind who believed that foreign ways should be imported wholesale into Turkey to the detriment of deep rooted Islamic values, and those who held that the acquisition of science and technology was not incompatible with religion. The monograph's emphasis is on how the age of Ataturk was an inevitable outcome of the reforms that had begun to take place long before his advent, from as far back as 1839. Among a tiny handful of documents appended to her monograph, the author includes a brief essay by Ayverdi about the change of the alphabet: 'We flirted with the Western civilisation very dangerously for centuries, and made our most dangerous mistake in the last quarter of the century, which is our groundless, unskilful and dangerous operation on the Turkish language.'

Much of what is available to us of Ayverdi's words needs extensive interpretation, as she seems constantly to veer towards abstractions. In the aforementioned essay we can assume that she is lamenting the loss of the Ottoman alphabet and the subsequent loss for future generations of important texts: a problem with which, as she points out, the Arabs and Iranians do not suffer.

Muderrisoglu's booklet, which is largely partisan, raises as many questions as it answers. It is best read in tandem with the recent essay 'Paradoxes of a Cold War Sufi Woman: Samiha Ayverdi between Islam, nationalism and modernity' by Ilner Ayturk and Laurent Mignon, published in the journal *New Perspectives on Turkey* (49 57-89 2013), which is a critique of Ayverdi's 'right wing' position, showing her as an elitist woman who scorned the masses she set out to enlighten, belonged to a posse of glamorous women uncomfortable with the undignified behaviour of plebeian Muslims in places of worship, and benefited hugely from the very society she despised, in terms of her social position as an independent female intellectual. This essay is also aware of the neglect Ayverdi's fiction has suffered – though perhaps of ambiguous literary merit, it nevertheless places women at its epicentre by giving them agency as the emblematic suffering lovers of Sufi lore, substituting the male as beloved object of endless desire. Though the writers see Ayverdi as Islamocentric, xenophobic and even racist, and point out her opportunistic failure to indict the superpowers with any degree of accuracy, they also accept her distance from Wahhabi ways of thinking and articulating Islam, and acknowledge her as the 'heroine of the Turkish right', a major influence on the 'renaissance of right-wing politics' which she witnessed to her quiet satisfaction before her death.

For all its tantalising elisions, the little of Ayverdi's work that is available in translation indicates a need for more of her work to be made available in translation. Perhaps an enterprising translator could begin with a selection of essays that mirrors the trajectory of her writing. Ayverdi, for all the contradictions in her position, was obviously a maverick whose thinking, though possibly inconsistent and at times lacking in cogency, engages with an entire centre of Turkish history, and – albeit from a distance – the contemporary history of the Middle East and Islam.

TRIBAL POWER

Hassan Mahamdallie

It is so easy to view the Arab Gulf states as uniquely soulless, artificial, despotic and ultimately illegitimate entities. Many assume, in stop-motion photography-style, that once the oil has stopped flowing the sky-scraping cities that have erupted out of the sand will just as quickly disintegrate back into the desert landscape. The imperious ruling elite will likewise tumble back into the nomadic camel-herding existence of their ancestors. Not quite, according to Miriam Cooke, Professor of Asian and Middle Eastern Studies at Duke University, and author of such feminist works as *Women Claim Islam* (2000) and *Opening the Gates* (2004). One could not ask for a more informed and sympathetic observer of the Arab world.

In *Tribal Modern*, she provides us with a novel insight into the rapid emergence and development of the Arab Gulf nation states. Cooke seeks to uncover the forces at work behind the seeming contradiction of the 'Tribal' and the 'Modern' in the Gulf. She reveals the societal superstructure scaffolding an economic system based on the vast wealth extracted from oil reserves, which have been used for 'nation building on tribal territories'. It is a process that has 'turned tribe into race into nation'.

Cooke's central argument is that it is a mistake in the context of the Gulf States to regard the tribal as an archaic or vestigial formation overtaken by modernity and technological advance. In fact, the tribe is making a vigorous comeback in the twenty-first century: 'the tribal signals racial privilege, social status, and exclusive entitlement to a share in national profits'. When the tribal comes face to face with modernity, there is no clash of conflicting values, no moral antagonism. Rather, it is a meeting of the minds: 'the desired effect of common aspirations'. Moreover, the tribal is not subsumed into modernity – it exists as a discreet and active component within the present-day Gulf capitalist set-up. Cooke asserts that 'the tribal is integral to the modern; it constitutes a crucial element in the Gulf's modernity'.

How can one explain this dynamic? Cooke uses an unexpected and somewhat paradoxical device – the Qur'anic concept of *barzakh*, the metaphysical space between life and the hereafter, as well as the physical space between salty and sweet, fresh water. She points out that the island of Bahrain is Arabic for two seas, a reference to the natural phenomenon by which fossil aquifers under the seabed push out a permanent and separate layer of fresh water that lies underneath the Gulf seawater. For Cooke *barzakh* provides the holding metaphor for the recent development of the region: 'the Tribal and the Modern in today's Gulf states cannot be disentangled. In the fifty-year *barzakh* linking and separating the oil sheikdoms and today's nation-states, each is shaping the other in a dynamic, cultural-political field in which apparently contradictory states remain in balance, the tribal does not compromise with the modern, nor does the modern erase the tribal'.

Miriam Cooke, *Tribal Modern, Branding New Nations in the Arab Gulf*, University of California Press, Oakland, 2014

Cooke also explains, referencing the Marxist historian Eric Hobsbawn's concept of 'the invention of tradition', how the Arab elite has sought to legitimise its rule by inventing 'pure' tribal bloodlines cleansed of all past foreign influences. The Gulf's ruling families are not unique in their endeavours to manufacture a historical 'authenticity' – Hobsbawn's concept was originally applied to British phenomena such as the airbrushing away of the British monarchy's Germanic roots and its re-invention as the entirely fictitious 'Windsor' family, as well as invented totems of Scottish nationalism such as the clan tartan.

So how do the denizens of the Gulf States themselves perceive tribal modern? Cooke asks her students. 'Of course! Tribal roots is everyone's new thing!' is the standard reply. The students explain how upon meeting one another for the first time they would immediately ask each other's tribal connection (a line of questioning seen as extremely rude in other tribal cultures such as Somali). For the students 'the tribe had to be elite, with an impressive lineage, for it to be really cool'. Thus, the 'tribe' is transformed from a social organisation by which nomadic peoples could negotiate territorial rights, access to resources and resolve disputes, into a racialised category conferring exclusive claim to superiority and access to political and economic power.

But like all founding myths the truth it obscures is much more interesting. The Arabian Gulf has historically been a crossroads connected via trade-routes to the Indian subcontinent, the East African coastal civilisations and East Asia. In this sense the migrant workers who labour in Dubai and other cities are only the latest in a line of wealth-creators stretching back millennium. It is ironic that cities like Dubai are today pouring vast resources into manufacturing a heritage based on a rather sparse and romanticised vision of desert culture revolving around falcons and camels, when its actual history reveals what many would regard as a rich and fascinating multicultural and multi-ethnic cosmopolitan past. But to admit this ancestry would be to undermine the invention of an authentic Arab past of racially pure tribes. As Cooke observes, it is taboo to discuss the Persian, African and Indian heritage comingled with the elite Arab bloodlines – thereby dissolving the past into sterile 'myths of millennial isolation'.

The next step is to fit tribe and race into the nation state. Those tribes who refused to give up a nomadic lifestyle that traditionally ranged across national boundaries have been effectively rendered stateless and without the benefits of citizenship. They have become known as the *Bedoon* – 'without'. Cooke quotes a *Bedoon* activist who complains that they 'cannot legally obtain birth, death, marriage or divorce certificates. The same applies to driving licences, identification cards and passports. They do not have access to public education, health care, housing or employment…Simply stated, the *Bedoon*, who are equal to about ten per cent of the Kuwaiti population, do not exist'.

For the tribal modern to work effectively it has to be policed rigorously, Cooke asserts. Laws regulate which marriages are permitted. Qatari Law No 21 bans categories of state employees, including ministers, diplomats, the military officer class and the police, from marrying foreigners. Spouses have to meet various qualifications based on a matrix of hierarchies on tribal, ethnic, and national lines. Couples who defy the rules can be forced to divorce. Proof of suitability inevitably boils down to biological and racial constructions, casting a very dark light on the essence of Gulf marriage laws, with historical echoes of eugenics and Nazi policies of racial purity. One upshot of course is a proliferation of first cousin marriages (30 per cent of all marriages in Qatar) and the accompanying danger of inherited genetic diseases.

Cooke spends time to describe and deconstruct the Gulf heritage 'brand'. This heritage is manufactured through banal, grand scale, projects such as Norman Foster's plan for the (zero carbon) Abu Dhabi Museum, which will feature 'five high-tech soaring pavilions, representing the feathers of a falcon's wing', or Jean Nouvel's design for the Qatar National Museum 'inspired' by a desert rose growing out of desert landscape. This '*barzakh* dynamic' represents a unique hypermodernity, argues Cooke. It is transforming the Gulf States from regional powers to global players: 'before oil their countries were unliveable, but today they have the wealth and power to assure luxurious lifestyles, continued independence, and growing international presence'.

I am not quite sure that a racialised identity, based on pure blood and social eugenics, can ensure anyone's independence. Anthropologists tend to have a slightly romantic notion of tribes. We ought to be aware that many of the contemporary problems of the Muslim world are a product of tribal allegiances. Think of Afghanistan and its warring tribes. Or how tribal factions have destroyed and shed so much blood in Iraq. Or the conflict in Syria which is essentially an all-out war of tribes. Nor am I convinced that the inhabitants of the Gulf State are all that 'modern'; after all, if modernity has any meaning, it is not limited to grand structures and wonders of imported technology. Modernity is essentially a conceptual category which requires acceptance of certain norms and values – such as embracing diversity, human rights, and shunning the Nazi era ideology of blood superiority. If ibn Khaldun was around, he would describe tribal modern as simply *asabiyyah* – generating bonds of cohesion but nevertheless obnoxious clannish behaviour that thwarts the emergence of civilisation. Moreover, I am not convinced that the *barzakh* metaphor is necessary or if it actually works.

The rapid emergence of the Arab Gulf states can be viewed, and explained, as a very particular configuration of twenty-first century, globalised, hyper-capitalism. The tribal modern lens is certainly a rewarding method by which one can discern the source of the region's dynamism. However, one is left wondering how unique an example it is on a historical level. As Hobsbawn pointed out, states have often found it necessary to mask or dampen their internal contradictions by constructing mythical pasts that attempt to unify a population behind the national project. The huge wealth generated by oil revenues has made it possible for the Arab elites to rapidly erect such an artifice – reconfiguring tribe into race into nation with relative ease.

It is worth considering that there are frameworks other than *barzakh* that one can bring to bear to describe the way by which seemingly contradictory elements of the old and new can sit together. Over one hundred years ago Russian Marxists sought to explain how seemingly backward countries and economies could leap-frog stages in capitalist development in a short space of time. The theory of 'uneven and combined development' was originally devised to explain how early twentieth century Russia could simultaneously exist in a state of feudal Czarist absolutism and at the same time undergo rapid industrialisation in its cities. Leon Trotsky put it this way: 'although compelled to follow after the advanced countries, a backward country does not take things in the same order. The privilege of historic backwardness — and such a privilege exists — permits, or rather compels, the adoption of whatever is ready in advance of any specified date, skipping a whole series of intermediate stages. Savages throw away their bows and arrows for rifles all at once, without travelling the road which lay between those two weapons in the past. The European colonists in America did not begin history all over again from the beginning. The fact that Germany and the United States have now economically outstripped England was made possible by the very backwardness of their capitalist development'. In Russia, uneven and combined development led to the co-existence of an archaic culture of primitive peasant production and a semi-feudal state combined with the culture of modern industrial society. This meant that cultural practices, institutions, traditions and ways of life belonging to both the very old and the very new were all combined, juxtaposed and linked together in a unique way. As we know from subsequent Russian history, this process did not mean the inherent tensions in that society were resolved, indeed they were exacerbated and magnified.

So we might say that although the tribal modern has given the Arab Gulf states an advantageous platform from which to launch itself on a global stage, it is also simultaneously importing the contradictions and fault-lines present in twentieth-century hyper-capitalism into its midst. The tribal may have been modernised but it is still a clannish mentality. Purity, religious or tribal, is always toxic.

ET CETERA

}

ON THE MUSLIM BROTHERHOOD

Abdelwahab El-Affendi

In a message issued by the Muslim Brotherhood in early December 2014, the movement appealed to the supporters of the military regime of Field Marshal Abdel Fattah Sissi to abandon him and re-join the ranks of true revolutionaries. Given the harvest of a year and a half of murder and mayhem, and a series of scandals and failures in all areas, the truth is out. Those who had supported Sissi 'with good intentions' should 'revert to the truth', following the example of the Pharaoh's sorcerers, who sided with Moses as soon as the truth became clear to them, regardless of the sacrifices.

As expected, this brought condemnation from critics who thought it outrageous for the group to liken itself to the Prophet Moses, while branding its opponents as followers of the infidel Pharaoh. A similar torrent of indictments was provoked in April 2012, when the current Brotherhood's 'Supreme Guide', Mohammed Badie, accused the Egyptian media of acting like the Pharaoh's sorcerers in seeking to distort the truth (in reference to media criticism of the Brotherhood's performance in parliament). However, this did not deter the movement's spokespersons from making the comparison again and again. Even a cursory search of its literature produces scores of instances of such use.

This appeal to that ancient story is revealing at many levels. The Egyptians are very fond of their history, and many pro-Mubarak intellectuals frequently used the Pharaonic reference to make the point that Egyptians love their tyrants. One argument went like this: all Prophets were sent to their peoples, except in Egypt, where the Prophet was sent to the king. This is an indication that Egyptian society has always been a hierarchical one, and will always need its Pharaoh.

The sorcerers were not as enthusiastically claimed or hailed, but their role is probably more interesting and more revealing about the nature of authority. In the Qur'anic story, with its many overlapping versions, the sorcerers were assigned a crucial role in refuting Moses' claim about his divine mission. Their anticipated public humiliation of the Hebrew upstart would provide conclusive proof of his false claims, and confirm the Pharaoh's own unassailable authority. In 'supporting the cause', they were also motivated by their own form of 'nationalistic' feelings. They clearly bought into the official narrative that the two Israelites were a threat to the social order, who wanted to 'uproot you from your land' and 'destroy your cherished way of life'. (This in spite of the clear demand of Moses to be permitted to leave Egypt with his people, rather than take it over, but superpowers always have a different way of telling the story!) Being judiciously opportunistic, the sorcerers also inquired in advance about the reward for success, and were promised a generous one, which would include high status.

However, the collective response of the sorcerers to their humiliating defeat was rather intriguing and very disappointing for the hapless Pharaoh: they decided unanimously to endorse Moses. This enraged the tyrant, who was more upset by this 'unauthorised' endorsement than by their dismal failure. This provides another intriguing insight into the nature of public authority. For it was the Pharaoh who set up the test for Moses, and it was up to him to assess the outcome and its consequences. In his own 'spin', the victory indicates nothing more than Moses being a better magician, probably the master-magician who taught those inferior performers. It was anyway up to the King to determine if, and when, people should endorse Moses, even if unquestionable proof of his authenticity could be found. The 'truth' here is not a matter for 'experts', no matter how knowledgeable, but a matter for royal power. Long before Foucault, the Pharaoh stated unequivocally that truth was a product of power, and not the other way round.

Going back to the Brotherhood and their claims, it is to be noted that while Moses had performed a good number of miracles, displacing the Pharaoh as Egypt's ruler was not part of his repertoire. One would have thought the project perfectly feasible. Having been raised as a royal prince, and with apparently some powerful allies in the court, it would not have been far-fetched for him to stake a claim to rule. Just as the sorcerers endorsed him, the people at large could have done so (that is precisely what had worried the Pharaoh). So why did that thought not cross his mind? More to the point, why was he not given that assignment?

On closer examination, it would appear that Prophet-rulers are a rare breed. Among all the prophets mentioned in the Qur'an, only David and Solomon became rulers. For the rest, either their people rejected them and were destroyed, or the prophet was killed or condemned to death. The Prophet Muhammad was the (partial) exception who proved the adage that a Prophet is more often than not rejected by his people and his homeland. For Muhammad was also forced out of his hometown, and did not become a 'King' anyway. It is to be noted that in all his missives to Emperors and Kings, he did not ask them to come under his authority, only to accept the divine message.

So while there may be lessons for Egypt's new hapless (and much less honest) sorcerers from the old story, there may also be some lessons for the would-be heirs to Moses. Given that they do not have the wherewithal to part the Red Sea or perform other miracles, their demands should be even more modest.

However, the main problem with the Brotherhood remains the lack of modesty and the near-pathological illusions of power. Paradoxically, the movement had swung in a very short period from paranoid displays of weakness and insecurity, to megalomaniac affirmation of omnipotence. Up to January 2012, the Guide vociferously opposed any suggestion for fielding a Brotherhood presidential candidate, saying in an interview that month that an Islamist president would expose Egypt to sanctions similar to those suffered by Gaza. The movement had earlier given repeated assurances that it will not seek a parliamentary majority. It did not completely respect those pledges. However, it still hounded out one of its most moderate (and sensible) leaders, Abdel Moneim Aboul Fotouh, for deciding to run for President as an independent.

The comparison between Gaza and Egypt was misinformed. Hamas did not face problems in Gaza because it was a democratically elected Islamist movement, but because it was an armed movement which wanted to work within the internationally-funded and Israeli-backed Palestinian National Authority (PNA). This posed a number of problems, the first of which is that the PNA was an Israeli-Palestinian partnership in accordance with the Oslo Accords, which Hamas rejects. As if this was not enough, Hamas decided in 2007 to mount a military coup and take over Gaza completely on its own. This put it at war with the official PNA and most other Palestinians factions. It is therefore incomprehensible to compare such a situation with a potentially freely elected government in a sovereign country!

In any case, by April 2012, the Brotherhood changed its mind and fielded a presidential candidate, Mohamed Morsi, who won the presidency by a very slim margin, even though he was running against one of Mubarak's former aides. In fact that candidate was forced out from his post as interim Prime Minister by revolutionary protesters who thought he represented the more sordid side of the old regime, and later faced corruption accusations. It was clear even then that a large section of Egyptians preferred Mubarak to Morsi. It was also clear that many who voted for Morsi did so mainly because they preferred him to one of Mubarak's most corrupt men. All this was a signal that the support for Morsi and Ikhwan was tentative and far from wholehearted or massive. However, the Brotherhood very soon began to act as if the whole Egyptian people were enthusiastic supporters. It allied itself with the more hardline Salafis, and systematically alienated everybody else. The movement and its front party, the Freedom and Justice Party (FJP), insisted on leading the government and transition alone, passing a controversial constitution and getting it endorsed through an equally controversial referendum. All proposals from the opposition to form a national unity government were rebuffed. In November 2012, Morsi committed his most fatal error. Even though he enjoyed full executive and legislative powers, he decided to pass a constitutional decree blocking any judicial challenge of his executive decisions and decrees, which meant that he also wanted to restrict judicial authority. Even though Morsi tried to justify this move as a temporary measure that would lapse once the new constitution was endorsed, it gave his enemies all the ammunition they needed to torpedo his presidency. To make matters worse, he did not appear to have consulted his close aides on this. His minister of justice heard the news from the media. By the end of the year, almost all his advisers resigned in disgust.

This hubris indicated a number of problems. For one thing, it confirmed everybody's fears about the secretive style of the Brotherhood. In spite of creating a legal political party (the FJP) which was its vehicle for political participation, it still maintained its secretive apparatus, which many feared was the one running the show. No one was bothering to hide this. For example, when the decision to field a presidential candidate was announced, the FJP was not even permitted to front the announcement presumably made in its name: the Guide and other Brotherhood leaders made the declaration without the benefit of that transparent fig-leaf.

More problematic was the demonstration of how the movement, in shifting from the paranoia of vulnerability to the arrogance of omnipotence, appeared oblivious to the limits of its power. The continuous diatribes against the media were just one indication about the movement's isolation among elite opinion-makers and its inability to deliver its message to the people. The 'sorcerers' refused to play ball. However, the real 'illusion' was not the one produce by the sorcerers, but the one entertained by the Brotherhood about having become the new Pharaoh. Nothing was further from the truth. At the time when the 'Supreme Guide' was berating the 'sorcerers', a military-appointed government, made up almost exclusively of old regime figures, held executive power. So while Islamists controlled parliament with their allies and were being blamed for the chaos and the economic and security deterioration, they had no power to remove that government.

But things got worse. Just two weeks before the June 2012 presidential elections, the parliament was dissolved by a court order, permitting legislative powers to revert to the Supreme Military Council (SMC). Morsi gained popular adulation with his deft move two months later to dissolve the SMC and appoint a new younger defence minister. However, his newly acquired self-confidence did not hide the fact that he remained as powerless as Iraqi and Egyptian monarchs during the British occupation. The military remained self-governing, and in control of a vast economic empire. The media (including the 'official' media) was against him, as was the judiciary. He had little control over the powerful and pervasive state security apparatus or the police, both still under firm control of Mubarak's men. Nor was he in possession of any tools to administer or control Egypt's collapsing economy. Unbeknownst to him, all these centres of power had begun to systematically conspire against him.

In reality, Morsi was nothing more than the head of an NGO headquartered at the presidential palace. His main asset remained the street. The old regime had collapsed under popular pressure, and was giving concession after concession as it lost its balance. However, the Brotherhood was instrumental in reducing, stopping and then reversing that momentum. In early 2011, it broke ranks with most other opposition forces when it sided with the SMC on a new constitution that was put to a referendum in March. During the competitive elections for parliament, even more fractures appeared in the solid revolutionary front. As it continued to push its unilateral agenda in government, in parliament, in the constitutional commission and on the streets, the Brotherhood lost almost all allies. By November, people were demonstrating in the streets against it, and even mounted violent attacks against its offices around the country. Morsi, the NGO-president, was unable to defend the centres. He was even unable to defend his own presidential palace, which was besieged with hostile and rather violent crowds. He had to be smuggled out of the palace as his presidential guard looked on, unwilling and unable to defend him.

The writing was on the wall; but this latter day Louis XVI was incapable of reading it. He rejected numerous overtures from opposition groups and mediators to salvage things by setting up a national unity government. Insisting on defiant unilateralism, he remained oblivious to the fact that, perhaps for the first time in its history, the Brotherhood had become a 'toxic brand'. It was clear that this was not just another setback like many the movement had faced throughout its history with characteristic stoicism and resignation. Having waited over eighty years in the wilderness (twice as long as the Israelites), it turned its greatest ever opportunity into a disaster. In the past, however, its enemies were unpopular regimes and its fate was met with popular indifference. This was an indictment in itself, and a sign of its self-imposed isolation. However, this time, it was facing popular anger and even hate. An even worse indictment was the fact that the regime many preferred to its rule is one of the ugliest and least appealing in Egyptian history.

The movement was advised by many of its sympathisers to call a halt to its political march and take time to reflect over the debacle it had brought on itself. It should leave it to the military and its allies to deal with the disasters zone Egypt had become, and attempt to regroup and rethink its strategies. The prominent Saudi journalist, Jamal Khashoggi, for example, pointed out the obvious fact that the movement is now hated and feared at home and abroad, and it has no chance of regaining power. So it should make another sacrifice by standing aside in order to give democracy a chance. The movement, instead, sought confrontation, with even more disastrous consequences.

In late December 2014, I received the movement's latest newsletter, containing an article by one of its intellectuals. The accompanying message asked: 'Isn't this project still providing the answers to the perplexed and tired in the face of the pressures of reality and fierce attack, and will continue to do so, God willing?' While the article in question, written by a prominent academic, was dated 2011, most of the references cited date from around the mid-1940s. It is so outdated it is an embarrassment. Its position on women is scandalous even by the movement's own practice today, while it nonchalantly prides itself in having created its own self-contained 'society' for its members which 'provided them with alternatives to everything it could find in Egyptian society'! Observe how they speak of 'Egyptian society' as something external, if not alien, to the movement.

It would appear from the circulation of such an anachronistic text at a time when the movement is fighting for its life, that it succeeded more than it had hoped for in building this disconnected society. It continues to live in a time warp with no link to the present or to the surrounding world. What is even more frightening is that it continues to believe that it has achieved success in spite of this lack of touch with reality.

It may be an exaggeration to speak of success, though. True, the Brotherhood's format, together with the comparable Jamaat Islami model in the Indian Subcontinent, has become the template for all mainstream Islamic movements. In fact, the two movements between them have cornered the 'Islamism' market. However, the model itself has not developed much. None of the movements have managed to make a political breakthrough. They may become the main opposition, or even the most popular political movement. But they could not accede to power, and they seem to lack not only the ability, but the will to do so. They are well aware that their programmes are unworkable, but they lack the ability to change them. They have no notion of self-criticism, and utterly fail to accept sympathetic criticism, even after such a disaster as the recent one in Egypt.

This is increasingly appearing to be a problem with Islamism as a phenomenon rather than with this movement or that. In the age of ISIL and similar mega-terror groups, the lines between violent dysfunctional and non-violent variety of Islamism get blurred. The Brotherhood wants to re-establish the caliphate, but never gets there. ISIL does establish the caliphate, but its success appears worse than the Brotherhood's failure. It is additionally a sad fact that groups like ISIL and Taliban keep springing up precisely because groups like Ikhwan and Jamaat seem to get nowhere, no matter how hard they try.

Both groups struggle to translate the core Islamic message, as they see it, into a practical programme fit for the modern era. But the translations repeatedly appear a travesty of the original text. This is an old problem, as noted by the seventh century sage al-Hassan al-Basri. Commenting on the policies of Ziyad, the first Umayyad Caliph Mu'awiya's ruthless governor of Iraq, al-Basri said that 'he wanted to emulate Omar (ibn al-Khattab)' but the consequences were disastrous for everybody. Just as Zaid erroneously mis-read the legendary firmness of Omar, the companion of the Prophet and Second Rightly Guided Caliph, as violence, the new Islamists present equally disastrous misreading of Islamic sources.

The Brotherhood's current narrative about themselves as God's elect, living apart from the 'Egyptian society', contrasts and overlaps with other modern Islamist narratives. The dominant Maududi-Qutb version (promoted by Abul ala Maududi, the founder of Jamaat-e-Islami and Syed Qutb, the chief ideologue of the Brotherhood) is that of the persecuted embryonic Muslim community in Mecca, waiting to migrate to the glories of Medina. However, the original narrative of Hassan al-Banna, the founder of the Muslim Brotherhood, implicitly harkens to the role of Omar ibn Abd al-Aziz, the righteous Umayyad Prince, who could 'magically' transform tyranny back into the Righteous Caliphate. But while such narratives remain problematic, the Pharaoh never disappoints, persistently playing his role to the script without fail. And as Sissi and Asad show, they are getting increasingly uglier and more inhuman. There are always too many of them and more than enough sorcerers. It is a pity that in this new replay, the Pharaoh and his sorcerers always win, and the Moses crew look less and less attractive. The miracle we await is the emergence of a new story, with new actors and a more reassuring ending.

A POWER LIST THAT IS NOT A LIST

Power is endlessly fascinating. Power is perennially enigmatic. The more complex society becomes the harder it is to define exactly where power resides. How do things happen? Why do things happen the way they do? Safe to say the vast majority of the world's population are unanimous in knowing, for sure, that they are not powerful but rather pawns in the hands of those who have and wield power over their lives. If only people knew their names, knew who these powerful people are, perhaps they could be confronted, and directly held accountable for the workings of power. Yes, let's confront the power structures directly. All we really, really need is a list that identifies, quantifies and ranks the people responsible, the real power holders, the names to conjure with who chart the course of other people' lives.

Thus the fascination with power lists. They come in all manner of categories, regularly published by newspapers and magazines, broadcast on radio, television and the internet. *Time* 100, the magazine's annual list of the most influential people in the world. *Forbes'* Hundred Most Powerful Women. Name a category and there will be a power list for you to play with – 50 Most Influential People in Sport/Hollywood/PR; 100 Most Powerful Gay and Lesbians; there are even various power lists of Muslims. All good fodder for the insatiable needs of opinion formers, significant members of the chattering classes, and our celebrity obsessed culture. A mention on a power list can be the passport to just such media exposure and thereby cement the impression of being a powerful name to conjure with. In this way lists mould and make more lists. And we all take notice. So, how better to conclude an edition devoted to the subject of power than with a power list of our own. We don't have to be formulaic. Who, for example are the world's most powerful Muslim women?

They have to be very *Critical Muslim* – slightly unexpected, rather chic, definitely cutting edge.

Well, there is Sheikha Al-Mayassa, sister of the Emir of Qatar, barely into her thirties, considered the most powerful woman in the art world. Armed with a £1 billion annual budget, the Sorbonne and Duke University educated Sheikha, is noted for her high-profile acquisitions including Cezanne's 'The Card Players' bought in 2012 for over £150 million and a Damien Hirst pill cabinet purchased for almost £10 million. Everyone knows Malala Yousafzai, the world's favourite goody two shoes; and the youngest recipient of the Nobel Peace Prize. She has even produced an autobiography while still a teenager! Surely, you have heard of the glamourous Amal Alamuddin, the human rights lawyer, who is powerful because she has married one of the most powerful men in Hollywood, George Clooney; and serves as an adviser to UN Special Envoy Kofi Annan and the King of Bahrain. We mustn't be sectarian. So let us include Maryam Mirzakhani, the Iranian-born, Harvard-educated mathematician and Stanford University professor. She has subverted religious, cultural and gender stereotypes to become the first woman to win the acclaimed Fields Medal for her work on geometric structures of surfaces and their deformations; and was one of the top ten 'people who mattered in 2014' identified by the influential science journal *Nature*. To make things a little bit more interesting, we could include the superhero Kamala Khan, created by two other powerful Muslim women, the Marvel Comics editor Sana Amanat and the brilliant writer G. Willow Wilson. Kamala is a second-generation Pakistani-American with shape-shifting powers, who negotiates her Muslim-ness in the same way that any teenage second-generation Muslim Pakistani-American girl may struggle with issues of identity and cultural conflict.

But let us pause for a moment. Let us sit upon the ground and calmly contemplate by means of our critical faculties what power lists actually tell us and what is so wrong about this list making genre.

A list by its very nature suggests priority, rank and precedence. A power list is inherently hierarchical. It explicitly puts forward the proposition that some are more powerful than others. But how are such judgements made? What distinguishes the potency of the power held by someone married to a Hollywood superstar as compared with a brilliant mathematician or a teenage Nobel laureate in peace? How powerful and influential is an oil-rich Sheikha from Qatar compared to the Queen of England or the Secretary

General of the United Nations? Are more people influenced by pop stars than authors, the literary legends of yesterday or today? Is an army general really powerful or do politicians hold the whip hand because they can determine when military might is to be unleashed? Surely all of these are invidious questions because they demonstrate how complicated the whole subject of power is. The hardest thing to know about power is precisely the priority, rank and precedence of one dimension of power as compared to another.

Power lists inevitably reflect the predilections of the list makers. List making is in its own way a power trip. Making a list is to exercise the power to confer notoriety and distribute public exposure. It is a very sophisticated version of parish pump gossip, reflecting publicly available information, a measure of tittle tattle and the titillation of thinking one has an insider's view of what's what in the world. The fact that it may all be smoke and mirrors never features on the list.

There is an old aphorism to the effect that power is not so much in the eye of the beholder as residing where we believe it to be. This is of course the Tinkerbell theory of power, and not to be entirely derided. The powerful in many ways get away with the liberties the public permit. Rank has its privileges and power its latitude and licence: the liberties power is allowed to get away with because of the intimidation, real or imaginary, it exudes. Power resides in being able to scoff at moral hazard – as we now all know to our cost. Banks and financial institutions that are too big to fail, now that is a definition of unmistakable, unmitigated power. No wonder they continue to behave much as before the nods at contrition doing little to disguise the fact that fat cat culture is purring along creamily.

As pawns we know power exists, like the banks much of its exercise is unmistakable. But how can power be curbed? How can we contain or constrain the routines of power that are patent abuses of best interests of the rest of society? That is not a conundrum which can be resolved by list making.

Now think back, if you will, to that hastily abandoned idea of a list of the most powerful Muslim women. Sadly, I have to admit that Muslim women do not rule the world (as of yet!). Though in contradiction to this self-evident statement Muslim countries have exceeded the global average in generating women prime ministers: Pakistan (one woman, twice);

Bangladesh (two women, serially), Turkey (one woman, sadly forgotten), Indonesia (one woman, who made a second attempt) – so we are only talking of the four most populous Muslim nations on earth! And the largest Muslim minority population is to be found in India, which also had a notable women leader. So how are the realities of female agency and power to be computed? Is it not equally true that while women can rise to important positions in politics, business, the media and academy in South Asia, across India outrage spurs a campaign to protect women from the increasing frequency and horror of gang rape; an invasion by foreign forces is justified by protecting the right of women to vote and be educated in Afghanistan, while the most common effect of Muslim clamour for Shariah power, particularly in Pakistan, is the application of *zina* laws which make women culpable for adultery under any and all circumstances, including rape, and always exonerate the men.

So would a power list of Muslim women be a harbinger of hope or a record of unfulfilled dreams which came true for those who managed to be part and parcel of the elite ranks of society and thereby had access to privileged advantage anyway? Lists can chart the potential and possibilities of ideas yet to come, there is power in the idea of what may yet come to be. There is little a power list can do to make it so.

Or is the purpose of such lists to stir the conscience and rouse the engagement of the public? Is a list designed to show us the power structures so that we can act upon them, confront them directly, know the culprits and assign culpability? In which case the question is do you ever feel incensed by reading a power list? Does it, has it, ever changed your view of the workings of power? Have you been inspired to consider the varied and diverse nature of where power resides and might be exerted? Has a list ever given you the urge to go and confront anyone directly? Have you been stirred and shaken by any power list to change your attitudes or actions? I would think not!

It is necessary to record an important reason for the impotence of power lists. Have you ever yet read a power list of any category with which you actually agreed? Shaken and stirred to social action, no. But shaken and stirred to fulminating irritation – almost inevitably! The makers of lists are, on the most cursory of glances, quite clearly buffoons, villains, dolts and innocents devoid of taste, discernment and sadly deficient in critical faculties. How could anyone possibly think a list accurately reflects a general and agreed ranking and hierarchy of anything? The world does not do such unanimity. As varied as the types of power that can be listed are the interpretations of who and how power is distributed, appropriated, and at work in the world. However much a list insists on its own view of the nature and importance, the power and potency of its rankings, all it really achieves is to stimulate the beholders dissent and alternate reading of reality. All that is enlisted is one's capacity to think for oneself and believe one's own judgement is infinitely superior. I think this makes the power list making genre the ultimate vanity project for both its makers and consumers, which is quite a feat!

Publishing power lists is essentially a journalistic tour de force. It intimates far more than it contains; it fascinates and irritates consumers making them think somehow it really matters in some way. And it generates and fills inordinate amounts of column inches. It is lazy work because it infers far more than it can possible mean. Yet the public's fascination with power lists is such that there never will be an end to filling whole supplements and issues with these specious flights of fancy.

So what of our power list of Muslim women? Well here's one Muslim woman exerting her power to foil you. Sorry, you shall not know, I will not divulge, and have sworn everyone to silence. True power does not advertise itself. If you want a list of powerful Muslim women – go make your own!

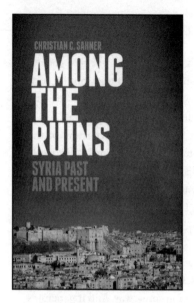

AMONG THE RUINS

SYRIA PAST AND PRESENT

CHRISTIAN C. SAHNER

ISBN: 9781849044004
£20.00 / Hardback / 240pp

As a civil war shatters a country and consumes its people, historian Christian Sahner offers a poignant account of Syria, where the past profoundly shapes its dreadful present.

Among the Ruins blends history, memoir and reportage, drawing on the author's extensive knowledge of Syria in ancient, medieval, and modern times, as well as his experiences living in the Levant on the eve of the war and in the midst of the 'Arab Spring'. These plotlines converge in a rich narrative of a country in constant flux — a place renewed by the very shifts that, in the near term, are proving so destructive.

Sahner focuses on five themes of interest to anyone intrigued and dismayed by Syria's fragmentation since 2011: the role of Christianity in society; the arrival of Islam; the rise of sectarianism and competing minorities; the emergence of the Ba'ath Party; and the current pitiless civil war.

Among the Ruins is a brisk and illuminating read, an accessible introduction to a country with an enormously rich past and a tragic present. For anyone seeking to understand Syria, this book should be their starting point.

'*Among the Ruins* is a uniquely vivid evocation of the past of Syria and a prescient record of its present state. Deeply humane and drawing on subjects from all walks of life, Sahner has a gift for presenting them against a past that is as varied and as ancient as the country itself. We are brought to the edge of the precipice over which, alas, a magnificently diverse society appears to have stumbled. We will be both better informed and wiser for reading it.' — Peter Brown, Rollins Professor Emeritus of History at Princeton University

WWW.HURSTPUBLISHERS.COM/BOOK/AMONG-THE-RUINS

41 GREAT RUSSELL ST, LONDON WC1B 3P
WWW.HURSTPUBLISHERS.COM
WWW.FBOOK.COM/HURSTPUBLISHERS
020 7255 2201

CITATIONS

Introduction: Searching for Power by Ziauddin Sardar and Merryl Wyn Davies

Adam Curtis's reflections on 2014 were broadcast on 'Charlie Brooker's 2014 Wipe' on BBC2, 30 December 2014 at 10pm. It can be viewed on YouTube.

On postnormal times, see Ziauddin Sardar, 'Welcome to Postnormal Times' *Futures* 42 (5) 435-444 June 2010; and 'Postnormal Times Revisited' *Futures* (to be published); and John Sweeny, 'Signs of Postnormal Times' *East-West Affairs*, 3+4, July-December 2013 5-12; and the special issue of Futures on 'Postnormal Times', edited by Merryl Wyn Davies 43 (2) March 2011. On the complexity of governance, see Jordi Serra, 'Postnormal Governance' *East-West Affairs* 5 January-March 2014; and Ziauddin Sardar, 'The Future of the Arab Spring in Postnormal Times' *American Journal of Islamic Social Sciences* 30 (4) 125-136 Fall 2013. Moises Naim's *The End of Power* is published by Basic Books (New York, 2013).

On the rise of Hindu Nationalism in India, see the 25 December 2014 Editorial, 'Religious Intolerance in India' in *New York Times*, which can be accessed at:

http://www.nytimes.com/2014/12/26/opinion/religious-intolerance-in-india.html?ref=opinion

Islam and the State by Malise Ruthven

Authors cited in this essay include: Ali A. Allawi *The Crisis of Islamic Civilization* (Yale University Press, New Haven, 2009) p 178; Wael B Hallaq *The Impossible State: Islam, Politics and Modernity's Moral Predicament* (Columbia University Press, New York, 2014), ppxi, 49, 51 and 89; Ashraf el-Sherif, 'The Egyptian Muslim Brotherhood's Failures' Carnegie Endowment July 2014, pp 7, 10 and 5; Diarmaid MacCulloch *Reformation: Europe's House Divided 1190-1700* (Penguin, London, 2003) p 487; Antony Black *The History of Islamic Political Thought – from the Prophet to the Present* (Edinburgh University Press, Edinburgh, 2001) p156; Aziz Al-Azmeh *Islams and Modernities* (Verso, London

1996, 2nd edn), p 151; Bassam Tibi *Islamism and Islam* (Yale University Press, New Haven, 2012) p 33.

The Pierre Bayle citation is from Ernst Cassirer, *The Philosophy of the Enlightenment*, trans. Fritz C. A. Koelln and James P. Pettegrove (Princeton University Press, Princeton, 1951), p 175; C F Robinson quote is from his Keynote Address to the Conference on 'Religious Wars in Early Modern Europe and Contemporary Islam' at Columbia University, New York, delivered on 23 October 2014; Rana Tanveer quote is from his paper 'Religious Conflicts in Pakistan and Role of Media', presented at a the same Conference. Ashraf el-Sherif quotes are from 'The Muslim Brotherhood and the Future of Political Islam in Egypt' Carnegie Endowment October 2014 p 5. David S Kirkpatrick article was published in *New York Times* of 7 September 2014. *The Economist* article appeared is in the issue of 13 December 2014, p58.

A weakness in Hallaq's essay is his failure to address the long drawn-out phenomenon of Ottoman-Turkish secularisation in the nineteenth and twentieth centuries, a process that weakens his claim that the 'socio-economic and political system regulated by the Sharia' was dismantled 'at the hands of colonialist Europe' [p ix]: the liberation movements that erupted in the Ottoman Balkans can hardly be described as 'colonialist'. These social movements often shifted their support between different Islamist parties as they saw fit, enabling the AKP to establish itself after its predecessors had been banned, in a pluralistic political context. Unlike the Brotherhood leaders, who tend to be engineers or doctors the AKP leaders and cadres have decades of political experience through participation in municipal, parliamentary, and executive politics.

Muhammad and Khadija by Kecia Ali

For form information about prophetic biography discussed in this essay, see Kecia Ali, *The Lives of Muhammad* (Harvard University Press, Cambridge, MA, 2014); and discussions about historical changes in gender roles, see *Sexual Ethics and Islam: Feminist Reflections on Qur'an, Hadith, and Jurisprudence* (Oneworld, Oxford 2006) and on the wife's sexual duties, also *Marriage and Slavery in Early Islam* (Harvard University Press, Cambridge, MA 2010). The discussion of the need for compelling alternative visions is found in a discussion of beauty in bell hooks, *Feminism is for Everybody* (South End Press, Boston, MA, 2000), p 35. On interpretation of Qur'an 4:1, see Aysha Hidayatullah, *Feminist Edges of the Qur'an* (Oxford University Press, New York, 2014). Louis-George Tin's *Invention of Heterosexual Culture* (MIT Press, Cambridge, MA, 2012) limits itself largely to European history; the quotation is from p149. Amira Sonbol's quotation comes from her contribution to Yvonne Yazbeck Haddad and John Esposito, *Daughters of Abraham: Feminist Thought in Judaism, Christianity and Islam* (University Press of Florida, Jacksonville, FL, 2002), page 142. Amanullah De Sondy's book is *The Crisis of Islamic Masculinities* (London: Bloomsbury, 2014). Look out for Debra Majeed's *Polygyny: What It Means When African American Muslim Women Share Their Husbands* (forthcoming from the University Press of Florida).

My brief foray into traditionalist chat rooms included a visit to http://www.ummah.net/forum/showthread.php?239847-Monogamy-is-also-a-sunnah

The Power of Education by Jeremy Henzell-Thomas

The World Exclusive on the loan of one of the Elgin Marbles to the Hermitage Museum appeared in *The Times* of 5 December 2014. Some concise reflections by Russell Bosworth on the legacy of Socrates can be found at http://www.philosophyworks.org/content/lives-plato-and-socrates (accessed 8/12/14). Plato's Apology translated by Benjamin Jowett can be accessed at http://classics.mit.edu/Plato/apology.html. The article from *Deutsche Welle* is entitled 'Knowledge is Power: Why Education Matters' and can be accessed at http://www.dw.de/knowledge-is-power-why-education-matters/a-15880356. Thomas Merton's reflections on the need to 'live out what we think' are expressed in his *Thoughts in Solitude* (Farrar Straus Giroux, 1993), and *Seeds*, selected and edited by Robert Inchausti, (Shambhala Publications, Inc., Boston, MA, 2002), 131. The essay by Ziauddin Sardar on freethinking is 'The Circumference of Free Thought', *Critical Muslim 12: Dangerous Freethinkers*, October-December 2014, 3-14. David Bohm's theory of quantum physics is set out in his *Wholeness and the Implicate Order* (Routledge, London, 1980). Ibn Khaldun's views on 'asabiyyah are examined in 'Asyiqin Abdul Halim et el., 'Ibn Khaldun's Theory of 'Asabiyyah and its Application in Modern Muslim Society', *Middle-East Journal of Scientific Research* 11:9 (2012), 1232-1237. The

Prophet's sayings on 'asabiyyah are noted by Muhammad Asad in his commentary on Qur'an 28:15 and 49:13.

Ibn 'Arabi's concept of continually unfolding implications is from the chapter of *al-Futuhat al-Makkiyya* concerning 'the people of spiritual bewliderment' (hayra) translated by James Winston Morris in his *The Reflective Heart: Discovering Spiritual Intelligence in Ibn 'Arabi's Meccan Illuminations* (Fons Vitae, Lousville, 2005), 81. Ahmed Moustafa and Stefan Sperl's *The Cosmic Script: Sacred Geometry and the Science of Arabic Penmanship* is published by Thames and Hudson, London, 2014. The quotation from Muhammad Asad about the impact of the Qur'an on the development of Western civilisation is from his Foreword to *The Message of the Qur'an* (The Book Foundation , Bath, 2004), vi. Other quotations from Asad are from his commentary in this work. Ziauddin Sardar's review in *The Guardian* of Sebastian Faulks's dismissal of the Qur'an is entitled 'Reading the Qur'an in the Dark' (27/8/09) can be accessed at http://www.theguardian.com/commentisfree/belief/2009/aug/27/sebastian-faulks-quran-islam. Pope Francis's address to the European Parliament on 25 November 2014 is available at: http://w2.vatican.va/content/francesco/en/speeches/2014/november/documents/papa-francesco_20141125_strasburgo-parlamento-europeo.html.

Excavations of the origin of words owe much to John Ayto, *Bloomsbury Dictionary of Word Origins* (Bloomsbury Publishing Limited, London, 1990), *Cassell's Dictionary of Word Histories* (Cassell, London, 2000), and *Chambers Dictionary of Etymology* (Chambers, Edinburgh, 1988).

On the Qur'anic basis for religious pluralism, see Reza Shah-Kazemi, 'The Metaphysics of Interfaith Dialogue: Sufi Perspectives on the Universality of the Qur'anic Message', in James Cutsinger (ed.), *Paths to the Heart: Sufism and the Christian East* (World Wisdom, Bloomington, Indiana, 2002). The quotation from Mahmoud Ayoub is from his essay, 'The Qur'an and Religious Pluralism' in Roger Boase (ed.) *Islam and Global Dialogue, Religious Pluralism and the Pursuit of Peace* (Ashgate, Aldershot, 2005), 273. The words of Rabbi Abraham Heschel are quoted by Prince Hasan Bin Talal in Rabbi Jonathan Magonet, *Talking to the Other: Jewish Interfaith Dialogue with Christians and Muslims* (I.B. Tauris, London, 2003), vii. The quotation from Nancy Kline is from her *Time to Think: Listening to Ignite the Human Mind* (Lock, London, 1999), 97. For recent theories on the extinction of the Neanderthals, see

'Why did the Neanderthals die out?' (*The Guardian*, 2/6/13) accessed on 1/12/14 at http://www.theguardian.com/science/2013/jun/02/why-did-neanderthals-die-out. Other works on pluralism to which I have referred include Diana L. Eck, *Encountering God* (Beacon Press, Boston, Boston, 1993), 198; Omid Safi (ed.), *Progressive Muslims on Justice, Gender and Pluralism* (Oneworld Publications, Oxford, 2003), 24; and Khalid Abou El Fadl, *The Place of Tolerance in Islam* (Beacon Press, Boston, 2002), 16. The progressive marginalisation of the humanities in mainstream education in the UK has been rigorously documented in *The Cambridge Primary Review* directed by Robin Alexander (see http://www.primaryreview.org.uk/).

On Plato's teaching on the superiority of dialectic over rhetoric, see R. Wardy, 'Rhetoric', in J. Brunschwig, and G. Lloyd (eds.), *Greek Thought: A Guide to Classical Knowledge* (The Belknap Press of Harvard University Press, Cambridge, Mass., 2000), 465. On dialectic as an advanced mode of human thought, see Karl Riegel, 'Dialectic Operations: The Final Period of Cognitive Development', *Human Development*, 16: 5 (1973), and James W. Fowler, *Stages of Faith: The Psychology of Human Development and the Quest for Meaning* (Harper and Row, San Francisco, CA, 1981). Roland Barth's critique of excessive 'teacher-talk' is in his *Learning by Heart* (Jossey-Bass, San Francisco, 2001). John Taylor Gatto's indictment of the system of state schooling in the USA is in his *Dumbing Us Down: The Hidden Curriculum of Compulsory Schooling* (New Society Publishers, 1992). For Neil Postman's critique of the false 'gods' blighting education see his *The End of Education: Redefining the Value of School* (Vintage Books, New York, 1996).

On the problem of 'narrative fallacies' see Nassim Nicholas Taleb, *The Black Swan: The Impact of the Highly Improbable* (Random House, New York, 2007) and Daniel Kahneman, *Thinking, Fast and Slow* (Penguin Books, London, 2012). Francis Bacon's *Meditationes Sacrae* (1597) can be read in a facsimile edition published by Kessinger Publishing Co., 1996 and 2010. Bacon's *The Four Idols* (originally in *Novum Organum*) appears in James D. Lester (ed.), *Plato's Heirs: Classic Essays* (NTC Publishing Group, Lincolnwood, 1996), 53-63. On the value of memorisation, see Michael Knox Beran, 'In Defense of Memorization', *City Journal*, Summer 2004. On the relationship between creativity and a body of knowledge, see Robert Weisberg, 'Creativity and Knowledge: A Challenge to Theories', in Robert J. Sternberg (ed.), *Handbook of Creativity* (Cambridge University Press,

Cambridge, 1999). The Ipsos MORI poll on public perceptions was based on 11,527 interviews in fourteen countries and was published in *The Times* on 30/10/14.

The report on the popularity of religious education amongst students in the UK is by L. Blaylock (ed.), *Listening to Young People in Secondary Religious Education*, Professional Council for Religious Education (PCfRE), September 2001. A. C. Grayling's dismissal of religious education as 'intellectual abuse' was voiced in a discussion on faith schools on BBC Radio 4's Moral Maze on 1 June, 2002. See also his article in *The Guardian*, 'Ghettoes of Superstition' (11/9/07) accessed on 5/12/14 at http://www.guardian.co.uk/commentisfree/2007/sep/11/ghettoesofsuperstition. The quote from Doris Lessing about indoctrination is from her novel, *The Golden Notebook* (Harper Perennial, 2007) and the quotation from Hannah Arendt about totalitarian education is from her *Totalitarianism* (Harcourt Brace Jovanovich, New York, 1968), 168.

The website '3 Ways to Develop Powers' is http://www.wikihow.com/Develop-Powers (accessed 5/12/14). Karim Douglas Crow's study 'Between wisdom and reason: Aspects of '*aql* (Mind-Cognition) in Early Islam', appeared in *Islamica* 3:1 (Summer 1999), 49-64. For Guy Claxton's influential views on different modes of thinking, see his *Hare Brain Tortoise Mind: Why Intelligence Increases When you Think Less* (Fourth Estate, London, 1997). F. David Peat explores indigenous science in his *Blackfoot Physics* (Fourth Estate, London, 1994). Harry Lewis's critique of the loss of meaning, purpose and ethical compass in modern liberal education in America is in his *Excellence Without A Soul: Does Liberal Education Have a Future?* (PublicAffairs, 2007) and the review quoted is by Derek Melleby on the CPYU (Center for Parent/Youth Understanding) website (accessed 26/8/14). The QS world university rankings for 2014/15 were accessed on 7/12/14 at http://www.topuniversities.com/qs-world-university-rankings.

On education, I have distilled here and there various ideas I have expressed in other works of my own, including the following: Foreword to Zahra Al Zeera, *Wholeness and Holiness in Education: An Islamic Perspective* (Richmond: International Institute for Islamic Thought, 2001); 'Passing Between the Clashing Rocks: The Heroic Quest for a Common and Inclusive Identity', *The Journal of Pastoral Care in Education*, 22:3 (2004), pp. 35-44; 'Thinking Skills: Engaging the Intellect Holistically', *Islamica*, 15

(2005); 'Thinking Outside the Box', *Islamica*, 16 (2006); 'Key Elements of Holistic Education', *Islamica*, 17 (2006); 'Muslim Youth and the Renewal of Core Human Values: The Centrality of Education', keynote address, AMSS Conference, Muslim Youth: Challenges, Opportunities and Expectations, University of Chester, 2009; 'Islam and Human Excellence', keynote address, Goldman Sachs Eid event, London, 30 September 2010; 'Islamic Education: Cosy Corner, Lame Duck, Model of Compliance, or Beacon of Excellence?', presentation incorporated into the section on education in Contextualising Islam in Britain II, a report compiled (with Professor Yasir Suleiman) for DCLG, University of Cambridge, 2012.

Michael Douglas interview can be read at: http://www.empireonline.com/interviews/interview.asp?IID=1090

Enlightening Engagement by Rahel Fischbach and Rachel Friedman

We have consulted the following sources on the history of Religious Studies: Donald Wiebe, *The Politics of Religious Studies: The Continuing Conflict with Theology in the Academy* (St. Martin's Press, New York, 1999); Joachim Wach, 'The Meaning and Task of the History of Religions (Religionswissenschaft),' in McCutcheon (ed), *The Insider/Outsider Problem in the Study of Religion: A Reader* (Cassell, New York 1999), the quotes are from pp. 82–94; and Tomoko Masuzawa, *The Invention of World Religions* (Chicago: University of Chicago Press, 2005). The student handbook of the religious studies program in Rabat is *Māṣṭir al-Madhāhib al-'Aqdiyya fil-Diyānāt* (Student Handbook; Rabat: Kulliyyat al-Ādāb wal-'Ulūm al-Ijtimā'iyya [College of Literatures and Social Sciences, Muhammad V University], 2008-2009). Regarding the history of Islam and Islamic education in Morocco, we consulted the following sources: Dale Eickelmann, 'Madrasas in Morocco: Their Vanishing Public Role,' in Hefner and Qasim Zaman (eds.) *Schooling Islam: the culture and politics of modern Muslim education* (Princeton University Press, Princeton, 2007, pp. 134-142); and Malika Zeghal, *Islamism in Morocco: Religion, authoritarianism, and electoral politics*, translated by George Holoch (Markus Wiener Publishers, Princeton, 2008). The philosophy texts we reference are: Hans-Georg Gadamer, *Truth and Method*, translated by Weinsheimer Marshall (Continuum, New York: 2004); William Schweiker, *Mimetic Reflection: A Study in Hermeneutics, Theology, and Ethics* (Fordham University Press, New York, 1992); and Jürgen Habermas, 'On Systematic Distorted Communication,' in *Inquiry* 13.2(1970), 205–218. The names of the Moroccan students have been changed to protect their anonymity.

The Turkish Medici by Mohamed Bakari

On recent Turkish politics see Soner Çağptay, *The Rise of Turkey: The Twenty-First Cerntury's First Muslim Power* (Potomac Books, Washington DC, 2014); Gerald Maclean, *Abdallah Gül and the Making of New Turkey* (Oneworld, Oxford, 2014);Kerem Oktem, *Angry Nation: Turkey Since 1989* (Zed Books, London, 2011); Banu Senay, *Beyond the Borders: Long-Distance Kemalism, State Politics and the Turkish Diaspora* (I.B. Tauris, London, 2013); Jenny White, *Muslim Nationalism and the New Turks* (Princeton University Press, Princeton, 2014). On the Golun movement, see M. Hakan Yavuz, *Towards Islamic Enlightenment: The Gülen Movement* (Oxford University Press, Oxford, 2013); and the Special Issue of *The Muslim World* 'Islam in the Contemporary World: The Contributions of Fetullah Gülen' 95 (3) 2005. For Ahmet Davutoglu's ideas see his *Civilizations and World Order: Geopolitics and Cultural Difference* (Lexington Books, Lanham MD, 2014).

Racialism in the Archipelago by Nazry Bahrawi

The quote from Sharon Siddique and Leo Suryadinata is from 'Bumiputra and Pribumi: Economic Nationalism (Indiginism) in Malaysia and Indonesia', *Pacific Affairs*, Vol. 54 No. 4 (Winter 1981-82), p. 665; the Michael MacDonald quote is from, *Why Race Matters in South Africa* (Harvard University Press, 2006) p.107; and Jacques Bertrand's quote is from *Nationalism and Ethnic Conflict in Indonesia* (Cambridge University Press, 2004) p 70. See also my essay, 'Incest Performed: The Neo-colonial Perversion of Translation in Malaysia' in *Translation and Global Asia: Relocating Cultural Production Network*, Uganda Sze-Pui Kwan and Lawrence Chong (eds) (Chinese University of Hong Kong, 2014).

Stokely Carmichael and Charles V. Hamilton *Black Power: The Politics of Liberation in America* is published by Jonathan Cape (London, 1968). The 'Race/Off" episode of The Daily Show can be seen on YouTube: ttps:// www.youtube.com/watch?v=T_98ojjIZDI

Governing Bosnia by Sejad Mekic

Various photographic images and video clips covering Bosnian protest can be viewed at: http://storify.com/euronews/bosnia-anti-government-protests-spread-to-sarajevo/embed.

Background information can be obtained from: Igor Štiks, 'We are all in this together: a civic awakening in Bosnia-Herzegovina', 12 June 2013, available at: https://www.opendemocracy.net/igor-%C5%A0tiks/%E2%80%98we-are-all-in-this-together%E2%80%99-civic-awakening-in-bosnia-herzegovina; Lana Pasic, 'Who is behind Bosnia's Riots?', Al-Jazeera, 10 February, available at: http://www.aljazeera.com/ indepth/ opinion/2014/02/who-behind-bosnia-riots-201429132930915905.html; Kurt Bassuener 'How Bosnia's Protest Movement Can Become Truly Transformative', *Balkan Insight*, 25 February 2014, available at: http://www.balkaninsight.com/en/blog/how-bosnia-s-protest-movement-can-become-truly-transformative; and Jasmin Mujanović, 'It's spring at last in Bosnia and Herzegovina', Al-Jazeera, 11 February 2014, available at: http://www.aljazeera.com/indepth/opinion/2014/02/it-spring-at-last-bosnia-herzegov-2014296537898443.html.

See also: N Malcolm, *Bosnia: A Short History* (London, 1994); M Malik, (ed) *Anti-Muslim Prejudice: Past and Present* (Routledge, London, 2013); M Pinson (ed) *The Muslims of Bosnia-Herzegovina* (Harvard University Press, Cambridge, 1994) and Paul Mojzes (ed) *Religion and the War in Bosnia* (Scholars Press, Atlanta, 1998)

Father, My Father by Hussain Ahmed

On Pakistan's military, see Ayesha Siddiqa, *Military Inc.: Inside Pakistan's Military Economy* (Pluto, London 2007); Shuja Nawaz, *Crossed Swords: Pakistan, Its Army and the Wars Within* (Oxford University Press, Karachi, 2009); and Aqil Shah, *The Army and Democracy: Military Politics in Pakistan* (Harvard University Press, Cambridge, Mass, 2014). From the perspective of the military itself see than former dictator Pervez Musharraf's *In the Line of Fire* (Simon and Schuster, London, 2006), clumsily named after a Clint Eastwood movie. And on US government's strong interest in maintaining Pakistan's military's continued prosperity, see former US Ambassador Husain Haqqani's *Magnificent Delusions:*

Pakistan, the United States, and an Epic History of Misunderstanding (PublicAffairs, NewYork, 2013).

Reports of the attack on Geo journalist first appeared in Dawn on 19 April 2014, 'Journalist Hamid Mir Injured in Gun Attack in Karachi', which can be accessed at: http://www.dawn.com/news/1100972. The full text of UK regulator Ofcom's judgment against ARY News can be found at: http://stakeholders.ofcom.org.uk/binaries/enforcement/broadcast-bulletins/obb269/obb269.pdf

For a fuller account of the pressures on newsrooms see Neha Ansari's 'Not Fit to Print: An Insider Account of Pakistani Censorship', *Foreign Policy*. FP.com, 20 Nov. 2014.

An Activist Speaks by Najah Kadhim

On the founder of Wahhabism, see the new study on his life and thought by Michael Crawford, *Ibn Abd al-Wahhab* (Oneworld, Oxford, 2014). On Salafi thought see the excellent *Global Salafism: Islam's New Religious Movement* by Roel Meijer (Hurst, London, 2009). President Morsi's constitution is discussed by Ziauddin Sardar in 'The Future of the Arab Spring in Postnormal Times' *American Journal of Islamic Social Sciences* 30 (4) 125-136 Fall 2013. A French translation of Abd al-Rahman al-Kawakibi's *The Nature of Despotism* has just been published as *Du despotisme et autres essais* (Sinbad, Paris, 2013). For the surveys and statistics see Shadi Hamid, *Temptation of Power* (Oxford University Press, 2014) pp 7-58.

A Theology of Moral Progress by Nader Hashemi

'RealTime with Bill Maher' was broadcast on HBO on 29 October 2010 and 3 October 2014, episodes 195 and 331, respectively. Chris Cuomo's diatribe against Raza Aslan can be viewed at: https://www.youtube.com/watch?v=B3ifuwnf-Ts. See also Michael R. Gordon and Kareem Fahim, 'Kerry Says Egypt's Military Was "Restoring Democracy" in Ousting Morsi,' *New York Times*, August 1, 2013; The White House, Office of the Press Secretary, 'Statement by the President on Syria,' August 31, 2013.

The quotation from Wilfred Cantwell Smith is from *Islam in Modern History* (Princeton: Princeton University Press, 1997) p 304.

Tribal Power by Hassan Mahamdallie

Miriam Cooke's *Women Claim Islam: Creating Islamic Feminist Through Literature* is published by Routledge (London, 2000) and *Opening the Gates: An Anthology of Arab Feminist Writing* by Indian University Press (Bloomington, 2004). The Leon Trotsky quotation is from *The History of the Russian Revolution* (Pluto Press, London, 1977), pp26-27. See also Ziauddin Sardar, 'The Master Race' *Critical Muslim 13: Race* (Hurst, London, 2015).

CONTRIBUTORS

Hussain Ahmed is a cultural anthropologist based in Karachi, Pakistan ● **Kecia Ali** is Associate Professor of Religion at Boston University ● **Nazry Bahrawi** is a research associate at the Middle East Institute, National University of Singapore ● **Mohamed Bakari** is Professor of English at Fatih University, Istanbul ● **Merryl Wyn Davies** is the Co-Director of the Muslim Institute and author of the seminal study *Knowing One Another* and *Introducing Anthropology* ● **Abdelwahab El-Affendi** is co-ordinator of the Democracy and Islam Programme at the Centre for the Study of Democracy, University of Westminster ● **Rahel Fischbach** is a PhD candidate in the Theology and Religious Studies Department at Georgetown University, Washington DC ● **Rachel Friedman** is a PhD candidate in the Department of Near Eastern Studies, University of California, Berkeley ● **Nader Hashemi** is the Director for Centre for Middle Eastern Studies, Josef Korbel School of International Studies, University of Denver ● **Jeremy Henzell-Thomas** is a Research Associate and former Visiting Fellow at the Centre of Islamic Studies, University of Cambridge ● **Aamer Hussein** is a well-known short story writer and Professorial Writing Fellow at the University of Southampton ● **Najah Kadhim** is the Chair of International Forum for Islamic Dialogue, London, and Senior Lecturer in Engineering at the University of Hertfordshire ● **Hassan Mahamdallie**, co-director of the Muslim Institute, is the author of *Defending Multiculturalism* and *Crossing the 'River of Fire': The Socialism of William Morris* ● **Sejad Mekic**, a Lecturer in Islamic Studies at the Muslim College (London) and Cambridge Muslim College, is the author of the forthcoming book, *A European Mufti in Communist Yugoslavia* ● **Avaes Mohammad** is a poet, playwright and performer with a background in the chemical sciences ● **Salim Nafar** is a Palestinian writer based in Gaza ● **Andre Naffis-Sahely** is a poet, critic and translator based in London ● **Laksmi Pamuntjak** is an Indonesian poet, novelist and food writer ● **Barnaby Rogerson**, writer and publisher, is the author of the widely acclaimed *The Prophet Muhammad: A Biography* ● **Malise Ruthven**, writer and academic, is the author of *Islam in the World* and other books ● **Boyd Tonkin** writes for *The Independent*.